Data Analytics with Spark Using Python

The Pearson Addison-Wesley Data and Analytics Series

Visit **informit.com/awdataseries** for a complete list of available publications.

The **Pearson Addison-Wesley Data and Analytics Series** provides readers with practical knowledge for solving problems and answering questions with data. Titles in this series primarily focus on three areas:

1. **Infrastructure:** how to store, move, and manage data
2. **Algorithms:** how to mine intelligence or make predictions based on data
3. **Visualizations:** how to represent data and insights in a meaningful and compelling way

The series aims to tie all three of these areas together to help the reader build end-to-end systems for fighting spam; making recommendations; building personalization; detecting trends, patterns, or problems; and gaining insight from the data exhaust of systems and user interactions.

Make sure to connect with us!
informit.com/socialconnect

Pearson
Addison-Wesley

Safari

Data Analytics with Spark Using Python

Jeffrey Aven

✦✦Addison-Wesley

Boston • Columbus • Indianapolis • New York • San Francisco • Amsterdam
Cape Town • Dubai • London • Madrid • Milan • Munich • Paris
Montreal • Toronto • Delhi • Mexico City • São Paulo • Sydney
Hong Kong • Seoul • Singapore • Taipei • Tokyo

Library of Congress Control Number: 2018938456

ISBN-13: 978-0-13-484601-9
ISBN-10: 0-13-484601-X

1 18

Editor-in-Chief
Greg Wiegand

Executive Editor
Trina MacDonald

Development Editor
Amanda Kaufmann

Managing Editor
Sandra Schroeder

Senior Project Editor
Lori Lyons

Technical Editor
Yaniv Rodenski

Copy Editor
Catherine D. Wilson

Project Manager
Dhayanidhi Karunanidhi

Indexer
Erika Millen

Proofreader
Jeanine Furino

Cover Designer
Chuti Prasertsith

Compositor
codemantra

Contents at a Glance

Table of Contents

II: Beyond the Basics

Preface

Spark is at the heart of the disruptive Big Data and open source software revolution. The interest in and use of Spark have grown exponentially, with no signs of abating. This book will prepare you, step by step, for a prosperous career in the Big Data analytics field.

Focus of the Book

This book focuses on the fundamentals of the Spark project, starting from the core and working outward into Spark's various extensions, related or subprojects, and the broader ecosystem of open source technologies such as Hadoop, Kafka, Cassandra, and more.

Although the foundational understanding of Spark concepts covered in this book—including the runtime, cluster and application architecture—are language independent and agnostic, the majority of the programming examples and exercises in this book are written in Python. The Python API for Spark (PySpark) provides an intuitive programming environment for data analysts, data engineers, and data scientists alike, offering developers the flexibility and extensibility of Python with the distributed processing power and scalability of Spark.

The scope of this book is quite broad, covering aspects of Spark from core Spark programming to Spark SQL, Spark Streaming, machine learning, and more. This book provides a good introduction and overview for each topic—enough of a platform for you to build upon any particular area or discipline within the Spark project.

Who Should Read This Book

This book is intended for data analysts and engineers looking to enter the Big Data space or consolidate their knowledge in this area. The demand for engineers with skills in Big Data and its preeminent processing framework, Spark, is exceptionally high at present. This book aims to prepare readers for this growing employment market and arm them with the skills employers are looking for.

Python experience is useful but not strictly necessary for readers of this book as Python is quite intuitive for anyone with any programming experience whatsoever. A good working knowledge of data analysis and manipulation would also be helpful. This book is especially well suited to data warehouse professionals interested in expanding their careers into the Big Data area.

How to Use This Book

This book is structured into two parts and eight chapters. Part I, "Spark Foundations," includes four chapters designed to build a solid understanding of what Spark is, how to deploy Spark, and how to use Spark for basic data processing operations:

- Chapter 1, "Introducing Big Data, Hadoop and Spark," provides a good overview of the Big Data ecosystem, including the genesis and evolution of the Spark project. Key properties of the Spark project are discussed, including what Spark is and how it is used, as well as how Spark relates to the Hadoop project.

- Chapter 2, "Deploying Spark," demonstrates how to deploy a Spark cluster, including the various Spark cluster deployment modes and the different ways you can leverage Spark.

- Chapter 3, "Understanding the Spark Cluster Architecture," discusses how Spark clusters and applications operate, providing a solid understanding of exactly how Spark works.
- Chapter 4, "Learning Spark Programming Basics," focuses on the basic programming building blocks of Spark using the Resilient Distributed Dataset (RDD) API.

Part II, "Beyond the Basics," includes the final four chapters, which extend beyond the Spark core into its uses with SQL and NoSQL systems, streaming applications, and data science and machine learning:

- Chapter 5, "Advanced Programming Using the Spark Core API," covers advanced constructs used to extend, accelerate, and optimize Spark routines, including different shared variables and RDD storage and partitioning concepts and implementations.
- Chapter 6, "SQL and NoSQL Programming with Spark," discusses Spark's integration into the vast SQL landscape as well as its integration with non-relational stores.
- Chapter 7, "Stream Processing and Messaging Using Spark," introduces the Spark streaming project and the fundamental DStream object. It also covers Spark's use with popular messaging systems such as Apache Kafka.
- Chapter 8, "Introduction to Data Science and Machine Learning Using Spark," provides an introduction to predictive modeling using Spark with R as well as the Spark MLlib subproject used to implement machine learning with Spark.

Book Conventions

Key terms or concepts are highlighted in italic. Code, object, and file references are displayed in a monospaced font.

Step-by-step exercises are provided to consolidate each topic.

Accompanying Code and Data for the Exercises

Sample data and source code for each of the exercises in this book is available at **http://sparkusingpython.com**. You can also view or clone the GitHub repository for this book at https://github.com/sparktraining/spark_using_python.

Register This Book

Register your copy of *Data Analytics with Spark Using Python* on the InformIT site for convenient access to updates and/or corrections as they become available. To start the registration process, go to informit.com/register and log in or create an account. Enter the product ISBN (9780134846019) and click Submit. Look on the Registered Products tab for an Access Bonus Content link next to this product, and follow that link to access any available bonus materials. If you would like to be notified of exclusive offers on new editions and updates, please check the box to receive email from us.

About the Author

Jeffrey Aven is an independent Big Data, open source software and cloud computing professional based out of Melbourne, Australia. Jeffrey is a highly regarded consultant and instructor and has authored several other books including *Teach Yourself Apache Spark in 24 Hours* and *Teach Yourself Hadoop in 24 Hours*.

Introduction

Spark is a first-class data processing platform and programming interface for Big Data which is inexorably linked to the Big Data technology wave. At the time of this writing, Spark is one of the most active open source projects under the Apache Software Foundation (ASF) framework, and it's one of the most active open source Big Data projects ever.

With so much interest in Spark from the analytics, data processing, and data science communities, it's important to understand what Spark is, what purpose it serves, what advantages it provides, and how to leverage Spark for Big Data analytics. This book covers all that.

Unlike many other publications dedicated to Spark, which almost exclusively use the Scala API, this book focuses on the Python API for Spark, or PySpark. Python was selected as the basis for this book because it is an intuitive, interpreted language that is widely known and easily learned by those who haven't used it. Moreover, Python is a very popular programming language with data scientists, a major constituency of the Spark community.

This book takes it from the top with Big Data and Spark and is suitable whether you have had zero exposure to Spark and Hadoop or have had some exposure but are looking to get a holistic understanding of how Spark operates and how best to leverage its vast capabilities.

Throughout the book you will learn about adjacent and complementary platforms, projects, and technologies such as Hadoop, HBase, Kafka, and many others, and see how they interact and integrate with Spark.

I have dedicated the past several years of my career to this subject area, teaching courses and consulting with clients on analytics and Big Data. I have seen the emergence and maturity of Spark and the Big Data and open source movements more generally and have been part of their assimilation into the enterprise. I have tried to synthesize my personal learning journey into this book.

I have supplied sample data and source code for each of the exercises in this book, which is available at http://sparkusingpython.com. You can also view or clone the GitHub repository for this book at https://github.com/sparktraining/spark_using_python.

I hope this book launches or assists in your journey to becoming a Big Data and Spark practitioner.

Spark Foundations

Introducing Big Data, Hadoop, and Spark

In pioneer days they used oxen for heavy pulling, and when one ox couldn't budge a log, they didn't try to grow a larger ox. We shouldn't be trying for bigger computers, but for more systems of computers.

Rear Admiral Grace Murray Hopper, American computer scientist

In This Chapter:

- Introduction to Big Data and the Apache Hadoop project
- Basic overview of the Hadoop core components (HDFS and YARN)
- Introduction to Apache Spark
- Python fundamentals required for PySpark programming, including functional programming basics

The Hadoop and Spark projects are inexorably linked to the Big Data movement. From their early beginnings at search engine providers and in academia to the vast array of current applications that range from data warehousing to complex event processing to machine learning and more, Hadoop and Spark have indelibly altered the data landscape.

This chapter introduces some basic distributed computing concepts, the Hadoop and Spark projects, and functional programming using Python, providing a solid platform to build your knowledge upon as you progress through this book.

Introduction to Big Data, Distributed Computing, and Hadoop

Before discussing Spark, it is important to take a step back and understand the history of what we now refer to as Big Data. To be proficient as a Spark professional, you need to understand not only

Hadoop and its use with Spark but also some of the concepts at the core of the Hadoop project, such as data locality, shared nothing, and MapReduce, as these are all applicable and integral to Spark.

A Brief History of Big Data and Hadoop

The set of storage and processing methodologies commonly known as Big Data emerged from the search engine providers in the early 2000s, principally Google and Yahoo!. The search engine providers were the first group of users faced with Internet scale problems, mainly how to process and store indexes of all the documents in the Internet universe. This seemed an insurmountable challenge at the time, even though the entire body of content in the Internet was a fraction of what it is today.

Yahoo! and Google independently set about developing a set of capabilities to meet this challenge. In 2003, Google released a whitepaper titled "The Google File System." Subsequently, in 2004, Google released another whitepaper, titled "MapReduce: Simplified Data Processing on Large Clusters." Around the same time, Doug Cutting, who is generally acknowledged as the initial creator of Hadoop, and Mike Cafarella were working on a web crawler project called Nutch, which was based on Cutting's open source Lucene project (now Apache Lucene). The Google whitepapers inspired Cutting to take the work he had done on the Nutch project and incorporate the storage and processing principles outlined in these whitepapers. The resulting product is what we know today as Hadoop. Later in 2006, Yahoo! decided to adopt Hadoop and hire Doug Cutting to work full time on the project. Hadoop joined the Apache Software Foundation in 2006.

The Apache Software Foundation

The Apache Software Foundation (ASF) is a nonprofit organization founded in 1999 to provide an open source software structure and framework for developers to contribute to projects. The ASF encourages collaboration and community involvement and protects volunteers from litigation. ASF is premised on the concept of meritocracy, meaning projects are governed by merit.

Contributors are developers who contribute code or documentation to projects. They are typically active on mailing lists and support forums, and they provide suggestions, criticism, and patches to address defects.

Committers are developers whose expertise merits giving them access to a commit code to the main repository for a project. Committers sign a contributor license agreement (CLA) and have an apache.org email address. Committers act as a committee to make decisions about projects.

More information about the Apache Software Foundation can be found at http://apache.org/.

Around the same time the Hadoop project was born, several other technology innovations were afoot, including the following:

- The rapid expansion of ecommerce
- The birth and rapid growth of the mobile Internet
- Blogs and user-driven web content
- Social media

These innovations cumulatively led to an exponential increase in the amount of data generated. This deluge of data accelerated the expansion of the Big Data movement and led to the emergence of other related projects, such as Spark, open source messaging systems such as Kafka, and NoSQL platforms such as HBase and Cassandra, all of which we'll discuss in detail later in this book.

But it all started with Hadoop.

Hadoop Explained

Hadoop is a data storage and processing platform initially based on a central concept: data locality. *Data locality* refers to the pattern of processing data where it resides by bringing the computation to the data rather than the typical pattern of requesting data from its location—for example, a database management system—and sending the data to a remote processing system or host.

With Internet-scale data—Big Data—it is no longer efficient, practical, or even possible in some cases to move the large volumes of data required for processing across the network at compute time.

Hadoop enables large datasets to be processed locally on the nodes of a cluster using a *shared nothing* approach, where each node can independently process a much smaller subset of the entire dataset without needing to communicate with other nodes. This characteristic is enabled through its implementation of a distributed filesystem.

Hadoop is schemaless with respect to its write operations; it is what's known as a *schema-on-read* system. This means it can store and process a wide range of data, from unstructured text documents, to semi-structured JSON (JavaScript Object Notation) or XML documents, to well-structured extracts from relational database systems.

Schema-on-read systems are a fundamental departure from the relational databases we are accustomed to, which are, in contrast, broadly categorized as schema-on-write systems, where data is typically strongly typed and a schema is predefined and enforced upon INSERT, UPDATE, or UPSERT operations.

NoSQL platforms, such as HBase or Cassandra, are also classified as schema-on-read systems. You will learn more about NoSQL platforms in Chapter 6, "SQL and NoSQL Programming with Spark."

Because the schema is not interpreted during write operations to Hadoop, there are no indexes, statistics, or other constructs often employed by database systems to optimize query operations and filter or reduce the amount of data returned to a client. This further necessitates data locality.

Hadoop is designed to find needles in haystacks by dividing and conquering large problems into sets of smaller problems and applying the concepts of data locality and shared nothing. Spark applies the very same concepts.

Core Components of Hadoop

Hadoop has two core components: *HDFS* (Hadoop Distributed File System) and *YARN* (Yet Another Resource Negotiator). HDFS is Hadoop's storage subsystem, whereas YARN can be thought of as Hadoop's processing, or resource scheduling, subsystem (see Figure 1.1).

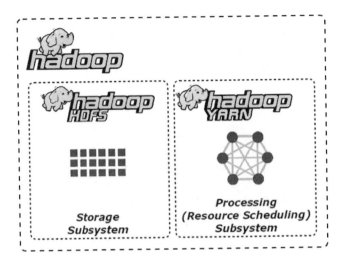

Figure 1.1   Hadoop core components.

Each component is independent of the other and can operate in its own cluster. However, when a HDFS cluster and a YARN cluster are collocated with each other, the combination of both systems is considered to be a Hadoop cluster. Spark can leverage both Hadoop core components, as discussed in more detail later in this chapter.

Cluster Terminology

A *cluster* is a collection of systems that work together to perform functions, such as computational or processing functions. Individual servers within a cluster are referred to as *nodes*.

Clusters can have many topologies and communication models; one such model is the master/slave model. Master/slave is a model of communication whereby one process has control over one or more other processes. In some systems, a master is selected from a group of eligible processes at runtime or during processing, while in other cases—such as with a HDFS or YARN cluster—the master and slave processes are pre-designated static roles for the lifetime of the cluster.

Any other projects that interact or integrate with Hadoop in some way—for instance, data ingestion projects such as Flume or Sqoop or data analysis tools such as Pig or Hive—are called Hadoop "ecosystem" projects. You could consider Spark an ecosystem project, but this is debatable because Spark does not require Hadoop to run.

HDFS: Files, Blocks, and Metadata

HDFS is a virtual filesystem where files are composed of *blocks* distributed across one or more *nodes* of the cluster. Files are split indiscriminately, according to a configured block size upon uploading data into the filesystem, in a process known as *ingestion*. The blocks are then distributed and replicated across cluster nodes to achieve fault tolerance and additional opportunities for processing data locally (the design goal of "bringing the computation to the data"). HDFS blocks are stored and managed on a slave node HDFS cluster process called the *DataNode*.

The DataNode process is the HDFS slave node daemon that runs on one or more nodes of the HDFS cluster. DataNodes are responsible for managing block storage and access for reading and writing of data, as well as for block replication, which is part of the data ingestion process, shown in Figure 1.2.

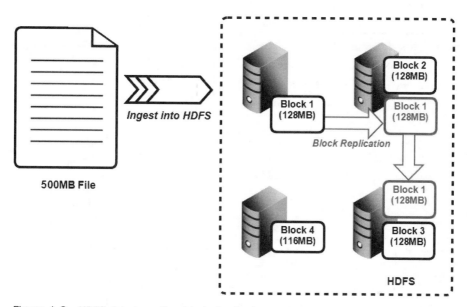

Figure 1.2   HDFS data ingestion, block distribution, and replication.

There are typically many hosts running the DataNode process in a fully distributed Hadoop cluster. Later you will see that the DataNode process provides input data in the form of partitions to distributed Spark worker processes for Spark applications deployed on Hadoop.

The information about the filesystem and its virtual directories, files, and the physical blocks that comprise the files is stored in the filesystem *metadata*. The filesystem metadata is stored in resident memory on the HDFS master node process known as the *NameNode*. The NameNode in a HDFS cluster provides durability to the metadata through a journaling function akin to a relational database transaction log. The NameNode is responsible for providing HDFS clients with block locations for read and write operations, with which the clients communicate directly with the DataNodes for data operations. Figure 1.3 shows the anatomy of an HDFS read operation, and Figure 1.4 shows the anatomy of a write operation in HDFS.

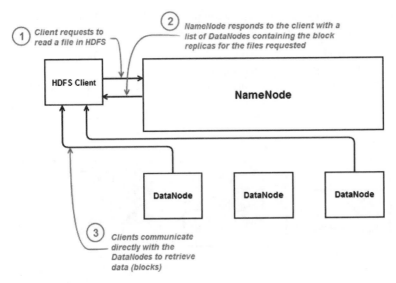

Figure 1.3   Anatomy of an HDFS read operation.

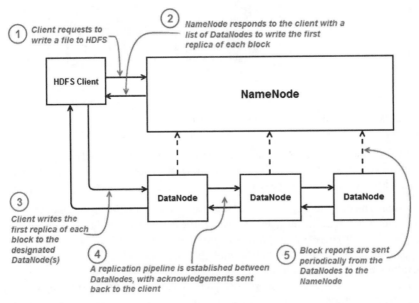

Figure 1.4   Anatomy of an HDFS write operation.

Application Scheduling Using YARN

YARN governs and orchestrates the processing of data in Hadoop, which usually is data sourced from and written to HDFS. The YARN cluster architecture is a master/slave cluster framework like HDFS, with a master node daemon called the *ResourceManager* and one or more slave node daemons called *NodeManagers* running on worker, or slave, nodes in the cluster.

The ResourceManager is responsible for granting cluster compute resources to applications running on the cluster. Resources are granted in units called *containers*, which are predefined combinations of CPU cores and memory. Container allotments, including minimum and maximum thresholds, are configurable on the cluster. Containers are used to isolate resources dedicated to a process or processes.

The ResourceManager also tracks available capacity on the cluster as applications finish and release their reserved resources, and it tracks the status of applications running on the cluster. The ResourceManager serves an embedded web UI on port 8088 of the host running this daemon, which is useful for displaying the status of applications running, completed, or failed on the cluster, as shown in Figure 1.5. You often use this user interface when managing the status of Spark applications running on a YARN cluster.

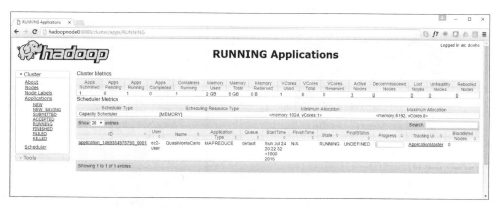

Figure 1.5   YARN ResourceManager user interface.

Clients submit applications, such as Spark applications, to the ResourceManager; the ResourceManager then allocates the first container on an available NodeManager in the cluster as a delegate process for the application called the *ApplicationMaster*; the ApplicationMaster then negotiates all further containers required to run tasks for the application.

The NodeManager is the slave node YARN daemon that manages containers on the slave node host. Containers are used to execute the tasks involved in an application. As Hadoop's approach to solving large problems is to "divide and conquer," a large problem is deconstructed into a set of tasks, many of which can be run in parallel; recall the concept of shared nothing. These tasks are run in containers on hosts running the NodeManager process.

Most containers simply run tasks. However, the ApplicationMaster has some additional responsibilities for managing an application. As discussed earlier in this chapter, the ApplicationMaster is the first container allocated by the ResourceManager to run on a NodeManager. Its job is to plan the application, including determining what resources are required—often based on how much data is being processed—and to work out resourcing for application stages, which you'll learn about shortly. The ApplicationMaster requests these resources from the ResourceManager on behalf of the application. The ResourceManager grants resources on the same or other NodeManagers to the ApplicationMaster to use for the lifetime of the specific application. The ApplicationMaster—in the case of Spark, as detailed later—monitors the progress of tasks, stages (groups of tasks that can be performed in parallel), and dependencies. The summary information is provided to the ResourceManager to display in its user interface, as shown earlier. A generalization of the YARN application submission, scheduling, and execution process is shown in Figure 1.6.

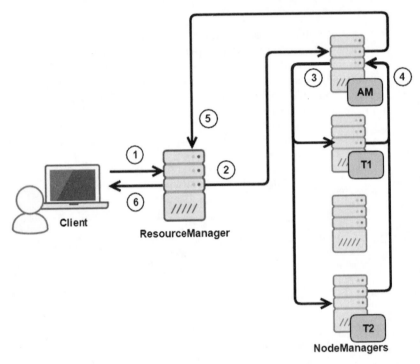

Figure 1.6   YARN application submission, scheduling, and execution (Hadoop 6.6).

The process pictured in Figure 1.6 works as follows:

1. A client submits an application to the ResourceManager.

2. The ResourceManager allocates an ApplicationMaster process on a NodeManager with sufficient capacity to be assigned this role.

3. The ApplicationMaster negotiates task containers with the ResourceManager to be run on NodeManagers—which can include the NodeManager on which the ApplicationMaster is running as well—and dispatches processing to the NodeManagers hosting the task containers for the application.

4. The NodeManagers report their task attempt status and progress to the ApplicationMaster.

5. The ApplicationMaster reports progress and the status of the application to the ResourceManager.

6. The ResourceManager reports application progress, status, and results to the client.

We will explore how YARN is used to schedule and orchestrate Spark programs running on a Hadoop cluster in Chapter 3, "Understanding the Spark Cluster Architecture."

Hadoop MapReduce

Following Google's release of the whitepaper "The Google File System" in 2003, which influenced the HDFS project, Google released another whitepaper, titled "MapReduce: Simplified Data Processing on Large Clusters," in December 2004. The MapReduce whitepaper gives a high-level description of Google's approach to processing—specifically indexing and ranking—large volumes of text data for search engine processing. MapReduce would become the programming model at the core of Hadoop and would ultimately inspire and influence the Spark project.

Introduction to Apache Spark

Apache Spark was created as an alternative to the implementation of MapReduce in Hadoop to gain efficiencies measured in orders of magnitude. Spark also delivers unrivaled extensibility and is effectively a Swiss Army knife for data processing, delivering SQL access, streaming data processing, graph and NoSQL processing, machine learning, and much more.

Apache Spark Background

Apache Spark is an open source distributed data processing project started in 2009 by Matei Zaharia at the University of California, Berkeley, RAD Lab. Spark was created as part of the Mesos research project, designed to look at an alternative resource scheduling and orchestration system to MapReduce. (For more information on Mesos, see http://mesos.apache.org/.)

Using Spark became an alternative to using traditional MapReduce on Hadoop, which was unsuited for interactive queries or real-time, low-latency applications. A major disadvantage of Hadoop's MapReduce implementation was its persistence of intermediate data to disk between the Map and Reduce processing phases.

As an alternative to MapReduce, Spark implements a distributed, fault-tolerant, in-memory structure called a Resilient Distributed Dataset (RDD). Spark maximizes the use of memory across multiple machines, significantly improving overall performance. Spark's reuse of these in-memory structures makes it well suited to iterative machine learning operations as well as interactive queries.

Spark is written in Scala, which is built on top of the Java Virtual Machine (JVM) and Java runtime. This makes Spark a cross-platform application capable of running on Windows as well as Linux; many consider Spark to be the future of data processing in Hadoop.

Spark enables developers to create complex, multi-stage data processing routines, providing a high-level API and fault-tolerant framework that lets programmers focus on logic rather than infrastructure or environmental issues, such as hardware failure.

As a top-level Apache Software Foundation project, Spark has more than 400 individual contributors and committers from companies such as Facebook, Yahoo!, Intel, Netflix, Databricks, and others.

Uses for Spark

Spark supports a wide range of applications, including the following:

- Extract-transform-load (ETL) operations
- Predictive analytics and machine learning
- Data access operations, such as SQL queries and visualizations
- Text mining and text processing
- Real-time event processing
- Graph applications
- Pattern recognition
- Recommendation engines

At the time of this writing, more than 1,500 organizations worldwide are using Spark in production, with some organizations running Spark on hundreds to thousands of cluster nodes against petabytes of data.

Spark's speed and versatility are further complemented by the numerous extensions now included with Spark, including Spark SQL, Spark Streaming, and SparkR, to name a few.

Programming Interfaces to Spark

As mentioned earlier in this chapter, Spark is written in Scala, and it runs in JVMs. Spark provides native support for programming interfaces including the following:

- Scala
- Python (using Python's functional programming operators)
- Java
- SQL
- R

In addition, Spark includes extended support for Clojure and other languages.

Submission Types for Spark Programs

Spark programs can run interactively or as batch jobs, including mini-batch and micro-batch jobs.

Interactive Submission

Interactive programming shells are available in Python and Scala. The PySpark and Scala shells are shown in Figures 1.7 and 1.8, respectively.

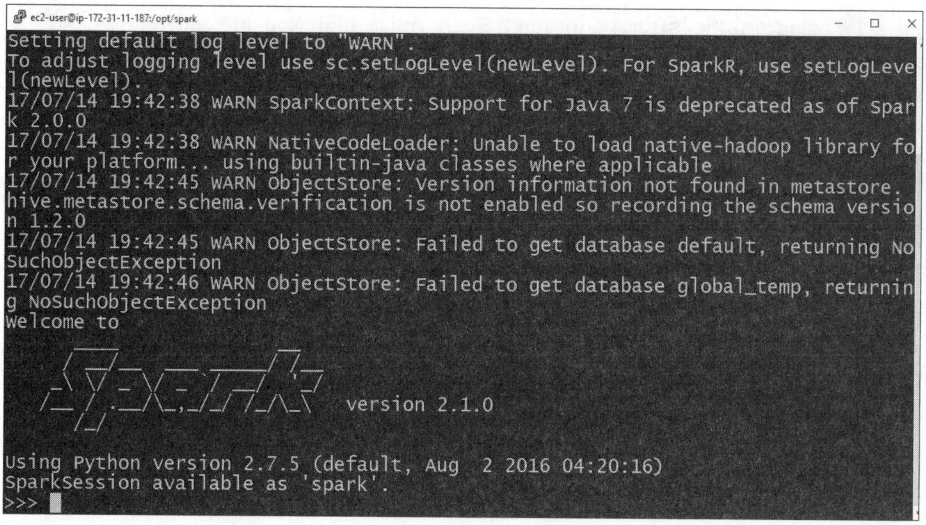

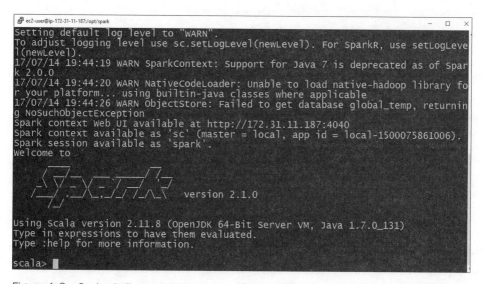

Figure 1.7   PySpark shell.

Figure 1.8   Scala shell.

Interactive R and SQL shells are included with Spark as well.

Non-interactive or Batch Submission

Non-interactive applications can be submitted using the spark-submit command, as shown in Listing 1.1.

Listing 1.1 **Using spark-submit to Run a Spark Application Non-interactively**

```
$SPARK_HOME/bin/spark-submit \
--class org.apache.spark.examples.SparkPi \
--master yarn-cluster \
--num-executors 4 \
--driver-memory 10g \
--executor-memory 10g \
--executor-cores 1 \
$SPARK_HOME/examples/jars/spark-examples*.jar 10
```

Input/Output Types for Spark Applications

Although Spark is mostly used to process data in Hadoop, Spark can be used with a multitude of other source and target systems, including the following:

- Local or network filesystems
- Object storage such as Amazon S3 or Ceph
- Relational database systems
- NoSQL stores, including Cassandra, HBase, and others
- Messaging systems such as Kafka

The Spark RDD

We will discuss the Spark Resilient Distributed Dataset (RDD) throughout this book, so it is worthwhile to introduce it now. The Spark RDD, the primary data abstraction structure for Spark applications, is one of the main differentiators between Spark and other cluster computing frameworks. Spark RDDs can be thought of as in-memory collections of data distributed across a cluster. Spark programs using the Spark core API consist of loading input data into an RDD, transforming the RDD into subsequent RDDs, and then storing or presenting the final output for an application from the resulting final RDD. (Don't worry ... there is much more about this in upcoming chapters of this book!)

Spark and Hadoop

As noted earlier, Hadoop and Spark are closely related to each other in their shared history and implementation of core parallel processing concepts, such as shared nothing and data locality. Let's look at the ways in which Hadoop and Spark are commonly used together.

HDFS as a Data Source for Spark

Spark can be deployed as a processing framework for data in Hadoop, typically in HDFS. Spark has built-in support for reading and writing to and from HDFS in various file formats, including the following:

- Native text file format
- Sequence file format
- Parquet format

In addition, Spark includes extended support for Avro, ORCFile formats, and others. Reading a file from HDFS using Spark is as easy as this:

```
textfile = sc.textFile("hdfs://mycluster/data/file.txt")
```

Writing data from a Spark application to HDFS is as easy as this:

```
myRDD.saveAsTextFile("hdfs://mycluster/data/output")
```

YARN as a Resource Scheduler for Spark

YARN is one of the most commonly used process schedulers for Spark applications. Because YARN is usually collocated with HDFS on Hadoop clusters, YARN is a convenient platform for managing Spark applications.

Also, because YARN governs available compute resources across distributed nodes in a Hadoop cluster, it can schedule Spark processing stages to run in parallel wherever possible. Furthermore, where HDFS is used as the input source for a Spark application, YARN can schedule map tasks to take full advantage of data locality, thereby minimizing the amount of data that needs to be transferred across the network during the critical initial stages of processing.

Functional Programming Using Python

Python is an amazingly useful language. Its uses range from automation to web services to machine learning and everything in between. Python has risen to be one of the most widely used languages today.

As a multi-paradigm programming language, Python combines imperative and procedural programming paradigms with full support for the object-oriented and functional paradigms.

The following sections examine the functional programming concepts and elements included in Python, which are integral to Spark's Python API (PySpark)—and are the basis of Spark programming throughout this book—including anonymous functions, common higher-order functions, and immutable and iterable data structures.

Data Structures Used in Functional Python Programming

Python RDDs in Spark are simply representations of distributed collections of Python objects, so it is important to understand the various data structures available in Python.

Lists

Lists in Python are zero-based indexed sequences of mutable values with the first value numbered zero. You can remove or replace elements in a list as well as append elements to the end of a list. Listing 1.2 shows a simple example of a list in Python.

Listing 1.2 **Lists**

```
>>> tempc = [38.4, 19.2, 12.8, 9.6]
>>> print(tempc[0])
38.4
>>> print(len(tempc))
4
```

As you can see from Listing 1.2, individual list elements are accessible using the index number in square brackets.

Importantly, lists support the three primary functional programming constructs—map(), reduce(), and filter()—as well as other built-in methods, including count(), sort(), and more. In this book we will spend a considerable amount of time working with Spark RDDs, which are essentially representations of Python lists. Listing 1.3 provides a basic example of a Python list and a map() function. Note that the map() function, which we will cover in more detail later, operates on an input list and returns a new list. This example is in pure Python; the equivalent PySpark operation has slightly different syntax.

Listing 1.3 **Python map() Function**

```
>>> tempf = map(lambda x: (float(9)/5)*x + 32, tempc)
>>> tempf
[101.12, 66.56, 55.040000000000006, 49.28]
```

Although Python lists are mutable by default, list objects contained within Python RDDs in Spark are immutable, as is the case with any objects created within Spark RDDs.

Sets are a similar object type available in Python; they are based upon the set mathematical abstraction. Sets are unordered collections of unique values supporting common mathematical set operations, such as union(), intersection(), and others.

Tuples

Tuples are an immutable sequence of objects, though the objects contained in a tuple can themselves be immutable or mutable. Tuples can contain different underlying object types, such as a mixture of string, int, and float objects, or they can contain other sequence types, such as sets and other tuples.

For simplicity, think of tuples as being similar to immutable lists. However, they are different constructs and have very different purposes.

Tuples are similar to records in a relational database table, where each record has a structure, and each field defined with an ordinal position in the structure has a meaning. List objects simply have an order, and because they are mutable by default, the order is not directly related to the structure.

Tuples consist of one or more values separated by commas enclosed in parentheses. Elements are accessed from Python tuples similarly to the way they are accessed from lists: using square brackets with a zero-based index referencing the specific element.

Tuple objects have methods for comparing tuples with other tuples, as well as returning the length of a tuple (the number of elements in the tuple). You can also convert a list in Python to a tuple by using the `tuple(list)` function.

Listing 1.4 shows the creation and usage of tuples in native Python.

Listing 1.4   **Tuples**

```
>>> rec0 = "Jeff", "Aven", 46
>>> rec1 = "Barack", "Obama", 54
>>> rec2 = "John F", "Kennedy", 46
>>> rec3 = "Jeff", "Aven", 46
>>> rec0
('Jeff', 'Aven', 46)
>>> len(rec0)
3
>>> print("first name: " + rec0[0])
first name: Jeff
# create tuple of tuples
>>> all_recs = rec0, rec1, rec2, rec3
>>> all_recs
(('Jeff', 'Aven', 46), ('Barack', 'Obama', 54),
('John F', 'Kennedy', 46), ('Jeff', 'Aven', 46))
# create list of tuples
>>> list_of_recs = [rec0, rec1, rec2, rec3]
>>> list_of_recs
[('Jeff', 'Aven', 46), ('Barack', 'Obama', 54),
('John F', 'Kennedy', 46), ('Jeff', 'Aven', 46)]
```

As you can see from Listing 1.4, it is very important to distinguish square brackets from parentheses because they have very different structural meanings.

Tuples are integral objects in Spark, as they are typically used to represent key/value pairs, which are often the fundamental unit of data in Spark programming.

Dictionaries

Dictionaries, or *dicts*, in Python are unordered mutable sets of key/value pairs. Dict objects are denoted by curly braces ({ }), which you can create as empty dictionaries by simply executing a command such as `my_empty_dict = {}`. Unlike with lists and tuples, where an element is accessed by its ordinal position in the sequence (its index), an element in a dict is accessed by its key. A key is separated from its value by a colon (:), whereas key/value pairs in a dict are separated by commas.

Dicts are useful because their elements are self-describing rather than relying on a predefined schema or ordinality. Dict elements are accessed by key, as shown in Listing 1.5. This listing also shows how to add or remove elements from a dict, and it shows some useful dict methods, including keys(), values(), cmp(), and len().

Listing 1.5 **Dictionaries**

```
>>> dict0 = {'fname':'Jeff', 'lname':'Aven', 'pos':'author'}
>>> dict1 = {'fname':'Barack', 'lname':'Obama', 'pos':'president'}
>>> dict2 = {'fname':'Ronald', 'lname':'Reagan', 'pos':'president'}
>>> dict3 = {'fname':'John', 'mi':'F', 'lname':'Kennedy', 'pos':'president'}
>>> dict4 = {'fname':'Jeff', 'lname':'Aven', 'pos':'author'}
>>> len(dict0)
3
>>> print(dict0['fname'])
Jeff
>>> dict0.keys()
['lname', 'pos', 'fname']
>>> dict0.values()
['Aven', 'author', 'Jeff']
# compare dictionaries
>>> cmp(dict0, dict1)
1 ## keys match but values dont
>>> cmp(dict0, dict4)
0 ## all key value pairs match
>>> cmp(dict1, dict2)
-1 ## some key value pairs match
```

Dicts can be used as immutable objects within a Python RDD.

Python Object Serialization

Serialization is the process of converting an object into a structure that can be unpacked (deserialized) at a later point in time on the same system or on a different system.

Serialization, or the ability to serialize and deserialize data, is a necessary function of any distributed processing system and features heavily throughout the Hadoop and Spark projects.

JSON

JSON (JavaScript Object Notation) is a common serialization format. JSON has extended well beyond JavaScript and is used in a multitude of platforms, with support in nearly every programming language. It is a common response structure returned from web services.

JSON is supported natively in Python using the json package. A package is a set of libraries or a collection of modules (which are essentially Python files). The json package is used to encode and decode JSON. A JSON object consists of key/value pairs (dictionaries) and/or arrays (lists), which can be nested within each other. The Python JSON object includes methods for searching, adding, and deleting keys; updating values; and printing objects. Listing 1.6 demonstrates creating a JSON object in Python and performing various actions.

Listing 1.6 **Using a JSON Object in Python**

```
>>> import json
>>> from pprint import pprint
>>> json_str = '''{
... "people" : [
... {"fname": "Jeff",
... "lname": "Aven",
... "tags": ["big data","hadoop"]},
... {"fname": "Doug",
... "lname": "Cutting",
... "tags": ["hadoop","avro","apache","java"]},
... {"fname": "Martin",
... "lname": "Odersky",
... "tags": ["scala","typesafe","java"]},
... {"fname": "John",
... "lname": "Doe",
... "tags": []}
... ]}'''
>>> people = json.loads(json_str)
>>> len(people["people"])
4
>>> print(people["people"][0]["fname"])
Jeff
# add tag item to the first person
people["people"][0]["tags"].append(u'spark')
# delete the fourth person
del people["people"][3]
# "pretty print" json object
pprint(people)
{u'people': [{u'fname': u'Jeff',
              u'lname': u'Aven',
              u'tags': [u'big data', u'hadoop', u'spark']},
             {u'fname': u'Doug',
              u'lname': u'Cutting',
              u'tags': [u'hadoop', u'avro', u'apache', u'java']},
             {u'fname': u'Martin',
              u'lname': u'Odersky',
              u'tags': [u'scala', u'typesafe', u'java']}]}
```

JSON objects can be used within RDDs in PySpark; we will look at this in detail a bit later in this book.

Pickle

Pickle is a serialization method that is proprietary to Python. Pickle is faster than JSON. However, it lacks the portability of JSON, which is a universally interchangeable serialization format.

The Python `pickle` module converts a Python object or objects into a byte stream that can be transmitted, stored, and reconstructed into its original state.

`cPickle`, as the name suggests, is implemented in C instead of Python, and thus it is much faster than the Python implementation. There are some limitations, however. The `cPickle` module does not support subclassing, which is possible using the `pickle` module. Pickling and unpickling an object in Python is a straightforward process, as shown in Listing 1.7. Notice that the load and dump idioms are analogous to the way you serialize and deserialize objects using JSON. The `pickle.dump` approach saves the pickled object to a file, whereas `pickle.dumps` returns the pickled representation of the object as a string that may look strange, although it is not designed to be human readable.

Listing 1.7 **Object Serialization Using Pickle in Python**

```
>>> import cPickle as pickle
>>> obj = { "fname": "Jeff", \
... "lname": "Aven", \
... "tags": ["big data","hadoop"]}
>>> str_obj = pickle.dumps(obj)
>>> pickled_obj = pickle.loads(str_obj)
>>> print(pickled_obj["fname"])
Jeff
>>> pickled_obj["tags"].append('spark')
>>> print(str(pickled_obj["tags"]))
['big data', 'hadoop', 'spark']
# dump pickled object to a string
>>> pickled_obj_str = pickle.dumps(pickled_obj)
# dump pickled object to a pickle file
>>> pickle.dump(pickled_obj, open('object.pkl', 'wb'))
```

The PickleSerializer is used in PySpark to load objects into a pickled format and to unpickle objects; this includes reading preserialized objects from other systems, such as SequenceFiles in Hadoop, and converting them into a format that is usable by Python.

PySpark includes two methods for handling pickled input and output files: `pickleFile` and `saveAsPickleFile`. `pickleFile` is an efficient format for storing and transferring files between PySpark processes. We will examine these methods later in this book.

Aside from its explicit use by developers, pickling is also used by many internal Spark processes in the execution of Spark applications in Python.

Python Functional Programming Basics

Python's functional support embodies all of the functional programming paradigm characteristics that you would expect, including the following:

- Functions as first-class objects and the fundamental unit of programming
- Functions with input and output only (Statements, which could result in side effects, are not allowed.)
- Support for higher-order functions
- Support for anonymous functions

The next few sections look at some of functional programming concepts and their implementation in Python.

Anonymous Functions and the `lambda` Syntax

Anonymous functions, or unnamed functions, are a consistent feature of functional programming languages such as Lisp, Scala, JavaScript, Erlang, Clojure, Go, and many more.

Anonymous functions in Python are implemented using the `lambda` construct rather than using the `def` keyword for named functions. Anonymous functions accept any number of input arguments but return just one value. This value could be another function, a scalar value, or a data structure such as a list.

Listing 1.8 shows two similar functions; one is a named function and one is an anonymous function.

Listing 1.8   **Named Functions and Anonymous Functions in Python**

```
# named function
>>> def plusone(x): return x+1
...
>>> plusone(1)
2
>>> type(plusone)
<type 'function'>
# anonymous function
>>> plusonefn = lambda x: x+1
>>> plusonefn(1)
2
>>> type(plusonefn)
<type 'function'>
>>> plusone.func_name
'plusone'
>>> plusonefn.func_name
'<lambda>'
```

As you can see in Listing 1.8, the named function `plusone` keeps a reference to the function name, whereas the anonymous function `plusonefn` keeps a `<lambda>` name reference.

Named functions can contain statements such as `print`, but anonymous functions can contain only a single or compound expression, which could be a call to another named function that is in scope. Named functions can also use the `return` statement, which is not supported with anonymous functions.

The true power of anonymous functions is evident when you look at higher-order functions, such as `map()`, `reduce()`, and `filter()`, and start chaining single-use functions together in a processing pipeline, as you do in Spark.

Higher-Order Functions

A higher-order function accepts functions as arguments and can return a function as a result. `map()`, `reduce()`, and `filter()` are examples of higher-order functions. These functions accept a function as an argument.

The `flatMap()`, `filter()`, `map()`, and `reduceByKey()` functions in Listing 1.9 are all examples of higher-order functions because they accept and expect an anonymous function as input.

Listing 1.9 **Examples of Higher-Order Functions in Spark**

```
>>> lines = sc.textFile("file:///opt/spark/licenses")
>>> counts = lines.flatMap(lambda x: x.split(' ')) \
...    .filter(lambda x: len(x) > 0) \
...    .map(lambda x: (x, 1)) \
...    .reduceByKey(lambda x, y: x + y) \
...    .collect()
>>> for (word, count) in counts:
...      print("%s: %i" % (word, count))
```

Functions that return functions as a return value are also considered higher-order functions. This characteristic defines callbacks implemented in asynchronous programming.

Don't stress ... We will cover all these functions in detail in Chapter 4, "Learning Spark Programming Basics." For now it is only important to understand the concept of higher-order functions.

Closures

Closures are function objects that enclose the scope at the time they were instantiated. This can include any external variables or functions used when the function was created. Closures "remember" the values by enclosing the scope.

Listing 1.10 is a simple example of closures in Python.

Listing 1.10   **Closures in Python**

```
>>> def generate_message(concept):
...      def ret_message():
...              return 'This is an example of ' + concept
...      return ret_message
...
>>> call_func = generate_message('closures in Python')
>>> call_func
<function ret_message at 0x7fd138aa55f0>
>>> call_func()
'This is an example of closures in Python'
# inspect closure
>>> call_func.__closure__
(<cell at 0x7fd138aaa638: str object at 0x7fd138aaa688>,)
>>> type(call_func.__closure__[0])
<type 'cell'>
>>> call_func.__closure__[0].cell_contents
'closures in Python'
# delete function
del generate_message
# call closure again
call_func()
'This is an example of closures in Python'
# the closure still works!
```

In Listing 1.10, the function `ret_message()` is the closure, and the value for `concept` is enclosed in the function scope. You can use the `__closure__` function member to see information about the closure. The references enclosed in the function are stored in a tuple of cells. You can access the cell contents by using the `cell_contents` function, as shown in this listing. To prove the concept of closures, you can delete the outer function, `generate_message`, and find that the referencing function, `call_func`, still works.

The concept of closures is important to grasp because closures can be of significant benefit in a distributed Spark application. Conversely, closures can have a detrimental impact as well, depending on how the function you are using is constructed and called.

Summary

In this chapter you have gained an understanding of the history, motivation, and uses of Spark, as well as a solid background on Hadoop, a project that is directly correlated to Spark. You have learned the basic fundamentals or HDFS and YARN, the core components of Hadoop, and how these components are used by Spark. This chapter discussed the beginnings of the Spark project along with how Spark is used. This chapter also provided a primer on basic functional programming concepts and their implementations in Python and PySpark. Many of the concepts introduced in this chapter are referenced throughout the remainder of this book.

2

Deploying Spark

The value of an idea lies in the using of it.

Thomas A. Edison, American inventor

In This Chapter:

- Overview of the different Spark deployment modes
- How to install Spark
- The contents of a Spark installation
- Overview of the various methods available for deploying Spark in the cloud

This chapter covers the basics of how Spark is deployed, how to install Spark, and how to get Spark clusters up and running. It discusses the various deployment modes and schedulers available for Spark clusters, as well as options for deploying Spark in the cloud. If you complete the installation exercises in this chapter, you will have a fully functional Spark programming and runtime environment that you can use for the remainder of the book.

Spark Deployment Modes

There are several common deployment modes for Spark, including the following:

- Local mode
- Spark Standalone
- Spark on YARN (Hadoop)
- Spark on Mesos

Each deployment mode implements the Spark runtime architecture—detailed in Chapter 3, "Understanding the Spark Cluster Architecture"—similarly, with differences only in the way resources are managed across one or many nodes in the computing cluster.

In the case of deploying Spark using an external scheduler such as YARN or Mesos, you need to have these clusters deployed, whereas running Spark in Local mode or using the Spark Standalone scheduler removes dependencies outside Spark.

All Spark deployment modes can be used for interactive (shell) and non-interactive (batch) applications, including streaming applications.

Local Mode

Local mode allows all Spark processes to run on a single machine, optionally using any number of cores on the local system. Using Local mode is often a quick way to test a new Spark installation, and it allows you to quickly test Spark routines against small datasets.

Listing 2.1 shows an example of submitting a Spark job in local mode.

Listing 2.1 **Submitting a Spark Job in Local Mode**

```
$SPARK_HOME/bin/spark-submit \
--class org.apache.spark.examples.SparkPi \
--master local \
$SPARK_HOME/examples/jars/spark-examples*.jar 10
```

You specify the number of cores to use in Local mode by supplying the number in brackets after the local directive. For instance, to use two cores, you specify local[2]; to use all the cores on the system, you specify local[*].

When running Spark in Local mode, you can access any data on the local filesystem as well as data from HDFS, S3, or other filesystems, assuming that you have the appropriate configuration and libraries available on the local system.

Although Local mode allows you to get up and running quickly, it is limited in its scalability and effectiveness for production use cases.

Spark Standalone

Spark Standalone refers to the built-in, or "standalone," scheduler. We will look at the function of a scheduler, or cluster manager, in more detail in Chapter 3.

The term *standalone* can be confusing because it has nothing to do with the cluster topology, as might be interpreted. For instance, you can have a Spark deployment in Standalone mode on a fully distributed, multi-node cluster; in this case, *Standalone* simply means that it does not need an external scheduler.

Multiple host processes, or services, run in a Spark Standalone cluster, and each service plays a role in the planning, orchestration, and management of a given Spark application running on the cluster. Figure 2.1 shows a fully distributed Spark Standalone reference cluster topology. (Chapter 3 details the functions that these services provide.)

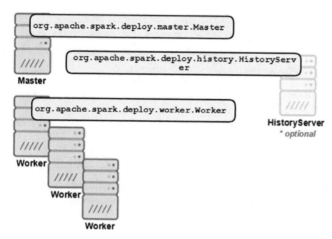

Figure 2.1   Spark Standalone cluster.

You can submit applications to a Spark Standalone cluster by specifying spark as the URI scheme, along with the designated host and port that the Spark Master process is running on. Listing 2.2 shows an example of this.

Listing 2.2   **Submitting a Spark Job to a Spark Standalone Cluster**

```
$SPARK_HOME/bin/spark-submit \
--class org.apache.spark.examples.SparkPi \
--master spark://mysparkmaster:7077 \
$SPARK_HOME/examples/jars/spark-examples*.jar 10
```

With Spark Standalone, you can get up and running quickly with few dependencies or environmental considerations. Each Spark release includes everything you need to get started, including the binaries and configuration files for any host to assume any specified role in a Spark Standalone cluster. Later in this chapter you will deploy your first cluster in Spark Standalone mode.

Spark on YARN

As introduced in Chapter 1, "Introducing Big Data, Hadoop, and Spark," the most common deployment method for Spark is using the YARN resource management framework provided with Hadoop. Recall that YARN is the Hadoop core component that allows you to schedule and manage workloads on a Hadoop cluster.

According to a Databricks annual survey (see https://databricks.com/resources/type/infographic-surveys), YARN and standalone are neck and neck, with Mesos trailing behind.

As first-class citizens in the Hadoop ecosystem, Spark applications can be easily submitted and managed with minimal incremental effort. Spark processes such as the Driver, Master, and Executors (covered in Chapter 3) are hosted or facilitated by YARN processes such as the ResourceManager, NodeManager, and ApplicationMaster.

The spark-submit, pyspark, and spark-shell programs include command line arguments used to submit Spark applications to YARN clusters. Listing 2.3 provides an example of this.

Listing 2.3   **Submitting a Spark Job to a YARN Cluster**

```
$SPARK_HOME/bin/spark-submit \
--class org.apache.spark.examples.SparkPi \
--master yarn \
--deploy-mode cluster \
$SPARK_HOME/examples/jars/spark-examples*.jar 10
```

There are two cluster deployment modes when using YARN as a scheduler: cluster and client. We will distinguish between the two in Chapter 3 when we look at the runtime architecture for Spark.

Spark on Mesos

Apache Mesos is an open source cluster manager developed at University of California, Berkeley; it shares some of its lineage with the creation of Spark. Mesos is capable of scheduling different types of applications, offering fine-grained resource sharing that results in more efficient cluster utilization. Listing 2.4 shows an example of a Spark application submitted to a Mesos cluster.

Listing 2.4   **Submitting a Spark Job to a Mesos Cluster**

```
$SPARK_HOME/bin/spark-submit \
--class org.apache.spark.examples.SparkPi \
--master mesos://mesosdispatcher:7077 \
--deploy-mode cluster \
--supervise \
--executor-memory 20G \
--total-executor-cores 100 \
$SPARK_HOME/examples/jars/spark-examples*.jar 1000
```

This book focuses on the more common schedulers for Spark: Spark Standalone and YARN. However, if you are interested in Mesos, a good place to start is http://mesos.apache.org.

Preparing to Install Spark

Spark is a cross-platform application that can be deployed on the following operating systems:

- Linux (all distributions)
- Windows
- Mac OS X

Although there are no specific hardware requirements, general Spark instance hardware recommendations are as follows:

- 8 GB or more of memory (Spark is predominantly an in-memory processing framework, so the more memory the better.)

- Eight or more CPU cores

- 10 GB or greater network speed

- Sufficient local disk space for storage, if required (SSD is preferred for RDD disk storage. If the instance is hosting a distributed filesystem such as HDFS, then a JBOD configuration of multiple disks is preferred. JBOD stands for "just a bunch of disks," referring to independent hard disks not in a RAID, or redundant array of independent disks, configuration.)

Spark is written in Scala, a language compiled to run on a Java virtual machine (JVM) with programming interfaces in Python (PySpark), Scala, and Java. The following are software prerequisites for installing and running Spark:

- Java (JDK preferably)

- Python, if you intend to use PySpark

- R, if you wish to use Spark with R; as discussed in Chapter 8, "Introduction to Data Science and Machine Learning Using Spark"

- Git, Maven, or SBT, which may be useful if you intend to build Spark from source or compile Spark programs

Getting Spark

Using a Spark release is often the easiest way to install Spark on a given system. Spark releases are downloadable from http://spark.apache.org/downloads.html. These releases are cross-platform: They target a JVM environment, which is platform agnostic.

Using the build instructions provided on the official Spark website, you could also download the source code for Spark and build it yourself for your target platform. This method is more complicated however.

If you download a Spark release, you should select the builds with Hadoop, as shown in Figure 2.2. The "with Hadoop" Spark releases do not actually include Hadoop, as the name may imply. These releases simply include libraries to integrate with the Hadoop clusters and distributions listed. Many of the Hadoop classes are required, regardless of whether you are using Hadoop with Spark.

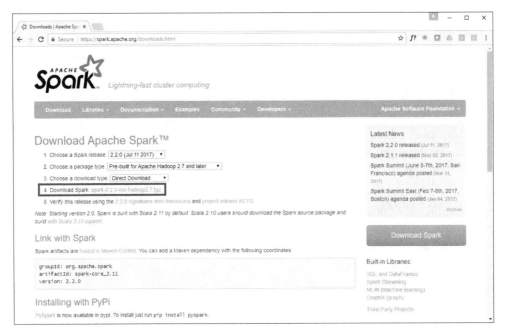

Figure 2.2   Downloading a Spark release.

Using the "Without Hadoop" Builds

You may be tempted to download the "without Hadoop," "user-provided Hadoop," or "spark-x.x.x-bin-without-hadoop.tgz" options if you are installing in Standalone mode and not using Hadoop. The nomenclature can be confusing, but this build expects many of the required classes that are implemented in Hadoop to be present on the system. Generally speaking, you are usually better off downloading one of the spark-x.x.x-bin-hadoopx.x builds.

Spark is typically available with most commercial Hadoop distributions, including the following:

- Cloudera Distribution of Hadoop (CDH)
- Hortonworks Data Platform (HDP)
- MapR Converged Data Platform

In addition, Spark is available from major cloud providers through managed Hadoop offerings, including AWS EMR, Google Cloud Dataproc, and Microsoft Azure HDInsight.

If you have a Hadoop environment, you may have everything you need to get started and can skip the subsequent sections on installing Spark.

Installing Spark on Linux or Mac OS X

Linux is the most common and easiest platform to install Spark on, followed by Mac OS X. Installation on these two platforms is similar because they share the same kernel and have a similar shell environment. This exercise shows how to install Spark on an Ubuntu distribution of Linux; however, the steps are similar for installing Spark on another distribution of Linux or on Mac OS X (only using different package managers, such as, yum). Follow these steps to install Spark on Linux:

1. **Install Java.** It is general practice to install a JDK (Java Development Kit), which includes the Java Runtime Engine (JRE) and tools for building and managing Java or Scala applications. To do so, run the following:

   ```
   $ sudo apt-get install openjdk-8-jdk-headless
   ```

   Test the installation by running `java -version` in a terminal session; you should see output similar to the following if the installation is successful:

   ```
   openjdk version "1.8.0_131"
   OpenJDK Runtime Environment (build 1.8.0_131-8u131-b11-2ubuntu1.17.04.3-b11)
   OpenJDK 64-Bit Server VM (build 25.131-b11, mixed mode)
   ```

   On macOS, the java installation command is as follows:

   ```
   $ brew cask install java
   ```

2. **Get Spark.** Download a release of Spark, using `wget` and the appropriate URL to download the release; you can obtain the actual download address from the http://spark.apache.org/downloads.html page shown in Figure 2.2. Although there is likely to be a later release available to you by the time you read this book, the following example shows a download of release 2.2.0:

   ```
   $ wget https://d3kbcqa49mib13.cloudfront.net/spark-2.2.0-bin-hadoop2.7.tgz
   ```

3. **Unpack the Spark release.** Unpack the Spark release and move it into a shared directory, such as /opt/spark:

   ```
   $ tar -xzf spark-2.2.0-bin-hadoop2.7.tgz
   $ sudo mv spark-2.2.0-bin-hadoop2.7 /opt/spark
   ```

4. **Set the necessary environment variables.** Set the SPARK_HOME variable and update the PATH variable as follows:

   ```
   $ export SPARK_HOME=/opt/spark
   $ export PATH=$SPARK_HOME/bin:$PATH
   ```

   You may wish to set these on a persistent or permanent basis (for example, using /etc/environment on an Ubuntu instance).

5. **Test the installation.** Test the Spark installation by running the built-in Pi Estimator example in Local mode, as follows:

   ```
   $ spark-submit --class org.apache.spark.examples.SparkPi \
   --master local \
   $SPARK_HOME/examples/jars/spark-examples*.jar 1000
   ```

If successful, you should see output similar to the following among a large amount of informational log messages (which you will learn how to minimize later in this chapter):

```
Pi is roughly 3.1414961114149613
```

You can test the interactive shells, `pyspark` and `spark-shell`, at the terminal prompt as well.

Congratulations! You have just successfully installed and tested Spark on Linux. How easy was that?

Installing Spark on Windows

Installing Spark on Windows can be more involved than installing Spark on Linux or Mac OS X because many of the dependencies, such as Python and Java, need to be addressed first. This example uses Windows Server 2012, the server version of Windows 8.1. You need a decompression utility capable of extracting `.tar.gz` and `.gz` archives because Windows does not have native support for these archives. 7-Zip, which you can obtain from http://7-zip.org/download.html, is a suitable program for this. When you have the needed compression utility, follow these steps:

1. **Install Python.** As mentioned earlier, Python is not included with Windows, so you need to download and install it. You can obtain a Windows installer for Python from https://www.python.org/getit/ or https://www.python.org/downloads/windows/. This example uses Python 2.7.10, so select `C:\Python27` as the target directory for the installation.

2. **Install Java.** In this example, you will download and install the latest Oracle JDK. You can obtain a Windows installer package from http://www.oracle.com/technetwork/java/javase/downloads/index.html. To confirm that Java has been installed correctly and is available in the system ta `PATH`, type `java -version` at the Windows command prompt; you should see the version installed returned.

3. **Download and unpack a Hadoop release.** Download the latest Hadoop release from http://hadoop.apache.org/releases.html. Unpack the Hadoop release (using 7-Zip or a similar decompression utility) into a local directory, such as `C:\Hadoop`.

4. **Install Hadoop binaries for Windows.** In order to run Spark on Windows, you need several Hadoop binaries compiled for Windows, including `hadoop.dll` and `winutils.exe`. The Windows-specific libraries and executables required for Hadoop are obtainable from https://mvnrepository.com/artifact/org.apache.hadoop/hadoop-winutils. Download the `hadoop-winutils` archive and unpack the contents to the `bin` subdirectory of your Hadoop release (`C:\Hadoop\bin`).

5. **Download and unpack Spark.** Download the latest Spark release from https://spark.apache.org/downloads.html, as shown in Figure 2.2. As discussed, use the "pre-built for Apache Hadoop" release corresponding to the Hadoop release downloaded in step 3. Unpack the Spark release into a local directory, such as `C:\Spark`.

6. **Disable IPv6.** Disable IPv6 for Java applications by running the following command as an administrator from the Windows command prompt:

```
C:\> setx _JAVA_OPTIONS "-Djava.net.preferIPv4Stack=true"
```

If you are using Windows PowerShell, you can enter the following equivalent command:

```
PS C:\>[Environment]::SetEnvironmentVariable("_JAVA_OPTIONS",
"-Djava.net.preferIPv4Stack=true", "User")
```

Note that you need to run these commands as a local administrator. For simplicity, this example shows applying all configuration settings at a *user* level. However, you can instead choose to apply any of the settings shown at a *machine* level—for instance, if you have multiple users on a system. Consult the documentation for Microsoft Windows for more information about this.

7. **Set the necessary environment variables.** Set the HADOOP_HOME environment variable by running the following command at the Windows command prompt:

```
C:\> setx HADOOP_HOME C:\Hadoop
```

Here is the equivalent using the Windows PowerShell prompt:

```
PS C:\>[Environment]::SetEnvironmentVariable("HADOOP_HOME", "C:\Hadoop", "User")
```

8. **Set up the local metastore.** You need to create a location and set the appropriate permissions to a local metastore. We discuss the role of the metastore specifically in Chapter 6, "SQL and NoSQL Programming with Spark," when we begin to look at Spark SQL. For now, just run the following commands from the Windows or PowerShell command prompt:

```
C:\> mkdir C:\tmp\hive
C:\> Hadoop\bin\winutils.exe chmod 777 /tmp/hive
```

9. **Test the installation.** Open a Windows command prompt or PowerShell session and change directories to the bin directory of your Spark installation, as follows:

```
C:\> cd C:\Spark\bin
```

At the subsequent prompt, enter the pyspark command to open an interactive Python Spark shell:

```
C:\Spark\bin> pyspark --master local
```

Figure 2.3 shows an example of what you should expect to see using Windows PowerShell.

Figure 2.3   PySpark in Windows PowerShell.

Enter quit() to exit the shell.

Now run the built-in Pi Estimator sample application by running the following from the command prompt:

```
C:\Spark\bin> spark-submit --class org.apache.spark.examples.SparkPi
  --master local C:\Spark\examples\jars\spark-examples*.jar 100
```

You now see a lot of informational logging messages; within these messages you should see something that resembles the following:

```
Pi is roughly 3.1413223141322315
```

Congratulations! You have just successfully installed and tested Spark on Windows.

Exploring the Spark Installation

It is worth getting familiar with the contents of the Spark installation directory, sometimes referred to as the SPARK_HOME. Table 2.1 provides an overview of the directories within the SPARK_HOME.

Table 2.1   **Spark Installation Contents**

Directory	Description
bin/	Contains all the commands/scripts to run Spark applications interactively through shell programs such as pyspark, spark-shell, spark-sql, and sparkR, or in batch mode using spark-submit.

Directory	Description
conf/	Contains templates for Spark configuration files, which you can use to set Spark configuration values (spark-defaults.conf.template), as well as a shell script used to set environment variables required for Spark processes (spark-env.sh.template). There are also configuration templates to control logging (log4j.properties.template), a metrics collection (metrics.properties.template), and a template for the slaves file (slaves.template), which controls which slave nodes can join the Spark cluster running in Standalone mode.
data/	Contains sample datasets used for testing the mllib, graphx, and streaming libraries within the Spark project (all of which are discussed later in this book).
examples/	Contains the source code and compiled assemblies (jar files) for all the examples shipped with the Spark release, including the Pi Estimator application used in previous examples. Sample programs are included in Java, Python, R, and Scala. You can also find the latest code for the included examples at https://github.com/apache/spark/tree/master/examples.
jars/	Contains the main assemblies for Spark as well as assemblies for support services used by Spark, such as snappy, py4j, parquet, and more. This directory is included in the CLASSPATH for Spark by default.
licenses/	Includes license files covering other included projects, such as Scala and JQuery. These files are for legal compliance purposes only and are not required to run Spark.
python/	Contains all the Python libraries required to run PySpark. You generally don't need to access these files directly.
R/	Contains the SparkR package and associated libraries and documentation. You will learn about SparkR in Chapter 8, "Introduction to Data Science and Machine Learning Using Spark."
sbin/	Contains administrative scripts to start and stop master and slave services for Spark clusters running in Standalone mode, locally or remotely, as well as start processes related to YARN and Mesos. You will use some of these scripts in the next section when you deploy a multi-node cluster in Standalone mode.
yarn/	Contains support libraries for Spark applications running on YARN. This includes the shuffle service, a support service Spark uses to move data between processes in a YARN cluster.

The remainder of this book references many of the directories listed in Table 2.1.

Deploying a Multi-Node Spark Standalone Cluster

Now that you have installed and tested a Spark installation in Local mode, it's time to unleash the true power of Spark by creating a fully distributed Spark cluster. For this exercise, you will use four Linux hosts to create a simple three-node cluster using the Standalone scheduler. Follow these steps:

1. **Plan a cluster topology and install Spark on multiple systems.** Because this is a distributed system, you need to install Spark, as shown in the previous exercises, on three additional hosts. In addition, you need to designate one host as the Spark Master and

the other hosts as Workers. For this exercise, the first host is named *sparkmaster*, and the additional hosts are names *sparkworker1*, *sparkworker2*, and *sparkworker3*.

2. **Configure networking.** All nodes in the Spark cluster need to communicate will all other hosts in the cluster. The easiest way to accomplish this is by using `hosts` files (entries for all hosts in `/etc/hosts` on each system). Ensure that each node can resolve the other. The `ping` command can be used for this; for example, here is how you use it from the *sparkmaster* host:

```
$ ping sparkworker1
```

3. **Create and edit a `spark-defaults.conf` file on each host.** To create and configure a `spark-defaults.conf` file on each node, run the following commands on the *sparkmaster* and *sparkworker* hosts:

```
$ cd $SPARK_HOME/conf
$ sudo cp spark-defaults.conf.template spark-defaults.conf
$ sudo sed -i "\$aspark.master\tspark://sparkmaster:7077" spark-defaults.conf
```

4. **Create and edit a `spark-env.sh` file on each host.** To create and configure a `spark-env.sh` file on each node, complete the following tasks on the *sparkmaster* and *sparkworker* hosts:

```
$ cd $SPARK_HOME/conf
$ sudo cp spark-env.sh.template spark-env.sh
$ sudo sed -i "\$aSPARK_MASTER_IP=sparkmaster" spark-env.sh
```

5. **Start the Spark Master.** On the *sparkmaster* host, run the following command:

```
$ sudo $SPARK_HOME/sbin/start-master.sh
```

Test the Spark Master process by viewing the Spark Master web UI at http://sparkmaster:8080/.

6. **Start the Spark Workers.** On each *sparkworker* node, run the following command:

```
$ sudo $SPARK_HOME/sbin/start-slave.sh spark://sparkmaster:7077
```

Check the Spark Worker UIs on http://sparkslave*N*:8081/.

7. **Test the multi-node cluster.** Run the built-in Pi Estimator example from the terminal of any node in the cluster:

```
$ spark-submit --class org.apache.spark.examples.SparkPi \
--master spark://sparkmaster:7077 \
--driver-memory 512m \
--executor-memory 512m \
--executor-cores 1 \
$SPARK_HOME/examples/jars/spark-examples*.jar 10000
```

You should see output similar to that from the previous exercises.

You could also enable passwordless SSH (Secure Shell) for the Spark Master to the Spark Workers. This is required to enable remote login for the slave daemon startup and shutdown actions.

Deploying Spark in the Cloud

The proliferation of public and private cloud technology, Software-as-a-Service (SaaS), Infrastructure-as-a-Service (IaaS), and Platform-as-a-Service (PaaS) have been game changers in terms of the way organizations deploy technology.

You can deploy Spark in the cloud to provide a fast, scalable, and elastic processing environment. Several methods are available to deploy Spark platforms, applications, and workloads in the cloud; the following sections explore them.

Amazon Web Services (AWS)

Amazon has spent years designing and building scalable infrastructure, platforms, services, and APIs to manage its vast business requirements. The majority of these services are exposed for public consumption (paid, of course!) through Amazon Web Services (AWS).

The AWS portfolio contains dozens of different services, from IaaS products such as Elastic Compute Cloud (EC2), storage services such as S3, and PaaS products such as Redshift. AWS compute resources can be provisioned on demand and paid for on an hourly basis. They are also available as "spot" instances, which use a market mechanism to offer lower usage costs by taking advantage of low-demand periods.

There are two primary methods for creating Spark clusters in AWS: EC2 and Elastic MapReduce (EMR). To use any of the AWS deployment options, you need a valid AWS account and API keys if you are using the AWS software development kit (SDK) or command line interface (CLI).

Spark on EC2

You can launch Spark clusters (or Hadoop clusters capable of running Spark) on EC2 instances in AWS. Typically this is done within a Virtual Private Cloud (VPC), which allows you to isolate cluster nodes from public networks. Deployment of Spark clusters on EC2 usually involves deployment of configuration management tools such as Ansible, Chef, Puppet, or AWS CloudFormation, which can automate deployment routines using an Infrastructure-as-Code (IaC) discipline.

In addition, there are several predeveloped Amazon Machine Images (AMIs) available in the AWS Marketplace; these have a pre-installed and configured release of Spark.

You can also create Spark clusters on containers by using the EC2 Container Service. There are numerous options to create these, from existing projects available in GitHub and elsewhere.

Spark on EMR

Elastic MapReduce (EMR) is Amazon's Hadoop-as-a-Service platform. EMR clusters are essentially Hadoop clusters with a variety of configurable ecosystem projects, such as Hive, Pig, Presto, Zeppelin, and, of course, Spark.

You can provision EMR clusters using the AWS Management Console or via the AWS APIs. Options for creating EMR clusters include number of nodes, node instance types, Hadoop distribution, and additional applications to install, including Spark.

EMR clusters are designed to read data and output results directly to and from S3. EMR clusters are intended to be provisioned on demand, run a discrete work flow or job flow, and terminate. They do have local storage, but they are not intended to run in perpetuity. Therefore, you should use this local storage only for transient data.

Listing 2.5 demonstrates creating a simple three-node EMR cluster with Spark and Zeppelin using the AWS CLI.

Listing 2.5   **Creating an EMR Cluster by Using the AWS CLI**

```
$ aws emr create-cluster \
--name "MyEMRCluster" \
--instance-type m1.xlarge \
--instance-count 3 \
--ec2-attributes KeyName=YOUR_KEY \
--use-default-roles \
--applications Name=Spark Name=Zeppelin-Sandbox
```

Figure 2.4 shows an EMR cluster console session.

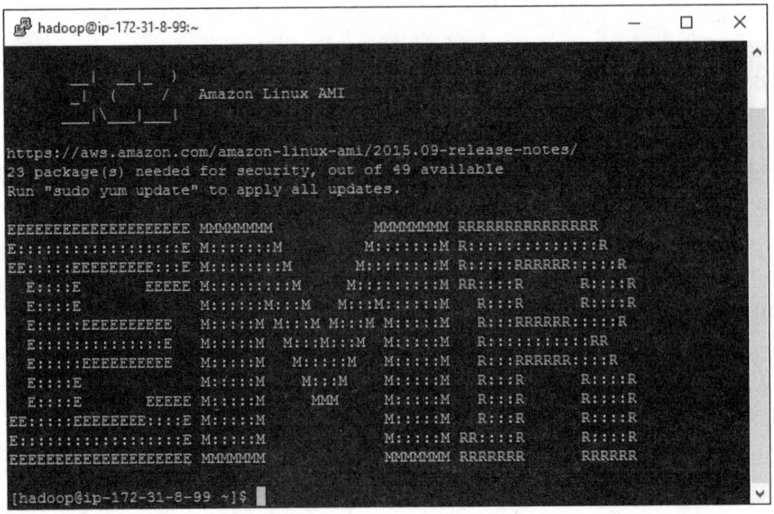

Figure 2.4   EMR console.

Figure 2.5 shows the Zeppelin notebook interface included with the EMR deployment, which can be used as a Spark programming environment.

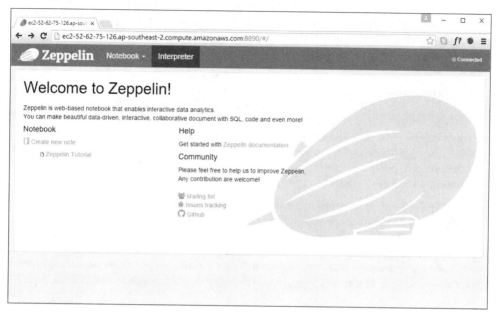

Figure 2.5   Zeppelin interface.

Using EMR is a quick and scalable deployment method for Spark. For more information about EMR, go to https://aws.amazon.com/elasticmapreduce/.

Google Cloud Platform (GCP)

Much like Amazon does with AWS, Google deploys its vast array of global services, such as Gmail and Maps, using its cloud computing platform known as the Google Cloud Platform (GCP). Google's cloud offering supports most of the services available in AWS, but the company has many other offerings as well, including making available TPUs (Tensor Processing Units).

TensorFlow

TensorFlow is an open source software library that Google created specifically for training *neural networks*, an approach to *deep learning*. Neural networks are used to discover patterns, sequences, and relations in much the same way that the human brain does.

As with AWS, you could choose to deploy Spark using Google's IaaS offering, Compute, which requires you to deploy the underlying infrastructure. However, there is a managed Hadoop and Spark platform available with GCP called Cloud Dataproc, and it may be an easier option.

Cloud Dataproc offers a similarly managed software stack to AWS EMR, and you can deploy it to a cluster of nodes.

Databricks

Databricks is an integrated cloud-based Spark workspace that allows you to launch managed Spark clusters and ingest and interact with data from S3 or other relational database or flat-file data sources, either in the cloud or from your environment. The Databricks platform uses your AWS credentials to create its required infrastructure components, so you effectively have ownership of these assets in your AWS account. Databricks provides the deployment, management, and user/application interface framework for a cloud-based Spark platform in AWS.

Databricks has several pricing plans available, with different features spanning support levels, security and access control options, GitHub integration, and more. Pricing is subscription based, with a flat monthly fee plus nominal utilization charges (charged per hour per node). Databricks offers a 14-day free trial period to get started. You are responsible for the instance costs incurred in AWS for Spark clusters deployed using the Databricks platform; however, Databricks allows you to use discounted spot instances to minimize AWS costs. For the latest pricing and subscription information, go to https://databricks.com/product/pricing.

Databricks provides a simple deployment and user interface, shown in Figure 2.6, which abstracts the underlying infrastructure and security complexities involved in setting up a secure Spark environment in AWS. The Databricks management console allows you to create notebooks, similar to the Zeppelin notebook deployed with AWS EMR. There are APIs available from Databricks for deployment and management as well. These notebooks are automatically associated with your Spark cluster and provide seamless programmatic access to Spark functions using Python, Scala, SQL, or R.

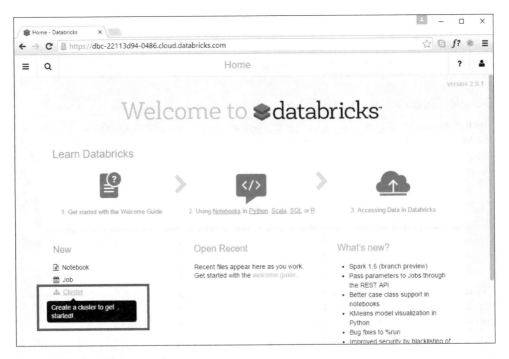

Figure 2.6   Databricks console.

Databricks has its own distributed filesystem called the Databricks File System (DBFS). DBFS allows you to mount existing S3 buckets and make them seamlessly available in your Spark work-space. You can also cache data on the solid-state disks (SSDs) of your worker nodes to speed up access. The `dbutils` library included in your Spark workspace allows you to configure and inter-act with the DBFS.

The Databricks platform and management console allows you to create data objects as tables—which is conceptually similar to tables in a relational database—from a variety of sources, includ-ing AWS S3 buckets, Java Database Connectivity (JDBC) data sources, the DBFS, or by uploading your own files using drag-and-drop functionality. You can also create jobs by using the Databricks console, and you can run them non-interactively on a user-defined schedule.

The core AMP Labs team that created—and continues to be a major contributor to—the Spark project founded the Databricks company and platform. Spark releases and new features are typi-cally available in the Databricks platform before they are shipped with other distributions, such as CDH or HDP. More information about Databricks is available at http://databricks.com.

Summary

In this chapter, you have learned how to install Spark and considered the various prerequisite requirements and dependencies. You have also learned about the various deployment modes available for deploying a Spark cluster, including Local, Spark Standalone, YARN, and Mesos. In the first exercise, you set up a fully functional Spark Standalone cluster. In this chapter you also looked at some of the cloud deployment options available for deploying Spark clusters, such as AWS EC2 or EMR clusters, Google Cloud Dataproc, and Databricks. Any of the deployments discussed or demonstrated in this chapter can be used for programming exercises throughout the remainder of this book—and beyond.

Understanding the Spark Cluster Architecture

It is not the beauty of a building you should look at; it's the construction of the foundation that will stand the test of time.

David Allan Coe, American songwriter

In This Chapter:

- Detailed overview of the Spark application and cluster components
- Spark resource schedulers and Cluster Managers
- How Spark applications are scheduled on YARN clusters
- Spark deployment modes

Before you begin your journey as a Spark programmer, you should have a solid understanding of the Spark application architecture and how applications are executed on a Spark cluster. This chapter closely examines the components of a Spark application, looks at how these components work together, and looks at how Spark applications run on Standalone and YARN clusters.

Anatomy of a Spark Application

A Spark application contains several components, all of which exist whether you're running Spark on a single machine or across a cluster of hundreds or thousands of nodes.

Each component has a specific role in executing a Spark program. Some of these roles, such as the client components, are passive during execution; other roles are active in the execution of the program, including components executing computation functions.

The components of a Spark application are the *Driver*, the *Master*, the *Cluster Manager*, and the *Executor(s)*, which run on worker nodes, or *Workers*. Figure 3.1 shows all the Spark components in the context of a Spark Standalone application. You will learn more about each component and its function in more detail later in this chapter.

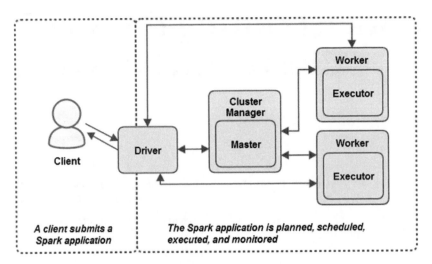

Figure 3.1   Spark Standalone cluster application components.

All Spark components, including the Driver, Master, and Executor processes, run in Java virtual machines (JVMs). A JVM is a cross-platform runtime engine that can execute instructions compiled into Java bytecode. Scala, which Spark is written in, compiles into bytecode and runs on JVMs.

It is important to distinguish between Spark's runtime application components and the locations and node types on which they run. These components run in different places using different deployment modes, so don't think of these components in physical node or instance terms. For instance, when running Spark on YARN, there would be several variations of Figure 3.1. However, all the components pictured are still involved in the application and have the same roles.

Spark Driver

The life of a Spark application starts and finishes with the Spark Driver. The Driver is the process that clients use to submit applications in Spark. The Driver is also responsible for planning and coordinating the execution of the Spark program and returning status and/or results (data) to the client. The Driver can physically reside on a client or on a node in the cluster, as you will see later.

SparkSession

The Spark Driver is responsible for creating the *SparkSession*. The SparkSession object represents a connection to a Spark cluster. The SparkSession is instantiated at the beginning of a Spark application, including the interactive shells, and is used for the entirety of the program.

Prior to Spark 2.0, entry points for Spark applications included the SparkContext, used for Spark core applications; the SQLContext and HiveContext, used with Spark SQL applications; and the StreamingContext, used for Spark Streaming applications. The SparkSession object introduced in Spark 2.0 combines all these objects into a single entry point that can be used for all Spark applications.

Through its SparkContext and SparkConf child objects, the SparkSession object contains all the runtime configuration properties set by the user, including configuration properties such as the Master, application name, number of Executors, and more. Figure 3.2 shows the SparkSession object and some of its configuration properties within a pyspark shell.

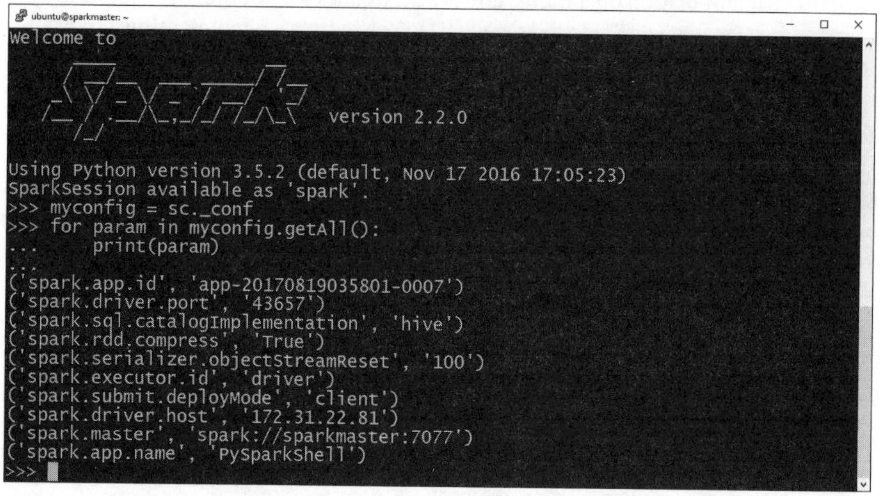

Figure 3.2   SparkSession properties.

SparkSession Name

The object name for the SparkSession instance is arbitrary. By default, the SparkSession instantiation in the Spark interactive shells is named spark. For consistency, you always instantiate the SparkSession as spark; however, the name is up to the developer's discretion.

Listing 3.1 demonstrates how to create a SparkSession within a non-interactive Spark application, such as a program submitted using spark-submit.

Listing 3.1   **Creating a SparkSession**

```
from pyspark.sql import SparkSession
spark = SparkSession.builder \
    .master("spark://sparkmaster:7077") \
    .appName("My Spark Application") \
```

```
    .config("spark.submit.deployMode", "client") \
    .getOrCreate()
numlines = spark.sparkContext.textFile("file:///opt/spark/licenses") \
    .count()
print("The total number of lines is " + str(numlines))
```

Application Planning

One of the main functions of the Driver is to plan the application. The Driver takes the application processing input and plans the execution of the program. The Driver takes all the requested *transformations* (data manipulation operations) and *actions* (requests for output or prompts to execute programs) and creates a *directed acyclic graph* (*DAG*) of *nodes*, each representing a transformational or computational step.

Directed Acyclic Graph (DAG)

A DAG is a mathematical construct that is commonly used in computer science to represent dataflows and their dependencies. DAGs contain vertices, or nodes, and edges. Vertices in a dataflow context are steps in the process flow. Edges in a DAG connect vertices to one another in a directed orientation and in such a way that it is impossible to have circular references.

A Spark application DAG consists of *tasks* and *stages*. A task is the smallest unit of schedulable work in a Spark program. A stage is a set of tasks that can be run together. Stages are dependent upon one another; in other words, there are *stage dependencies*.

In a process scheduling sense, DAGs are not unique to Spark. For instance, they are used in other Big Data ecosystem projects, such as Tez, Drill, and Presto for scheduling. DAGs are fundamental to Spark, so it is worth being familiar with the concept.

Application Orchestration

The Driver also coordinates the running of stages and tasks defined in the DAG. Key driver activities involved in the scheduling and running of tasks include the following:

- Keeping track of available resources to execute tasks
- Scheduling tasks to run "close" to the data where possible (the concept of data locality)

Other Functions

In addition to planning and orchestrating the execution of a Spark program, the Driver is also responsible for returning the results from an application. These could be return codes or data in the case of an action that requests data to be returned to the client (for example, an interactive query).

The Driver also serves the application UI on port 4040, as shown in Figure 3.3. This UI is created automatically; it is independent of the code submitted or how it was submitted (that is, interactive using pyspark or non-interactive using spark-submit).

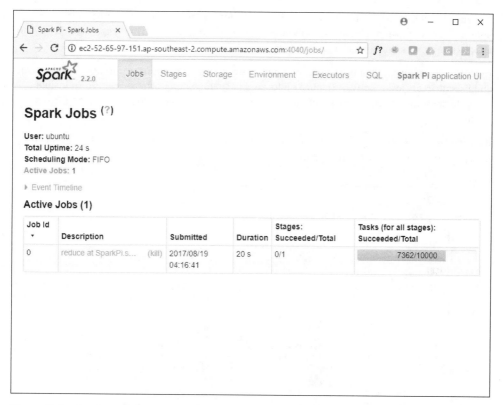

Figure 3.3   Spark application UI.

If subsequent applications launch on the same host, successive ports are used for the application UI (for example, 4041, 4042, and so on).

Spark Workers and Executors

Spark Executors are the processes on which Spark DAG tasks run. Executors reserve CPU and memory resources on slave nodes, or Workers, in a Spark cluster. An Executor is dedicated to a specific Spark application and terminated when the application completes. A Spark program normally consists of many Executors, often working in parallel.

Typically, a Worker node—which hosts the Executor process—has a finite or fixed number of Executors allocated at any point in time. Therefore, a cluster—being a known number of nodes—has a finite number of Executors available to run at any given time. If an application requires Executors in excess of the physical capacity of the cluster, they are scheduled to start as other Executors complete and release their resources.

As mentioned earlier in this chapter, JVMs host Spark Executors. The JVM for an Executor is allocated a *heap*, which is a dedicated memory space in which to store and manage objects.

The amount of memory committed to the JVM heap for an Executor is set by the property spark.executor.memory or as the --executor-memory argument to the pyspark, spark-shell, or spark-submit commands.

Executors store output data from tasks in memory or on disk. It is important to note that Workers and Executors are aware only of the tasks allocated to them, whereas the Driver is responsible for understanding the complete set of tasks and the respective dependencies that comprise an application.

By using the Spark application UI on port 404x of the Driver host, you can inspect Executors for the application, as shown in Figure 3.4.

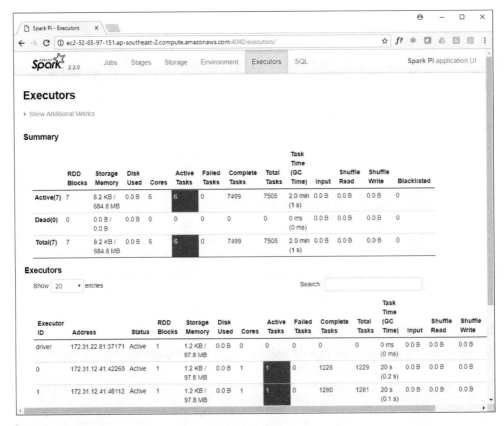

Figure 3.4   Executors tab in the Spark application UI.

For Spark Standalone cluster deployments, a worker node exposes a user interface on port 8081, as shown in Figure 3.5.

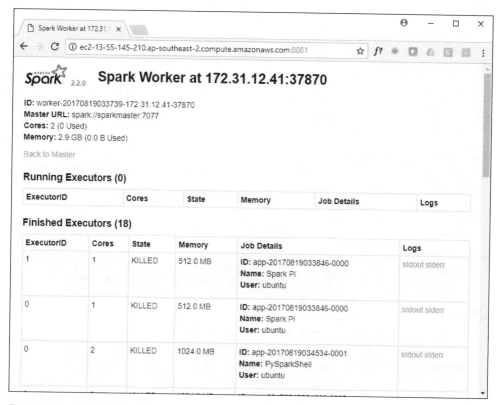

Figure 3.5   Spark Worker UI.

The Spark Master and Cluster Manager

The Spark Driver plans and coordinates the set of tasks required to run a Spark application. The tasks themselves run in Executors, which are hosted on Worker nodes.

The Master and the Cluster Manager are the central processes that monitor, reserve, and allocate the distributed cluster resources (or containers, in the case of YARN or Mesos) on which the Executors run. The Master and the Cluster Manager can be separate processes, or they can combine into one process, as is the case when running Spark in Standalone mode.

Spark Master

The Spark Master is the process that requests resources in the cluster and makes them available to the Spark Driver. In all deployment modes, the Master negotiates resources or containers with Worker nodes or slave nodes and tracks their status and monitors their progress.

When running Spark in Standalone mode, the Spark Master process serves a web UI on port 8080 on the Master host, as shown in Figure 3.6.

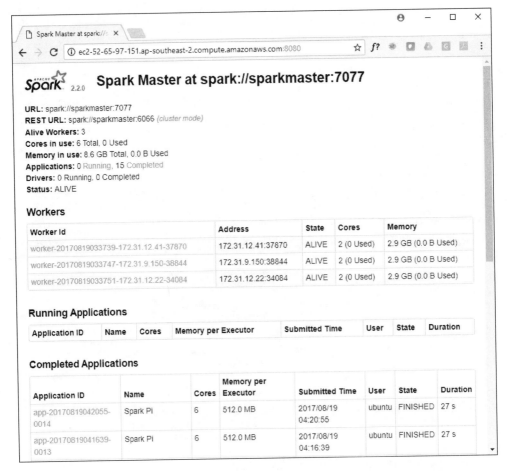

Figure 3.6   Spark Master UI.

Spark Master Versus Spark Driver

It is important to distinguish the runtime functions of the Driver and the Master. The name *Master* may be inferred to mean that this process is governing the execution of the application—but this is not the case. The Master simply requests resources and makes those resources available to the Driver. Although the Master monitors the status and health of these resources, it is not involved in the execution of the application and the coordination of its tasks and stages. That is the job of the Driver.

Cluster Manager

The Cluster Manager is the process responsible for monitoring the Worker nodes and reserving resources on these nodes upon request by the Master. The Master then makes these cluster resources available to the Driver in the form of Executors.

As discussed earlier, the Cluster Manager can be separate from the Master process. This is the case when running Spark on Mesos or YARN. In the case of Spark running in Standalone mode, the Master process also performs the functions of the Cluster Manager. Effectively, it acts as its own Cluster Manager.

A good example of the Cluster Manager function is the YARN ResourceManager process for Spark applications running on Hadoop clusters. The ResourceManager schedules, allocates, and monitors the health of containers running on YARN NodeManagers. Spark applications then use these containers to host Executor processes, as well as the Master process if the application is running in `cluster` mode; we will look at this shortly.

Spark Applications Using the Standalone Scheduler

In Chapter 2, "Deploying Spark," you learned about the Standalone scheduler as a deployment option for Spark. You also deployed a fully functional multi-node Spark Standalone cluster in one of the exercises in Chapter 2. As discussed earlier, in a Spark cluster running in Standalone mode, the Spark Master process performs the Cluster Manager function as well, governing available resources on the cluster and granting them to the Master process for use in a Spark application.

Spark Applications Running on YARN

As discussed previously, Hadoop is a very popular and common deployment platform for Spark. Some industry pundits believe that Spark will soon supplant MapReduce as the primary processing platform for applications in Hadoop. Spark applications on YARN share the same runtime architecture but have some slight differences in implementation.

ResourceManager as the Cluster Manager

In contrast to the Standalone scheduler, the Cluster Manager in a YARN cluster is the YARN ResourceManager. The ResourceManager monitors resource usage and availability across all nodes in a cluster. Clients submit Spark applications to the YARN ResourceManager. The ResourceManager allocates the first container for the application, a special container called the *ApplicationMaster*.

ApplicationMaster as the Spark Master

The ApplicationMaster is the Spark Master process. As the Master process does in other cluster deployments, the ApplicationMaster negotiates resources between the application Driver and the Cluster Manager (or ResourceManager in this case); it then makes these resources (containers) available to the Driver for use as Executors to run tasks and store data for the application. The ApplicationMaster remains for the lifetime of the application.

Deployment Modes for Spark Applications Running on YARN

Two deployment modes can be used when submitting Spark applications to a YARN cluster: Client mode and Cluster mode. Let's look at them now.

Client Mode

In Client mode, the Driver process runs on the client submitting the application. It is essentially unmanaged; if the Driver host fails, the application fails. Client mode is supported for both interactive shell sessions (pyspark, spark-shell, and so on) and non-interactive application submission (spark-submit). Listing 3.2 shows how to start a pyspark session using the Client deployment mode.

Listing 3.2 **YARN Client Deployment Mode**

```
$SPARK_HOME/bin/pyspark \
--master yarn-client \
--num-executors 1 \
--driver-memory 512m \
--executor-memory 512m \
--executor-cores 1
# OR
$SPARK_HOME/bin/pyspark \
--master yarn \
--deploy-mode client \
--num-executors 1 \
--driver-memory 512m \
--executor-memory 512m \
--executor-cores 1
```

Figure 3.7 provides an overview of a Spark application running on YARN in Client mode.

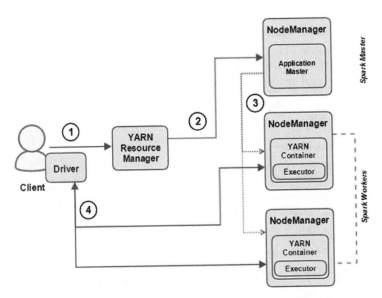

Figure 3.7 Spark application running in YARN Client mode.

The steps shown in Figure 3.7 are described here:

1. The client submits a Spark application to the Cluster Manager (the YARN ResourceManager). The Driver process, SparkSession, and SparkContext are created and run on the client.

2. The ResourceManager assigns an ApplicationMaster (the Spark Master) for the application.

3. The ApplicationMaster requests containers to be used for Executors from the ResourceManager. With the containers assigned, the Executors spawn.

4. The Driver, located on the client, then communicates with the Executors to marshal processing of tasks and stages of the Spark program. The Driver returns the progress, results, and status to the client.

The Client deployment mode is the simplest mode to use. However, it lacks the resiliency required for most production applications.

Cluster Mode

In contrast to the Client deployment mode, with a Spark application running in YARN Cluster mode, the Driver itself runs on the cluster as a subprocess of the ApplicationMaster. This provides resiliency: If the ApplicationMaster process hosting the Driver fails, it can be re-instantiated on another node in the cluster.

Listing 3.3 shows how to submit an application by using `spark-submit` and the YARN Cluster deployment mode. Because the Driver is an asynchronous process running in the cluster, Cluster mode is not supported for the interactive shell applications (`pyspark` and `spark-shell`).

Listing 3.3 **YARN Cluster Deployment Mode**

```
$SPARK_HOME/bin/spark-submit \
--master yarn-cluster \
--num-executors 1 \
--driver-memory 512m \
--executor-memory 512m \
--executor-cores 1
$SPARK_HOME/examples/src/main/python/pi.py 10000
# OR
$SPARK_HOME/bin/spark-submit \
--master yarn \
--deploy-mode cluster \
--num-executors 1 \
--driver-memory 512m \
--executor-memory 512m \
--executor-cores 1
$SPARK_HOME/examples/src/main/python/pi.py 10000
```

Figure 3.8 provides an overview of a Spark application running on YARN in Cluster mode.

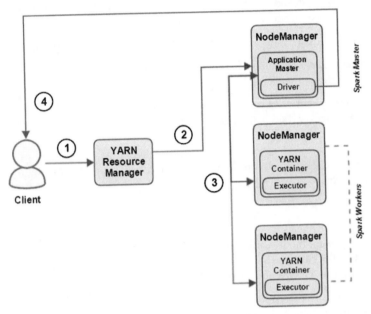

Figure 3.8   Spark application running in YARN Cluster mode.

The steps shown in Figure 3.8 are described here:

1. The client, a user process that invokes spark-submit, submits a Spark application to the Cluster Manager (the YARN ResourceManager).

2. The ResourceManager assigns an ApplicationMaster (the Spark Master) for the application. The Driver process is created on the same cluster node.

3. The ApplicationMaster requests containers for Executors from the ResourceManager. Executors are spawned within the containers allocated to the ApplicationMaster by the ResourceManager. The Driver then communicates with the Executors to marshal processing of tasks and stages of the Spark program.

4. The Driver, running on a node in the cluster, returns progress, results, and status to the client.

The Spark application web UI, as shown previously, is available from the ApplicationMaster host in the cluster; a link to this user interface is available from the YARN ResourceManager UI.

Local Mode Revisited

In Local mode, the Driver, the Master, and the Executor all run in a single JVM. As discussed earlier in this chapter, this is useful for development, unit testing, and debugging, but it has limited use for running production applications because it is not distributed and does not scale. Furthermore, failed tasks in a Spark application running in Local mode are not re-executed by default. You can override this behavior, however.

When running Spark in Local mode, the application UI is available at http://localhost:4040. The Master and Worker UIs are not available when running in Local mode.

Summary

In this chapter, you have learned about the Spark runtime application and cluster architecture, the components or a Spark application, and the functions of these components. The components of a Spark application include the Driver, Master, Cluster Manager, and Executors. The Driver is the process that the client interacts with when launching a Spark application, either through one of the interactive shells or through the `spark-submit` script. The Driver is responsible for creating the SparkSession object (the entry point for any Spark application) and planning an application by creating a DAG consisting of tasks and stages. The Driver communicates with a Master, which in turn communicates with a Cluster Manager to allocate application runtime resources (containers) on which Executors will run. Executors are specific to a given application and run all tasks for the application; they also store output data from completed tasks. Spark's runtime architecture is essentially the same regardless of the cluster resource scheduler used (Standalone, YARN, Mesos, and so on).

Now that we have explored Spark's cluster architecture, it's time to put the concepts into action starting in the next chapter.

4

Learning Spark Programming Basics

Talk is cheap. Show me the code.

Linus Torvalds, Finnish-American creator of Linux

In This Chapter:

- Resilient Distributed Datasets (RDDs)
- How to load data into Spark RDDs
- Transformation and actions on RDDs
- How to perform operations on multiple RDDs

Now that we've covered Spark's runtime architecture and how to deploy Spark, it's time to learn Spark programming in Python, starting with the basics. This chapter discusses a foundational concept in Spark programming and execution: Resilient Distributed Datasets (RDDs). You will also learn how to work with the Spark API, including the fundamental Spark transformations and actions and their usage. This is an intense chapter, but by the end of it, you will have all the basic building blocks you need to create any Spark application.

Introduction to RDDs

A Resilient Distributed Dataset (RDD) is the most fundamental data object used in Spark programming. RDDs are datasets within a Spark application, including the initial dataset(s) loaded, any intermediate dataset(s), and the final resultant dataset(s). Most Spark applications load an RDD with external data and then create new RDDs by performing operations on the existing RDDs; these operations are *transformations*. This process is repeated until an output operation is ultimately required—for instance, to write the results of an application to a filesystem; these types of operations are *actions*.

RDDs are essentially distributed collections of objects that represent the data used in Spark programs. In the case of PySpark, RDDs consist of distributed Python objects, such as lists, tuples, and dictionaries. Objects within RDDs, such as elements in a list, can be of any object type, including primitive data types such as integers, floating point numbers, and strings, as well as complex types such as tuples, dictionaries, or other lists. If you are using the Scala or Java APIs, RDDs consist of collections of Scala and Java objects, respectively.

Although there are options for persisting RDDs to disk, RDDs are predominantly stored in memory, or at least they are intended to be stored in memory. Because one of the initial uses for Spark was to support machine learning, Spark's RDDs provided a restricted form of shared memory that could make efficient reuse of data for successive and iterative operations.

Moreover, one of the main downsides of Hadoop's implementation of MapReduce was its persistence of intermediate data to disk and the copying of this data between nodes at runtime. Although the MapReduce distributed processing method of sharing data did provide resiliency and fault tolerance, it was at the cost of latency. This design limitation was one of the major catalysts for the Spark project. As data volumes increased along with the necessity for real-time data processing and insights, Spark's mainly in-memory processing framework based on RDDs grew in popularity.

The term *Resilient Distributed Dataset* is an accurate and succinct descriptor for the concept. Here's how it breaks down:

- **Resilient:** RDDs are resilient, meaning that if a node performing an operation in Spark is lost, the dataset can be reconstructed. This is because Spark knows the lineage of each RDD, which is the sequence of steps to create the RDD.

- **Distributed:** RDDs are distributed, meaning the data in RDDs is divided into one or many partitions and distributed as in-memory collections of objects across Worker nodes in the cluster. As mentioned earlier in this chapter, RDDs provide an effective form of shared memory to exchange data between processes (Executors) on different nodes (Workers).

- **Dataset:** RDDs are datasets that consist of records. Records are uniquely identifiable data collections within a dataset. A record can be a collection of fields similar to a row in a table in a relational database, a line of text in a file, or multiple other formats. RDDs are created such that each partition contains a unique set of records and can be operated on independently. This is an example of the *shared nothing* approach discussed in Chapter 1.

Another key property of RDDs is their immutability, which means that after they are instantiated and populated with data, they cannot be updated. Instead, new RDDs are created by performing transformations such as map or `filter` functions, discussed later in this chapter, on existing RDDs.

Actions are the other operations performed on RDDs. Actions produce output that can be in the form of data from an RDD returned to a Driver program, or they can save the contents of an RDD to a filesystem (local, HDFS, S3, or other). There are many other actions as well, including returning a count of the number of records in an RDD.

Listing 4.1 shows a sample Spark program loading data into an RDD, creating a new RDD using a filter transformation, and then using an action to save the resultant RDD to disk. We will look at each of these operations in this chapter.

Listing 4.1   **Sample PySpark Program to Search for Errors in Log Files**

```
# load log files from local filesystem
logfilesrdd = sc.textFile("file:///var/log/hadoop/hdfs/hadoop-hdfs-*")
# filter log records for errors only
onlyerrorsrdd = logfilesrdd.filter(lambda line: "ERROR" in line)
# save onlyerrorsrdd as a file
onlyerrorsrdd.saveAsTextFile("file:///tmp/onlyerrorsrdd")
```

You can find more detail about RDD concepts in the University of California, Berkeley, paper "Resilient Distributed Datasets: A Fault-Tolerant Abstraction for In-Memory Cluster Computing," https://amplab.cs.berkeley.edu/publication/resilient-distributed-datasets-a-fault-tolerant-abstraction-for-in-memory-cluster-computing/.

Loading Data into RDDs

RDDs are effectively created after they are populated with data. This can be the result of transformations on an existing RDD being written into a new RDD as part of a Spark program.

To start any Spark routine, you need to initialize at least one RDD with data from an external source. This initial RDD is then used to create further intermediate RDDs or the final RDD through a series of transformations and actions. The initial RDD can be created in several ways, including the following:

- Loading data from a file or files
- Loading data from a data source, such as a SQL or NoSQL datastore
- Loading data programmatically
- Loading data from a stream, as discussed in Chapter 7, "Stream Processing and Messaging Using Spark"

Creating an RDD from a File or Files

Spark provides API methods to create RDDs from a file, files, or the contents of a directory. Files can be of various formats, from unstructured text files, to semi-structured files such as JSON files, to structured data sources such as CSV files. Spark also supports several common serialized binary encoded formats, such as SequenceFiles and protocol buffers (protobufs), as well as columnar file formats such as Parquet and ORC (which we will discuss later).

Spark and File Compression

Spark includes native support for several lossless compression formats. Spark can seamlessly read from common compressed file formats, including GZIP and ZIP (or any other compressed archives created using the DEFLATE compression method), as well as BZIP2 compressed archives.

Spark also provides native codecs, which are libraries for compressing and decompressing data, that enable both reading and writing of compressed files. Built-in codecs include LZ4 and LZF, which are LZ77-based lossless compression formats, and Snappy.

Snappy is a fast, splittable, low-CPU data compression and decompression library from Google that is commonly used in the Hadoop core and ecosystem projects. Snappy is used by default for compressing data internal to Spark, such as the data in RDD partitions exchanged across the network between Workers.

Splittable Versus Non-splittable Compression Formats

It's important to distinguish between splittable and non-splittable compression formats when using distributed processing platforms such as Spark or Hadoop.

Splittable compression formats are indexed so they can split—typically on block boundaries—without compromising the integrity of the archive. Non-splittable formats are not indexed and cannot split. This means that a non-splittable archive must be readable in its entirety on one system because it cannot be distributed.

Although common desktop compression formats such as ZIP and GZIP can achieve high rates of compression, they are not splittable. This may be okay for small files containing lookup data, but for larger datasets, splittable compression formats such as Snappy or LZO are preferable. In some cases, you are better off decompressing files altogether before ingesting them into a distributed filesystem such as HDFS.

Data Locality with RDDs

By default, Spark tries to read data into an RDD from the nodes close to it. Because Spark usually accesses distributed partitioned data, such as data from HDFS or S3, to optimize transformation operations, it creates partitions to hold the underlying blocks from the distributed filesystem. Figure 4.1 depicts how blocks from a file in a distributed filesystem such as HDFS are used to create RDD partitions on Workers, which are collocated with the data.

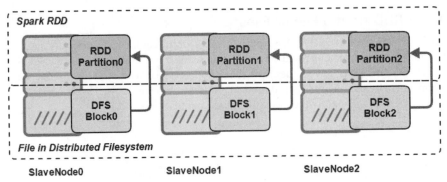

Figure 4.1   Loading an RDD from a text file in a distributed filesystem.

Loading RDDs from a Local Filesystem

If you are not using a distributed filesystem—for instance, if you are creating an RDD from a file on your local filesystem—you need to ensure that the file you are loading is available in the same relative path on all worker nodes in the cluster. Otherwise, you will get the following error:

```
java.io.FileNotFoundException: File does not exist
```

For this reason, it's preferable to use a distributed filesystem such as HDFS or S3 as a file-based source for Spark RDDs; in this case, you upload a file from your local filesystem to the distributed system first and then create the RDD from the distributed object, if possible. Another alternative approach to using a local filesystem is to use a shared network filesystem instead.

Methods for Creating RDDs from a Text File or Files

The Spark methods for creating an RDD from a file or files support several filesystems. The scheme in the URI specifies these filesystems. This scheme is the prefix followed by://. You see this all the time with Internet resources referred to by the scheme http:// or https://. Table 4.1 summarizes schemes and URI structures for common filesystems supported by Spark.

Table 4.1   **Filesystem Schemes and URI Structures**

Filesystem	URI Structure
Local filesystem	file:///path
HDFS*	hdfs://hdfs_path
Amazon S3*	s3://bucket/path (also used are s3a and s3n)
OpenStack Swift*	swift://container.PROVIDER/path

* Requires filesystem configuration parameters to be set.

You can use text files and the methods described in the following sections to create RDDs.

textFile()

Syntax:

```
sc.textFile(name, minPartitions=None, use_unicode=True)
```

The `textFile()` method is used to create RDDs from files (compressed or uncompressed), directories, or glob patterns (file patterns with wildcards).

The `name` argument specifies the path or glob to be referenced, including the filesystem scheme, as shown in Table 4.1.

The `minPartitions` argument determines the number of partitions to create. By default, if you are using HDFS, each block of the file (typically 128MB) creates a single partition, as demonstrated in Figure 4.1. You can request more partitions than there are blocks; however, any number of partitions specified that is less than the number of blocks will revert to the default behavior of one block to one partition.

The use_unicode argument specifies whether to use Unicode or UTF-8 as the character encoding scheme.

The minPartitions and use_unicode arguments are optional as they have default values configured. In most cases, it's not necessary to supply these parameters explicitly unless you need to override the defaults.

Consider the Hadoop filesystem directory shown in Figure 4.2.

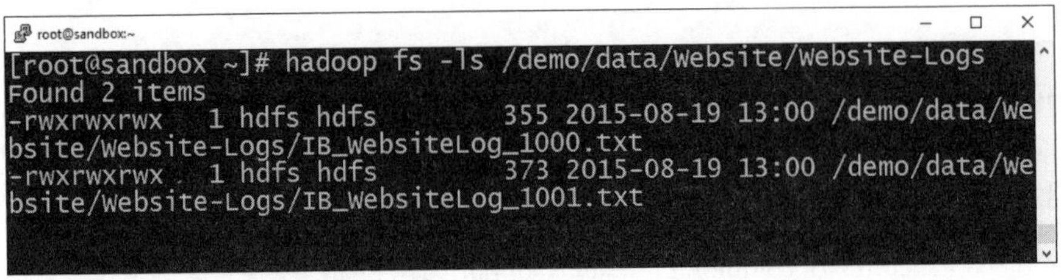

Figure 4.2   HDFS directory listing.

To read files in HDFS from Spark, the HADOOP_CONF_DIR environment variable must be set on all worker nodes of the cluster. The Hadoop config directory contains all the information used by Spark to connect to the appropriate HDFS cluster. You can set this automatically by using the spark-env.sh script located in the conf/ directory of each Spark installation. The command used to set this variable on Linux systems is as follows:

```
export HADOOP_CONF_DIR=/etc/hadoop/conf
```

Listing 4.2 provides examples of the textFile() method loading the data from the HDFS directory pictured in Figure 4.2.

Listing 4.2   **Creating RDDs Using the `textFile()` Method**

```
# load the contents of the entire directory
logs = sc.textFile("hdfs:///demo/data/Website/Website-Logs/")
# load an individual file
logs = sc.textFile("hdfs:///demo/data/Website/Website-Logs/IB_WebsiteLog_1001.txt")
# load a file or files using a glob pattern
logs = sc.textFile("hdfs:///demo/data/Website/Website-Logs/*_1001.txt")
```

In each of the examples in Listing 4.2, an RDD named logs is created, with each line of the file represented as a record.

wholeTextFiles()

Syntax:

```
sc.wholeTextFiles(path, minPartitions=None, use_unicode=True)
```

The wholeTextFiles() method lets you read a directory containing multiple files. Each file is represented as a record consisting of a key containing the filename and a value containing the contents of the file. In contrast, when reading all files in a directory with the textFile() method, each line of each file represents a separate record with no context of the line's file origin. Typically with event processing, the originating filename is not required because the record contains a timestamp field.

As each record contains the contents of the entire file with the wholeTextFiles() method, this method is intended for use with small files. The minPartitions and use_unicode arguments behave similarly to the textFile() method.

Using the HDFS directory shown in Figure 4.2, Listing 4.3 provides an example of the wholeTextFiles() method.

Listing 4.3   Creating RDDs by Using the wholeTextFiles() Method

```
# load the contents of the entire directory into key/value pairs
logs = sc.wholeTextFiles("hdfs:///demo/data/Website/Website-Logs/")
```

To demonstrate the difference between the textFile() and wholeTextFiles() methods in Spark, let's look at an example. This is an example you can try for yourself on any Spark installation. The Spark installation includes a directory named licenses that contains license files for all the open source projects used within the Spark project (for example, Scala).

Using the licenses directory as a source of text files to load different RDDs, Listing 4.4 shows the difference between the textFile() and wholeTextFiles() methods.

Listing 4.4   Comparing the textFile() and wholeTextFiles() Methods

```
# load the contents of the entire directory into an RDD named licensefiles
licensefiles = sc.textFile("file:///opt/spark/licenses/")
# inspect the object created
licensefiles
# returns:
#   file:///opt/spark/licenses/ MapPartitionsRDD[1] at textFile at
#   NativeMethodAccessorImpl.java:0
licensefiles.take(1)
# returns a list containing the first line of the first file read in the directory:
#   [u'The MIT License (MIT)']
licensefiles.getNumPartitions()
# there is a partition created for each file in the directory, in this case the
# return value is 36
licensefiles.count()
# this action will count the combined total number of lines in all the files, in
# this case the return value is 1075

# now let's perform a similar exercise using the same directory using the
# wholeTextFiles() method instead
```

```
licensefile_pairs = sc.wholeTextFiles("file:///opt/spark/licenses/")
# inspect the object created
licensefile_pairs
# returns:
#    org.apache.spark.api.java.JavaPairRDD@3f714d2d
licensefile_pairs.take(1)
# returns the first key/value pair as a list of tuples, with the key being each file
# and the value being the entire contents of that file:
#    [(u'file:/opt/spark/licenses/LICENSE-scopt.txt', u'The MIT License (MIT)\n...)..]
licensefile_pairs.getNumPartitions()
# this method will create a single partition (1) containing key/value pairs for each
# file in the directory
licensefile_pairs.count()
# this action will count the number of files or key/value pairs
# in this case the return value is 36
```

Creating an RDD from an Object File

Spark supports several common object file implementations. The term *object files* refers to serialized data structures that are not normally human readable and that are designed to provide structure and context to data, making access to data more efficient for the requesting platform.

Sequence files are encoded serialized files commonly used in Hadoop. You can create RDDs by using the `sequenceFile()` method. There is also a similar method called `hadoopFile()`. (For brevity, we won't cover sequence files in detail in this book because it would require more knowledge about serialization in Hadoop, which is beyond the book's scope.)

In addition, there is support for reading and writing Pickle files, a special serialization format for Python. Similar functionality is available for serialized Java objects with the `objectFile()` method.

Spark also has native support for JSON files, which we will look at shortly.

Creating an RDD from a Data Source

It is commonly required to load data from a database into an RDD in a Spark program as a source of historical data, master data, or reference or lookup data. This data can come from a variety of host systems and database platforms, including Oracle, MySQL, Postgres, and SQL Server.

As with the creation of RDDs using external files, RDDs created using data from an external database—a MySQL database, for example—attempt to move the data into multiple partitions across multiple Workers. This maximizes parallelism during processing, especially during the initial stages. In addition, if you divide the table, typically by key space, into different partitions, the partitions can load in parallel as well, and each partition is responsible for fetching a unique set of rows. This concept is depicted in Figure 4.3.

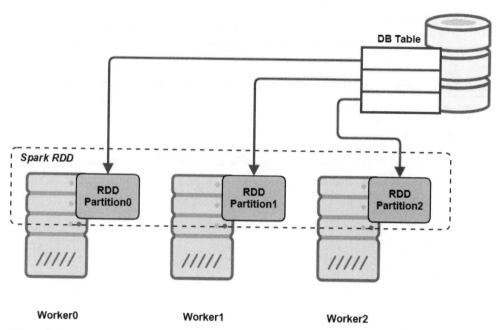

Figure 4.3   Loading an RDD from a table in a relational database.

The preferred methods of creating an RDD from a relational database table or query involve using functions from the SparkSession object. Recall that this is the main entry point for working with all types of data in Spark, including tabular data. The SparkSession exposes a read function, which returns a DataFrameReader object. You can then use this object to read data in a DataFrame, a special type of RDD previously referred to as a SchemaRDD. (Chapter 6, "SQL and NoSQL Programming with Spark," covers DataFrames in more detail.)

The read() method has a jdbc function that can connect to and collect data from any JDBC-compliant data source.

Java Database Connectivity (JDBC)

Java Database Connectivity (JDBC) is a popular Java API for accessing different (mainly relational) database management systems (DBMSs), managing functions such as connecting to and disconnecting from a DBMS and running queries. Database vendors typically provide drivers or connectors to provide access to their database platforms via JDBC. Because Spark processes run in Java virtual machines (JVMs), JDBC is natively available to Spark.

Consider a MySQL Server called mysqlserver with a database named employees with a table called employees. The employees table has a primary key named emp_no that is a logical candidate to use for dividing the key space from the table into multiple partitions. To access the MySQL database via JDBC, you need to launch `pyspark` providing the `mysql-connector.jar` in the driver class path. Connectors, such as the `mysql-connector.jar`, are generally available from your target database platform vendor's website. An example of this is shown in Listing 4.5.

Listing 4.5   **Launching `pyspark` and Supplying the JDBC MySQL Connector JAR File**

```
# download the latest jdbc connector for your target database, include as follows:
$SPARK_HOME/bin/pyspark \
--driver-class-path mysql-connector-java-5.*-bin.jar \
--master local
```

Once you have launched an interactive or non-interactive Spark application, including the relevant JDBC connection library for your target database, you can use the `jdbc` method of the DataFrame reader object.

read.jdbc()

Syntax:

```
spark.read.jdbc(url, table,
    column=None,
    lowerBound=None,
    upperBound=None,
    numPartitions=None,
    predicates=None,
    properties=None)
```

The `url` and `table` arguments specify the target database and table to read.

The `column` argument helps Spark choose the appropriate column, preferably a `long` or `int` datatype, to create the number of partitions specified by `numPartitions`. The `upperBound` and `lowerBound` arguments are used in conjunction with the `column` argument to assist Spark in creating the partitions. These represent the minimum and maximum values for the specified column in the source table. If any one of these arguments is supplied with the `read.jdbc()` function, all must be supplied.

The optional argument `predicates` allows for including `WHERE` conditions to filter unneeded records while loading partitions. You can use the `properties` argument to pass parameters to the JDBC API, such as the database user credentials; if supplied, this argument must be a Python dictionary, a set of name/value pairs representing the various configuration options.

Listing 4.6 shows the creation of an RDD using the `read.jdbc()` method.

Listing 4.6   **Loading Data from a JDBC Data Source by Using `read.jdbc()`**

```
employeesdf = spark.read.jdbc(url="jdbc:mysql://localhost:3306/employees",
    table="employees",column="emp_no",numPartitions="2",lowerBound="10001",
    upperBound="499999",properties={"user":"<user>","password":"<pwd>"})
employeesdf.rdd.getNumPartitions()
# should return 2 as we specified numPartitions=2
```

The `read.jdbc()` function returns a DataFrame (a special Spark object against which SQL queries can be executed), as shown in Listing 4.7.

Listing 4.7   **Running SQL Queries Against Spark DataFrames**

```
sqlContext.registerDataFrameAsTable(employeesdf, "employees")
df2 = spark.sql("SELECT emp_no, first_name, last_name FROM employees LIMIT 2")
df2.show()
# will return a 'pretty printed' result set similar to:
#+------+----------+---------+
#|emp_no|first_name|last_name|
#+------+----------+---------+
#| 10001|    Georgi|  Facello|
#| 10002|   Bezalel|   Simmel|
#+------+----------+---------+
```

> **Creating Too Many Partitions Using the `read.jdbc()` Function**
>
> Be careful not to specify too many partitions when loading a DataFrame from a relational data source. Each partition running on each individual worker node connects to the DBMS independently and queries its designated portion of the dataset. If you have hundreds or thousands of partitions, this could be misconstrued as a distributed denial-of-service (DDoS) attack on the host database system.

Creating RDDs from JSON Files

JSON (JavaScript Object Notation) is a popular data-interchange format. JSON is a "self-describing" format, which is human readable and commonly used to return responses from web services and RESTful APIs. JSON objects are treated as data sources and accessed using the `read.json()` method that is exposed through the SparkSession entry point.

`read.json()`

Syntax:

```
spark.read.json(path, schema=None)
```

The `path` argument specifies the full path to the JSON file you are using as a data source. You can use the optional `schema` argument to specify the target schema for creating the DataFrame.

Consider a JSON file named `people.json` that contains the names and, optionally, the ages of people. This file happens to be in the `examples` directory of the Spark installation, as shown in Figure 4.4.

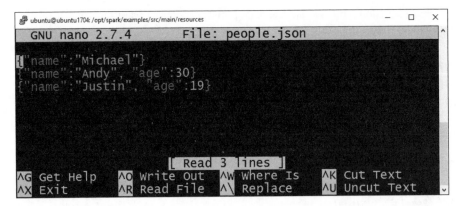

Figure 4.4   JSON file.

Listing 4.8 demonstrates the creation of a DataFrame named people using the people.json file.

Listing 4.8   **Creating and Working with a DataFrame Created from a JSON File**

```
people = spark.read.json("/opt/spark/examples/src/main/resources/people.json")
# inspect the object created
people
# notice that a DataFrame is created which includes the following schema:
# DataFrame[age: bigint, name: string]
# this schema was inferred from the object
people.dtypes
# the dtypes method returns the column names and datatypes in this case it returns:
#[('age', 'bigint'), ('name', 'string')]
people.show()
# you should see the following output
#+----+-------+
#| age|   name|
#+----+-------+
#|null|Michael|
#|  30|   Andy|
#|  19| Justin|
#+----+-------+
# as with all DataFrames you can create use them to run SQL queries as follows
sqlContext.registerDataFrameAsTable(people, "people")
df2 = spark.sql("SELECT name, age FROM people WHERE age > 20")
df2.show()
# you should see the resultant output below
#+----+---+
#|name|age|
#+----+---+
#|Andy| 30|
#+----+---+
```

Creating an RDD Programmatically

It is possible to create an RDD programmatically from data in your program, whether the data is in lists, arrays, or collections. The data from your collection is partitioned and distributed in much the same way as it is using the previous methods. However, creating RDDs this way can be limiting because it requires all of the dataset to exist or be created in memory on one system. The following sections describe methods exposed by the SparkContext that allow you to create RDDs from lists in your program.

parallelize()

Syntax:

```
sc.parallelize(c, numSlices=None)
```

The parallelize() method assumes that you have a list created already and that you supply it as the c (for collection) argument. The numSlices argument specifies the desired number of partitions to create. An example of the parallelize() method is shown in Listing 4.9.

Listing 4.9 **Creating an RDD by Using the parallelize() Method**

```
parallelrdd = sc.parallelize([0, 1, 2, 3, 4, 5, 6, 7, 8])
parallelrdd
# notice the type of RDD created:
# ParallelCollectionRDD[0] at parallelize at PythonRDD.scala:423
parallelrdd.count()
# this action will return 9 as this is the number of elements in our collection
parallelrdd.collect()
# will return the parallel collection as a list as follows:
# [0, 1, 2, 3, 4, 5, 6, 7, 8]
```

range()

Syntax:

```
sc.range(start, end=None, step=1, numSlices=None)
```

The range() method generates a list for you and creates and distributes the RDD. The start, end, and step arguments define the sequence of values, and numSlices specifies the desired number of partitions. An example of the range() method is shown in Listing 4.10.

Listing 4.10 **Creating an RDD by Using the range() Method**

```
# create an RDD with 1000 integers starting at 0 in increments of 1
# across 2 partitions
range_rdd = sc.range(0, 1000, 1, 2)
range_rdd
# note the PythonRDD type, as range is a native Python function
# PythonRDD[1] at RDD at PythonRDD.scala:43
range_rdd.getNumPartitions()
```

```
# should return 2 as we requested numSlices=2
range_rdd.min()
# should return 0 as this was out start argument
range_rdd.max()
# should return 999 as this is 1000 increments of 1 starting from 0
range_rdd.take(5)
# should return [0, 1, 2, 3, 4]
```

Operations on RDDs

Now that you have learned how to create RDDs from files in various filesystems, from relational
data sources, and programmatically, let's look at the types of operations you can perform against
RDDs and some of the key RDD concepts.

Key RDD Concepts

Recall that *transformations* in Spark are functions that operate on an RDD and return a new RDD,
whereas *actions* operate against an RDD and return a value or perform an output operation.
We will look at many examples of both shortly, but first we need to introduce two concepts:
coarse-grained transformations and lazy evaluation.

Coarse-Grained Versus Fine-Grained Transformations

Operations performed against RDDs are considered to be coarse grained as they apply a function
(a map or filter function, for example, which we will discuss shortly) against every element in
the dataset, and they return a new dataset with the transformations applied. In contrast to coarse-
grained transformations, fine-grained transformations can manipulate a single record or data
cell, such as single-row updates in a relational database or put operations in a NoSQL database.
Coarse-grained transformations are conceptually similar to Hadoop's implementation of the
MapReduce programming model.

Transformations, Actions, and Lazy Evaluation

Transformations are operations performed against RDDs that result in the creation of new RDDs.
Common transformations include map and filter functions. The following example shows a
new RDD created from a transformation of an existing RDD:

```
originalrdd = sc.parallelize([0, 1, 2, 3, 4, 5, 6, 7, 8])
newrdd = originalrdd.filter(lambda x: x % 2)
```

originalrdd originated from a parallelized collection of numbers. The filter() transformation
was then applied to each element in the originalrdd to bypass even numbers in the collection.
This transformation results in the RDD called newrdd.

In contrast to transformations, which return new RDD objects, actions return values or data
to the driver program. Common actions include reduce(), collect(), count(), and
saveAsTextFile(). The following example uses the collect() action to display the contents of
newrdd:

```
newrdd.collect() # will return [1, 3, 5, 7]
```

Spark uses *lazy evaluation*, also called *lazy execution*, in processing Spark programs. Lazy evaluation defers processing until an action is called (that is, when output is required). This is easily demonstrated using an interactive shell, where you can enter one or more transformation methods to RDDs one after the other without any processing starting. Instead, each statement is parsed for syntax and object references only. After requesting an action such as count() or saveAsText-File(), a DAG is created along with logical and physical execution plans. The Driver then orchestrates and manages these plans across Executors.

This lazy evaluation allows Spark to combine operations where possible, thereby reducing processing stages and minimizing the amount of data transferred between Spark Executors in a process called *shuffling*.

RDD Persistence and Reuse

RDDs are created and exist predominantly in memory on Executors. By default, RDDs are transient objects that exist only while they are required. After they transform into new RDDs and aren't needed for any other operations, they are removed permanently. This may be problematic if an RDD is required for more than one action because it must be reevaluated in its entirety each time. An option to address this is to cache or persist the RDD by using the persist() method. Listings 4.11 and 4.12 demonstrate the effects of persisting an RDD.

Listing 4.11 **Using an RDD for Multiple Actions Without Persistence**

```
numbers = sc.range(0, 1000000, 1, 2)
evens = numbers.filter(lambda x: x % 2)
noelements = evens.count()
# processes evens RDD
print "There are %s elements in the collection" % (noelements)
# returns "There are 500000 elements in the collection"
listofelements = evens.collect()
# REPROCESSES evens RDD
print "The first five elements include " + (str(listofelements[0:5]))
# returns "The first five elements include [1, 3, 5, 7, 9]"
```

Listing 4.12 **Using an RDD for Multiple Actions with Persistence**

```
numbers = sc.range(0, 1000000, 1, 2)
evens = numbers.filter(lambda x: x % 2)
evens.persist()
# instructs Spark to persist evens RDD when the next action requires it
noelements = evens.count()
# processes and persists evens RDD in memory
print "There are %s elements in the collection" % (noelements)
# returns "There are 500000 elements in the collection"
listofelements = evens.collect()
# does NOT have to recompute the evens RDD
print "The first five elements include " + (str(listofelements[0:5]))
# returns "The first five elements include [1, 3, 5, 7, 9]"
```

After a request to persist the RDD using the persist() method (note that there is a similar cache() method as well), the RDD remains in memory on all the nodes in the cluster where it is computed after the first action called on it. You can see the persisted RDD in your Spark application UI in the Storage tab, as shown in Figure 4.5.

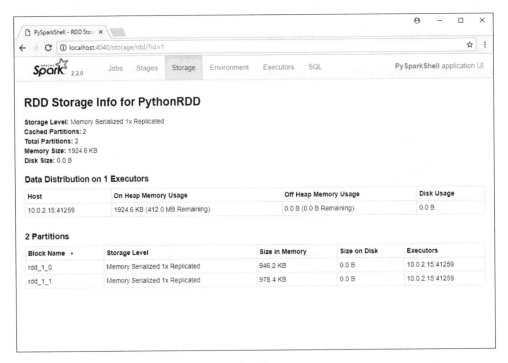

Figure 4.5   Storage tab in the Spark application UI.

RDD Lineage

Spark keeps track of each RDD's lineage—that is, the sequence of transformations that resulted in the RDD. As discussed previously, every RDD operation recomputes the entire lineage by default unless RDD persistence is requested.

In an RDD's lineage, each RDD has a parent RDD and/or a child RDD. Spark creates a directed acyclic graph (DAG) consisting of dependencies between RDDs. RDDs are processed in stages, which are sets of transformations. RDDs and stages have dependencies that can be narrow or wide.

Narrow dependencies, or *narrow operations*, are categorized by the following traits:

- Operations can collapse into a single stage; for instance, a map() and filter() operation against elements in the same dataset can be processed in a single pass of each element in the dataset.

- Only one child RDD depends on the parent RDD; for instance, an RDD is created from a text file (the parent RDD), with one child RDD to perform the set of transformations in one stage.

- No shuffling of data between nodes is required.

Narrow operations are preferred because they maximize parallel execution and minimize shuffling, which is quite expensive and can be a bottleneck.

Wide dependencies of wide *operations*, in contrast, have the following traits:

- Operations define new stages and often require shuffling.

- RDDs have multiple dependencies; for instance, a join() operation (covered shortly) requires an RDD to be dependent upon two or more parent RDDs.

Wide operations are unavoidable when grouping, reducing, or joining datasets, but you should be aware of the impacts and overhead involved with these operations.

Lineage can be visualized by using the DAG Visualization option link from the Jobs or Stages detail page in the Spark application UI. Figure 4.6 shows a DAG with multiple stages as a result of a wide operation (reduceByKey() in this case).

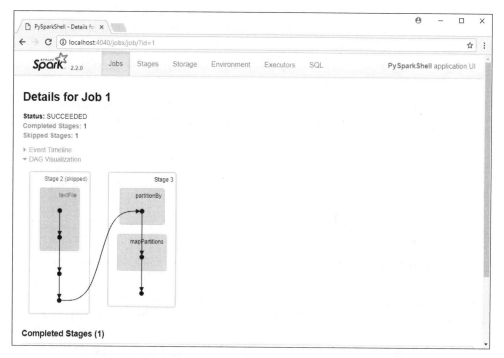

Figure 4.6   DAG visualization in the Spark application UI.

Fault Tolerance with RDDs

Spark records the lineage of each RDD, including the lineage of all parent RDDs and parents' parents, and so on. Any RDD with all of its partitions can be reconstructed to the state it was in at the time of the failure, which could have resulted from a node failure, for example. Because RDDs are distributed, they can tolerate and recover from the failure of any single node.

Non-deterministic Functions and Fault Tolerance

The use of non-deterministic functions in a Spark program—that is, functions that can produce different output given the same inputs, such as `random()`—will impact the ability to re-create RDDs in a consistent, repeatable state. This is further complicated if you use the non-deterministic function as a condition, which affects the logic or flow of the program. Use caution when implementing non-deterministic functions.

You can avert long recovery periods for complex processing operations by checkpointing, or saving the data to a persistent file-based object. (Chapter 5, "Advanced Programming Using the Spark Core API," discusses checkpointing.)

Types of RDDs

Aside from the base RDD class that contains members (properties or attributes and functions) common to all RDDs, there are some specific RDD implementations that enable additional operators and functions. These additional RDD types include the following:

- **PairRDD:** An RDD of key/value pairs. You have already seen this type of RDD as it is automatically created by using the `wholeTextFiles()` method.

- **DoubleRDD:** An RDD consisting of a collection of double values only. Because the values are of the same numeric type, several additional statistical functions are available, including `mean()`, `sum()`, `stdev()`, `variance()`, and `histogram()`, among others.

- **DataFrame (formerly known as SchemaRDD):** A distributed collection of data organized into named and typed columns. A DataFrame is equivalent to a relational table in Spark SQL. DataFrames originated with the `read.jdbc()` and `read.json()` functions discussed earlier.

- **SequenceFileRDD:** An RDD created from a SequenceFile, either compressed or uncompressed.

- **HadoopRDD:** An RDD that provides core functionality for reading data stored in HDFS using the v1 MapReduce API.

- **NewHadoopRDD:** An RDD that provides core functionality for reading data stored in Hadoop—for example, files in HDFS, sources in HBase, or S3—using the new MapReduce API (org.apache.hadoop.mapreduce).

- **CoGroupedRDD:** An RDD that cogroups its parents. For each key in parent RDDs, the resulting RDD contains a tuple with the list of values for that key. (We will discuss the `cogroup()` function later in this chapter.)

- **JdbcRDD:** An RDD resulting from a SQL query to a JDBC connection. It is available in the Scala API only.

- **PartitionPruningRDD:** An RDD used to prune RDD partitions or other partitions to avoid launching tasks on all partitions. For example, if you know the RDD is partitioned by range, and the execution DAG has a filter on the key, you can avoid launching tasks on partitions that don't have the range covering the key.

- **ShuffledRDD:** The resulting RDD from a shuffle, such as repartitioning of data.

- **UnionRDD:** An RDD resulting from a `union()` operation against two or more RDDs.

There are other RDD variants, including ParallelCollectionRDD and PythonRDD, which are created from the `parallelize()` and `range()` functions discussed previously.

Throughout this book, in addition to the base RDD class, you will mainly use the PairRDD, DoubleRDD, and DataFrame RDD classes, but it's worthwhile to be familiar with all the various RDD types. Documentation and more information about the types of RDDs can be found in the Spark Scala API documentation at https://spark.apache.org/docs/latest/api/scala/index.html.

Basic RDD Transformations

The most commonly used Spark functions include `map()`, `flatMap()`, `filter()`, and `distinct()`, which are covered in the following sections. You will also learn about the `groupBy()` and `sortBy()` functions, which are commonly implemented by other functions. Grouping data is a normal precursor to performing aggregation or summary functions such as summing, counting, and so on. Sorting data is another useful operation for preparing output or for looking at the top or bottom records in a dataset. The `groupBy()` and `sortBy()` functions should be familiar to you if you have experience in relational database programming because they are analogous to the `GROUP BY` and `ORDER BY` functions in SQL.

map()

Syntax:

```
RDD.map(<function>, preservesPartitioning=False)
```

The `map()` transformation is the most basic of all transformations. It evaluates a named or anonymous function for each element within a dataset partition. One or many `map()` functions can run asynchronously because they shouldn't produce any side effects, maintain state, or attempt to communicate or synchronize with other `map()` operations. That is, they are *shared nothing* operations.

The `preservesPartitioning` argument is an optional Boolean argument intended for use with RDDs with a partitioner defined—typically a key/value pair RDD (as discussed later in this chapter) in which a key is defined and grouped by a key hash or key range. If this parameter is set to `True`, the partitions stay intact. This parameter can be used by the Spark scheduler to optimize subsequent operations, such as joins based on the partitioned key.

Consider Figure 4.7, where the map() transformation evaluates a function for each input record and emits a transformed output record. In this case, the split function takes a string and produces a list, and each string element in the input data maps to a list element in the output. The result, in this case, is a list of lists.

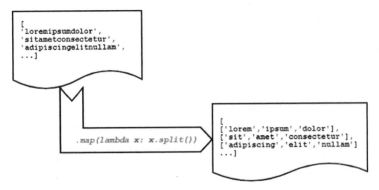

Figure 4.7   The map() transformation.

flatMap()

Syntax:

RDD.flatMap(<function>, preservesPartitioning=False)

The flatMap() transformation is similar to the map() transformation in that it runs a function against each record in the input dataset. However, flatMap() "flattens" the output, meaning it removes a level of nesting. For example, given a list containing lists of strings, flattening would result in a single list of strings—"flattening" all of the nested lists. Figure 4.8 shows the effect of a flatMap() transformation using the same anonymous (lambda) function as the map() operation shown in Figure 4.7. Notice that instead of each string producing a respective list object, all elements are flattened into one list. In other words, flatMap(), in this case, produces one combined list as output, in contrast to the list of lists in the map() example.

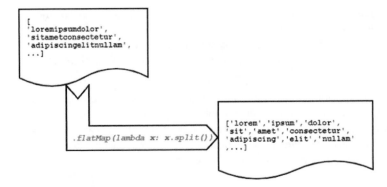

Figure 4.8   The flatMap() transformation.

The preservesPartitioning argument works the same in flatMap() as it does in the map() function.

filter()

Syntax:

```
RDD.filter(<function>)
```

The `filter` transformation evaluates a Boolean expression, usually expressed as an anonymous function, against each element in the dataset. The Boolean value returned determines whether the record is included in the resultant output RDD. This is another common transformation used to remove from RDD records that are not required for intermediate processing and that are not included in the final output.

Listing 4.13 shows an example of using the `map()`, `flatMap()`, and `filter()` transformations together to convert input text to uppercase. It uses `map()` and `flatMap()` to split the text into a combined list of words and then uses `filter()` to filter the list to return only words that are greater than four characters long.

Listing 4.13 **The `map()`, `flatMap()`, and `filter()` Transformations**

```
licenses = sc.textFile('file:///opt/spark/licenses')
words = licenses.flatMap(lambda x: x.split(' '))
words.take(5)
# returns [u'The', u'MIT', u'License', u'(MIT)', u'']
lowercase = words.map(lambda x: x.lower())
lowercase.take(5)
# returns [u'the', u'mit', u'license', u'(mit)', u'']
longwords = lowercase.filter(lambda x: len(x) > 12)
longwords.take(2)
# returns [u'documentation', u'merchantability,']
```

There is a standard axiom in the world of Big Data programming: "Filter early, filter often." This refers to the fact that there is no value in carrying records or fields through a process where they are not needed. Both the `filter()` and `map()` functions can be used to achieve this objective. That said, in many cases Spark—through its key runtime characteristic of lazy execution—attempts to optimize routines for you even if you do not explicitly do this yourself.

distinct()

Syntax:

```
RDD.distinct(numPartitions=None)
```

The `distinct()` transformation returns a new RDD containing distinct elements from the input RDD. It is used to remove duplicates, where *duplicates* are defined as having all elements or fields within a record that are the same as other records in the dataset. The numPartitions argument can redistribute data to a target number of partitions; if this is not supplied or is left at the default, the number of partitions returned by the `distinct()` transformation is identical to the number of partitions from the RDD operated against.

Listing 4.14 demonstrates the use of the `distinct()` function.

Listing 4.14 **The `distinct()` Transformation**

```
licenses = sc.textFile('file:///opt/spark/licenses')
words = licenses.flatMap(lambda x: x.split(' '))
lowercase = words.map(lambda x: x.lower())
allwords = lowercase.count()
distinctwords = lowercase.distinct().count()
print "Total words: %s, Distinct Words: %s" % (allwords, distinctwords)
# returns "Total words: 11484, Distinct Words: 892"
```

groupBy()

Syntax:

```
RDD.groupBy(<function>, numPartitions=None)
```

The `groupBy()` transformation returns an RDD of items grouped by a specified function. The `<function>` argument is an anonymous or named function used to nominate a key by which to group all elements or to specify an expression to evaluate against elements to determine a group, such as when grouping elements by odd or even numbers of a numeric field in the data.

You can use the `numPartitions` argument to create a specified number of partitions automatically by computing hashes of the key space from the output of the grouping function. For instance, if you want to group an RDD by the days in a week and process each day separately, specify `numPartitions=7`. You will see `numPartitions` specified in numerous Spark transformations, where its behavior is analogous.

Listing 4.15 demonstrates the use of the `groupBy()` function. Notice that `groupBy()` returns an *iterable* object; we will look at how to handle this type of object later in this chapter.

Listing 4.15 **Grouping Data in Spark by Using the `groupBy()` Function**

```
licenses = sc.textFile('file:///opt/spark/licenses')
words = licenses.flatMap(lambda x: x.split(' ')) \
                .filter(lambda x: len(x) > 0)
groupedbyfirstletter = words.groupBy(lambda x: x[0].lower())
groupedbyfirstletter.take(1)
# returns:
# [('l', <pyspark.resultiterable.ResultIterable object at 0x7f678e9cca20>)]
```

> **Consider Other Functions for Grouping Data**
>
> If your ultimate intention in using `groupBy()` is to aggregate values, such as when performing a `sum()` or `count()` operation, you should opt for more efficient operators for this purpose in Spark, including `aggregateByKey()` and `reduceByKey()`, which we will discuss shortly. The `groupBy()` transformation does not perform any aggregation prior to shuffling data, resulting in more data being shuffled. Furthermore, `groupBy()` requires that all values for a given key fit into memory. The `groupBy()` transformation is useful in some cases, but you should consider these factors before deciding to use this function.

sortBy()

Syntax:

```
RDD.sortBy(<keyfunc>, ascending=True, numPartitions=None)
```

The sortBy() transformation sorts an RDD by the <keyfunc> argument (a named or anonymous function) that nominates the key for a given dataset. It sorts according to the sort order of the key object type. For instance, int and double data types are sorted numerically, whereas String types are sorted in lexicographical order.

The ascending argument is a Boolean argument that defaults to True and specifies the sort order to be used. A descending sort order is specified by setting ascending=False.

An example of the sortBy() function is shown in Listing 4.16.

Listing 4.16 **Sorting Data by Using the sortBy() Function**

```
readme = sc.textFile('file:///opt/spark/README.md')
words = readme.flatMap(lambda x: x.split(' ')) \
               .filter(lambda x: len(x) > 0)
sortbyfirstletter = words.sortBy(lambda x: x[0].lower(), ascending=False)
sortbyfirstletter.take(5)
# returns ['You', 'you', 'You', 'you', 'you']
```

Basic RDD Actions

Recall that actions in Spark either return values, as is the case with count(); return data, as is the case with collect(); or save data externally, as is the case with saveAsTextFile(). In all cases, actions force computation of an RDD and all of its parents. Some actions return either a count, an aggregation of the data, or part or all of the data in an RDD. In contrast, foreach() is an action that performs a *function* on each element of an RDD. The following sections look at some of the basic actions in the core Spark API.

count()

Syntax:

```
RDD.count()
```

The count() action takes no arguments and returns a long value, which represents the count of the elements in the RDD. Listing 4.17 shows a simple count() example. Note that with actions that take no arguments, you need to include empty parentheses, (), after the action name.

Listing 4.17 **The count() Action**

```
licenses = sc.textFile('file:///opt/spark/licenses')
words = licenses.flatMap(lambda x: x.split(' '))
words.count()
# returns 11484
```

collect()

Syntax:

```
RDD.collect()
```

The collect() action returns a list that contains all the elements in an RDD to the Spark Driver. Because collect() does not restrict the output, which can be quite large and can potentially cause out-of-memory errors on the Driver, it is typically useful for only small RDDs or development. Listing 4.18 demonstrates the collect() action.

Listing 4.18 **The collect() Action**

```
licenses = sc.textFile('file:///opt/spark/licenses')
words = licenses.flatMap(lambda x: x.split(' '))
words.collect()
# returns [u'The', u'MIT', u'License', u'(MIT)', u'', u'Copyright', ...]
```

take()

Syntax:

```
RDD.take(n)
```

The take() action returns the first n elements of an RDD. The elements taken are not in any particular order; in fact, the elements returned from a take() action are non-deterministic, meaning they can differ if the same action is run again, particularly in a fully distributed environment. There is a similar Spark function, takeOrdered(), which takes the first n elements ordered based on a key supplied by a key function.

For RDDs that span more than one partition, take() scans one partition and uses the results from that partition to estimate the number of additional partitions needed to satisfy the number requested.

Listing 4.19 shows an example of the take() action.

Listing 4.19 **The take() Action**

```
licenses = sc.textFile('file:///opt/spark/licenses')
words = licenses.flatMap(lambda x: x.split(' '))
words.take(3)
# returns [u'The', u'MIT', u'License']
```

top()

Syntax:

```
RDD.top(n, key=None)
```

The top() action returns the top n elements from an RDD, but unlike with take(), with top() the elements are ordered and returned in descending order. Order is determined by the object type, such as numeric order for integers or dictionary order for strings.

The key argument specifies the key by which to order the results to return the top n elements. This is an optional argument; if it is not supplied, the key will be inferred from the elements in the RDD.

Listing 4.20 shows the top three distinct words sorted from a text file in descending lexicographical order.

Listing 4.20 **The `top()` Action**

```
readme = sc.textFile('file:///opt/spark/README.md')
words = readme.flatMap(lambda x: x.split(' '))
words.distinct().top(3)
# returns [u'your', u'you', u'with']
```

first()

Syntax:

```
RDD.first()
```

The `first()` action returns the first element in this RDD. Similar to the `take()` and `collect()` actions and unlike the `top()` action, `first()` does not consider the order of elements and is a non-deterministic operation, especially in fully distributed environments.

As you can see from Listing 4.21, the primary difference between `first()` and `take(1)` is that `first()` returns an atomic data element, and `take()` (even if n = 1) returns a list of data elements. The `first()` action is useful for inspecting the output of an RDD as part of development or data exploration.

Listing 4.21 **The `first()` Action**

```
readme = sc.textFile('file:///opt/spark/README.md')
words = readme.flatMap(lambda x: x.split(' ')) \
       .filter(lambda x: len(x) > 0)
words.distinct().first()
# returns a string: u'project.'
words.distinct().take(1)
# returns a list with one string element: [u'project.']
```

The `reduce()` and `fold()` actions are aggregate actions, each of which executes a commutative and/or an associative operation, such as summing a list of values, against an RDD. *Commutative* and *associative* are the operative terms here. This makes the operations independent of the order in which they run, and this is integral to distributed processing because the order isn't guaranteed. Here is the general form of the commutative characteristics:

$$x + y = y + x$$

And here is the general form of the associative characteristics:

$$(x + y) + z = x + (y + z)$$

The following sections look at the main Spark actions that perform aggregations.

reduce()

Syntax:

RDD.reduce(<function>)

The reduce() action reduces the elements of an RDD using a specified commutative and/or associative operator. The <function> argument specifies two inputs (lambda x, y: ...) that represent values in a sequence from the specified RDD. Listing 4.22 shows an example of a reduce() operation to produce a sum against a list of numbers.

Listing 4.22 **Summing Values in an RDD by Using the reduce() Action**

```
numbers = sc.parallelize([1,2,3,4,5,6,7,8,9])
numbers.reduce(lambda x, y: x + y)
# returns 45
```

fold()

Syntax:

RDD.fold(zeroValue, <function>)

The fold() action aggregates the elements of each partition of an RDD and then performs the aggregate operation against the results for all, using a given function and a zeroValue. Although reduce() and fold() are similar in function, they differ in that fold() is not commutative, and thus an initial and final value (zeroValue) is required. A simple example is a fold() action with zeroValue=0, as shown in Listing 4.23.

Listing 4.23 **The fold() Action**

```
numbers = sc.parallelize([1,2,3,4,5,6,7,8,9])
numbers.fold(0, lambda x, y: x + y)
# returns 45
```

The fold() action in Listing 4.23 looks exactly the same as the reduce() action in Listing 4.22. However, Listing 4.24 demonstrates a clear functional difference in the two actions. The fold() action provides a zeroValue that is added to the beginning and end of the function supplied as input to the fold() action, generalized here:

```
result  =  zeroValue  +  ( 1 + 2 ) + 3 . . .  + zeroValue
```

This allows fold() to operate on an empty RDD, whereas reduce() produces an exception with an empty RDD.

Listing 4.24 **The fold() Action Compared with reduce()**

```
empty = sc.parallelize([])
empty.reduce(lambda x, y: x + y)
# returns:
# ValueError: Cannot reduce() empty RDD
empty.fold(0, lambda x, y: x + y)
# returns 0
```

There is also a similar `aggregate()` action in the Spark RDD API.

foreach()

Syntax:

```
RDD.foreach(<function>)
```

The `foreach()` action applies a function specified in the `<function>` argument, anonymous or named, to all elements of an RDD. Because `foreach()` is an action rather than a transformation, you can perform functions otherwise not possible or intended in transformations, such as a `print()` function. Although Python `lambda` functions don't allow you to execute a `print()` statement directly, you can use a named function that executes `print()` instead. Listing 4.25 shows an example of this.

Listing 4.25 **The `foreach()` Action**

```
def printfunc(x):
    print(x)
licenses = sc.textFile('file:///opt/spark/licenses')
longwords = licenses.flatMap(lambda x: x.split(' ')) \
            .filter(lambda x: len(x) > 12)
longwords.foreach(lambda x: printfunc(x))
# returns:
# ...
# Redistributions
# documentation
# distribution.
# MERCHANTABILITY
# ...
```

Transformations on PairRDDs

Key/value pair RDDs, or simply PairRDDs, contain records consisting of keys and values. The keys can be simple objects such as integer or string objects or complex objects such as tuples. The values can range from scalar values to data structures such as lists, tuples, dictionaries, or sets. This is a common data representation in multi-structured data analysis on schema-on-read and NoSQL systems. PairRDDs and their constituent functions are integral to functional Spark programming. These functions are broadly classified into four categories:

- Dictionary functions
- Functional transformations
- Grouping, aggregation, and sorting operations
- Join functions, which we discuss specifically in the next section

Dictionary functions return a set of keys or values from a key/value pair RDD. Examples include keys() and values().

Earlier in this chapter we looked at other aggregate operations, including reduce() and fold(). These are conceptually similar in that they aggregate values in an RDD based on a key, but there is a fundamental difference: reduce() and fold() are *actions*, which means they force computation and produce a result, whereas reduceByKey() and foldByKey(), which we discuss shortly, are *transformations*, meaning they are lazily evaluated and return a new RDD.

keys()

Syntax:

```
RDD.keys()
```

The keys() function returns an RDD with the keys from a key/value pair RDD or the first element from each tuple in a key/value pair RDD. Listing 4.26 demonstrates using the keys() function.

Listing 4.26 **The keys() Function**

```
kvpairs = sc.parallelize([('city','Hayward')
                         ,('state','CA')
                         ,('zip',94541)
                         ,('country','USA')])
kvpairs.keys().collect()
# returns ['city', 'state', 'zip', 'country']
```

values()

Syntax:

```
RDD.values()
```

The values() function returns an RDD with values from a key/value pair RDD or the second element from each tuple in a key/value pair RDD. Listing 4.27 demonstrates using the values() function.

Listing 4.27 **The values() Function**

```
kvpairs = sc.parallelize([('city','Hayward')
                         ,('state','CA')
                         ,('zip',94541)
                         ,('country','USA')])
kvpairs.values().collect()
# returns ['Hayward', 'CA', 94541, 'USA']
```

keyBy()

Syntax:

```
RDD.keyBy(<function>)
```

The keyBy() transformation creates a tuple consisting of a key and a value from the elements in the RDD by applying a function specified by the <function> argument. The value is the complete tuple from which the key was derived.

Consider a list of locations as tuples with a schema of city, country, location_no. Say that you want the location_no field to be your key. The example in Listing 4.28 demonstrates the use of the keyBy() function to create new tuples in which the first element is the key and the second element, the value, is a tuple containing all fields from the original tuple.

Listing 4.28 **The keyBy() Transformation**

```
locations = sc.parallelize([('Hayward', 'USA', 1)
                           ,('Baumholder','Germany', 2)
                           ,('Alexandria','USA', 3)
                           ,('Melbourne','Australia', 4)])
bylocno = locations.keyBy(lambda x: x[2])
bylocno.collect()
# returns:
#[(1, ('Hayward', 'USA', 1)), (2, ('Baumholder', 'Germany', 2)),
# (3, ('Alexandria', 'USA', 3)), (4, ('Melbourne', 'Australia', 4))]
```

Recall that x[2] in Listing 4.28 refers to the third element in list x, as Python list elements are ordinal numbers, starting with 0.

Functional transformations available for key/value pair RDDs work similarly to the more general functional transformations you learned about earlier. The difference is that these functions operate specifically on either the key or value element within a tuple—the key/value pair, in this case. Functional transformations include mapValues() and flatMapValues().

mapValues()

Syntax:

RDD.mapValues(<function>)

The mapValues() transformation passes each value in a key/value pair RDD through a function (a named or anonymous function specified by the <function> argument) without changing the keys. Like its generalized equivalent map(), mapValues() outputs one element for each input element.

The original RDD's partitioning is not affected.

flatMapValues()

Syntax:

RDD.flatMapValues(<function>)

The flatMapValues() transformation passes each value in a key/value pair RDD through a function without changing the keys and produces a flattened list. It works exactly like flatMap(), which we looked at earlier, returning zero to many output elements per input element.

Much as with mapValues(), with flatMapValues() the original RDD's partitioning is retained.

The easiest way to contrast mapValues() and flatMapValues() is to look at a practical example. Consider a text file containing a city and a pipe-delimited list of temperatures, as shown here:

```
Hayward,71|69|71|71|72
Baumholder,46|42|40|37|39
Alexandria,50|48|51|53|44
Melbourne,88|101|85|77|74
```

Listing 4.29 simulates the loading of this data into an RDD and uses mapValues() to create a list of key/value pair tuples containing the city and a list of temperatures for the city. It shows the use of flatMapValues() with the same function against the same RDD to create tuples containing the city and a number for each temperature recorded for the city.

A simple way to describe this is that mapValues() creates one element per city containing the city name and a list of five temperatures for the city, whereas flatMapValues() *flattens* the lists to create five elements per city with the city name and a temperature value.

Listing 4.29 **The mapValues() and flatMapValues() Transformations**

```
locwtemps = sc.parallelize(['Hayward,71|69|71|71|72',
                            'Baumholder,46|42|40|37|39',
                            'Alexandria,50|48|51|53|44',
                            'Melbourne,88|101|85|77|74'])
kvpairs = locwtemps.map(lambda x: x.split(','))
kvpairs.take(4)
# returns :
# [['Hayward', '71|69|71|71|72'],
#  ['Baumholder', '46|42|40|37|39'],
#  ['Alexandria', '50|48|51|53|44'],
#  ['Melbourne', '88|101|85|77|74']]
locwtemplist = kvpairs.mapValues(lambda x: x.split('|')) \
                      .mapValues(lambda x: [int(s) for s in x])
locwtemplist.take(4)
# returns :
# [('Hayward', [71, 69, 71, 71, 72]),
#  ('Baumholder', [46, 42, 40, 37, 39]),
#  ('Alexandria', [50, 48, 51, 53, 44]),
#  ('Melbourne', [88, 101, 85, 77, 74])]
locwtemps = kvpairs.flatMapValues(lambda x: x.split('|')) \
                   .map(lambda x: (x[0], int(x[1])))
locwtemps.take(3)
# returns :
# [('Hayward', 71), ('Hayward', 69), ('Hayward', 71)]
```

Grouping, aggregation, and sorting operations are functionally analogous to their more generalized forms discussed earlier in this chapter (groupBy() and sortBy()), again with the difference being that these functions operate specifically on RDDs composed of key/value pairs.

> **Be Cautious of the Repartitioning and Shuffling Effects of Some Functions**
>
> Be aware that some functions, such as groupByKey() and reduceByKey(), may result in a repartitioning or require shuffling. Shuffling is a relatively expensive operation because it requires the movement of data between Spark Executors, often located on different Worker nodes. These operations are often necessary and unavoidable, but in some cases, by understanding the planning and execution of an RDD's lineage, you may be able to optimize these operations. We discuss partitioning in more detail in Chapter 5.

groupByKey()

Syntax:

RDD.groupByKey(numPartitions=None, partitionFunc=<hash_fn>)

The groupByKey() transformation groups the values for each key in a key/value pair RDD into a single sequence.

The numPartitions argument specifies how many partitions—how many groups, that is—to create. The partitions are created using the partitionFunc argument, which defaults to Spark's built-in hash partitioner. If numPartitions is None, which is the default, then the configured system default number of partitions is used (spark.default.parallelism).

Consider the output from Listing 4.29. If you want to calculate the average temperature by city, you first need to group all the values together by their city and then compute the averages. Listing 4.30 shows how to use groupByKey() to accomplish this.

Listing 4.30 **The groupByKey() Transformation**

```
# continued from Listing 4.29
grouped = locwtemps.groupByKey()
grouped.take(1)
# returns:
# [('Melbourne', <pyspark.resultiterable.ResultIterable object at 0x7f121ce11390>)]
avgtemps = grouped.mapValues(lambda x: sum(x)/len(x))
avgtemps.collect()
# returns:
# [('Melbourne', 85), ('Baumholder', 40), ('Alexandria', 49), ('Hayward', 70)]
```

Notice that groupByKey() returns a resultiterable object for the grouped values. An *iterable* object in Python is a sequence object that can loop over. Many functions in Python accept iterables as input, such as the sum() and len() functions.

> **Consider Using reduceByKey() or foldByKey() Instead of groupByKey()**
>
> If you group values for the purposes of aggregation, such as by using a sum() or count() for each key, then using reduceByKey() or foldByKey() provides much better performance in many cases. This is because the results of the aggregation function are combined before the shuffle, resulting in a reduced amount of data being shuffled.

reduceByKey()

Syntax:

```
RDD.reduceByKey(<function>, numPartitions=None, partitionFunc=<hash_fn>)
```

The reduceByKey() transformation merges the values for the keys by using an associative function. The reduceByKey() method is called on a dataset of key/value pairs and returns a dataset of key/value pairs, aggregating values for each key. This function is expressed as follows:

$$v_n, v_{n+1} => v_{result}$$

The numPartitions and partitionFunc arguments behave exactly the same as in the group-ByKey() function. The numPartitions value is effectively the number of reduce tasks to execute, and you can increase this to obtain a higher degree of parallelism. The numPartitions value also affects the number of files produced with saveAsTextFile() or other file-producing Spark actions. For instance, numPartitions=2 produces two output files when the RDD saves to disk.

Listing 4.31 takes the same input key/value pairs and produces the same results (average temperatures per city) as the previous groupByKey() example—but using the reduceByKey() function instead. This method is preferred for reasons we will discuss shortly.

Listing 4.31 **Using the reduceByKey() Function to Average Values by Key**

```
# continued from Listing 4.29
temptups = locwtemps.mapValues(lambda x: (x, 1))
# creates tuples (city, (temp, 1))
inputstoavg = temptups.reduceByKey(lambda x, y: (x[0]+y[0], x[1]+y[1]))
# sums temperatures by city
averages = inputstoavg.map(lambda x: (x[0], x[1][0]/x[1][1]))
# divides the sum of temperatures by key by the number of readings
averages.take(4)
# returns :
# [('Baumholder', 40.8),
#  ('Melbourne', 85.0),
#  ('Alexandria', 49.2),
#  ('Hayward', 70.8)]
```

Averaging is not an associative operation; you can get around this by creating tuples containing the sum total of values for each key and the count for each key—operations that are associative and commutative—and then computing the average as a final step, as shown in Listing 4.31.

Note that reduceByKey() is efficient because it combines values locally on each Executor before each of the combined lists sends to a remote Executor or Executors running the final reduce stage. This is a shuffle operation.

Because the same associative and commutative function are run on the local Executor or Worker and again on a remote Executor or Executors, taking a sum function, for example, you can think of this as adding a list of sums as opposed to summing a bigger list of individual values. Because there is less data sent in the shuffle phase, reduceByKey() using a sum function generally performs better than groupByKey() followed by a sum() function.

foldByKey()

Syntax:

```
RDD.foldByKey(zeroValue, <function>, numPartitions=None,
partitionFunc=<hash_fn>)
```

The foldByKey() transformation is functionally similar to the fold() action discussed in the previous section. However, foldByKey() is a transformation that works with predefined key/value pair elements (see Listing 4.32). Both foldByKey() and fold() provide a zeroValue argument of the same type to be used if the RDD is empty.

The function supplied is in the generalized aggregate function form:

$$v_n, v_{n+1} => v_{result}$$

This is the same generalization used by the reduceByKey() transformation.

The numPartitions and the partitionFunc arguments have the same effect as they do with the groupByKey() and reduceByKey() transformations.

Listing 4.32 **A foldByKey() Example to Find Maximum Value by Key**

```
#continued from Listing 4.29
maxbycity = locwtemps.foldByKey(0, lambda x, y: x if x > y else y)
maxbycity.collect()
# returns :
# [('Baumholder', 46), ('Melbourne', 101), ('Alexandria', 53), ('Hayward', 72)]
```

There is also a similar method called aggregateByKey() in the Spark RDD API.

sortByKey()

Syntax:

```
RDD.sortByKey(ascending=True, numPartitions=None, keyfunc=<function>)
```

The sortByKey() transformation sorts a key/value pair RDD by the predefined key. The sort order is dependent on the underlying key object type, where numeric types are sorted numerically and so on. The difference between sort(), discussed earlier, and sortByKey() is that sort() requires you to identify the key by which to sort, whereas sortByKey() is aware of the key already.

Keys are sorted in the order provided by the ascending argument, which defaults to True. The numPartitions argument specifies how many resultant partitions to output using a range partitioning function. The keyfunc argument is an optional parameter to use if you want to derive a key from passing the predefined key through another function, as in this example:

```
keyfunc=lambda k: k.lower()
```

Listing 4.33 shows the use of the sortByKey() transformation. The first example shows a simple sort based on the key: a string representing the city name, sorted alphabetically. In the second example, the keys and values are inverted to make the temperature the key and then use sortByKey() to list the temperatures in descending numeric order, with the highest temperatures first.

Listing 4.33 **The sortByKey() Transformation**

```
# continued from Listing 4.29
sortedbykey = locwtemps.sortByKey()
sortedbykey.take(4)
# returns:
# [('Alexandria', 50), ('Alexandria', 48), ('Alexandria', 51), ('Alexandria', 53)]
sortedbyval = locwtemps.map(lambda x: (x[1],x[0])) \
                        .sortByKey(ascending=False)
sortedbyval.take(4)
# returns:
# [(101, 'Melbourne'), (88, 'Melbourne'), (85, 'Melbourne'), (77, 'Melbourne')]
```

MapReduce and Word Count Exercise

MapReduce is a platform- and language-independent programming model or design pattern at the heart of most Big Data and NoSQL platforms. Although many abstractions of MapReduce exist, such as Pig and Hive, which allow you to process data without explicitly implementing map or reduce functions, understanding the concepts behind MapReduce is fundamental to truly understanding distributed programming and data processing in Spark.

Word Count, a sample program often referred to as the "Hello World" of MapReduce, is a simple algorithm often used to represent and demonstrate the MapReduce programming model. If you have previously read any Hadoop or Spark training material or tutorials, you are probably tired of seeing Word Count examples, or you may be scratching your head, trying to understand the fixation with counting words.

Word Count is the most prevalent example used when describing the MapReduce programming model because it is easy to understand and demonstrates all the components of the MapReduce model. Many real-life problems solved with MapReduce are simply adaptations or derivations of Word Count (for instance, counting occurrences of events in a large corpus of log files, or text mining functions such as *TF-IDF* [*Term Frequency-Inverse Document Frequency*]). When you understand Word Count, you understand MapReduce, and the problem-solving possibilities are endless. Let's walk through a simple example using Spark now:

1. Using your single-node Spark installation, download the shakespeare.txt file (works of Shakespeare) from this link:

   https://s3.amazonaws.com/sparkusingpython/shakespeare/shakespeare.txt

   You can use wget or curl to download this file.

2. Place the file in the /opt/spark/data directory of your Spark installation:

   ```
   $ sudo mv shakespeare.txt /opt/spark/data
   ```

   Note that if you have HDFS available to you (for example, with AWS EMR, Databricks, or a Hadoop distribution that includes Spark), you can upload the file to HDFS and use it as an alternative.

3. Open a PySpark shell in local mode:

```
$ pyspark --master local
```

If you have a Hadoop cluster or distributed Spark Standalone cluster accessible, you are free to use it instead by specifying one of the following:

```
--master yarn
--master spark://<yoursparkmaster>:7077
```

Note that if your Python binary is not python (for instance, it may be py or python3 depending upon your release), you need to direct Spark to the correct file. This can be done using the following environment variable settings:

```
$ export PYSPARK_PYTHON=python3
$ export PYSPARK_DRIVER_PYTHON=python3
```

4. From your PySpark session, import the Python re (Regular Expression) module, which you will use to tokenize the file:

```
import re
```

5. Load the shakespeare.txt file into an RDD named doc:

```
doc = sc.textFile("file:///opt/spark/data/shakespeare.txt")
```

6. Filter empty lines from the RDD, split lines by whitespace, and flatten the lists of words into one list:

```
flattened = doc.filter(lambda line: len(line) > 0) \
    .flatMap(lambda line: re.split('\W+', line))
```

7. Inspect the flattened RDD:

```
flattened.take(6)
```

8. Map text to lowercase, remove empty strings, and then convert to key/value pairs in the form (word, 1):

```
kvpairs = flattened.filter(lambda word: len(word) > 0) \
  .map(lambda word:(word.lower(),1))
```

9. Inspect the kvpairs RDD. Notice that the RDD created is a *PairRDD* representing a collection of key/value pairs:

```
kvpairs.take(5)
```

10. Count each word and sort results in reverse alphabetic order:

```
countsbyword = kvpairs.reduceByKey(lambda v1, v2: v1 + v2) \
  .sortByKey(ascending=False)
```

11. Inspect the countsbyword RDD:

```
countsbyword.take(5)
```

12. Find the top five most-used words:

```
# invert the kv pair to make the count the key and sort
topwords = countsbyword.map(lambda x: (x[1],x[0])) \
.sortByKey(ascending=False)
```

13. Inspect the `topwords` RDD:

```
topwords.take(5)
```

Note how the `map()` function is used in step 12 to invert the key and value. This is a common approach to performing an operation known as *secondary sort*, which is a means to sort values that are not sorted by default.

Now exit your pyspark session by pressing Ctrl+D.

14. Now put it all together and run it as a complete Python program by using `spark-submit`. First, minimize the amount of logging by creating and configuring a `log4j.properties` file in the `conf` directory of your Spark installation. Do this by executing the following command from a Linux terminal (or an analogous operation if you are using another operating system):

```
sed \
"s/log4j.rootCategory=INFO, console/log4j.rootCategory=ERROR, console/" \
$SPARK_HOME/conf/log4j.properties.template \
> $SPARK_HOME/conf/log4j.properties
```

15. Create a new file named `wordcounts.py` and add the following code to the file:

```
import sys, re
from pyspark import SparkConf, SparkContext
conf = SparkConf().setAppName('Word Counts')
sc = SparkContext(conf=conf)

# check command line arguments
if (len(sys.argv) != 3):
    print("""\
This program will count occurrences of each word in a document or documents
and return the counts sorted by the most frequently occurring words

Usage:  wordcounts.py <input_file_or_dir> <output_dir>
""")
    sys.exit(0)
else:
    inputpath = sys.argv[1]
    outputdir = sys.argv[2]

# count and sort word occurrences
wordcounts = sc.textFile("file://" + inputpath) \
                .filter(lambda line: len(line) > 0) \
                .flatMap(lambda line: re.split('\W+', line)) \
```

```
                   .filter(lambda word: len(word) > 0) \
                   .map(lambda word:(word.lower(),1)) \
                   .reduceByKey(lambda v1, v2: v1 + v2) \
                   .map(lambda x: (x[1],x[0])) \
                   .sortByKey(ascending=False) \
                   .persist()
    wordcounts.saveAsTextFile("file://" + outputdir)
    top5words = wordcounts.take(5)
    justwords = []
    for wordsandcounts in top5words:
        justwords.append(wordsandcounts[1])
    print("The top five words are : " + str(justwords))
    print("Check the complete output in " + outputdir)
```

16. Execute your program by using the following command:

```
$ spark-submit --master local \
wordcounts.py \
$SPARK_HOME/data/shakespeare.txt \
$SPARK_HOME/data/wordcounts
```

You should see the top five words displayed in the console. Check the output directory `$SPARK_HOME/data/wordcounts`; you should see one file in this directory (`part-00000`) because you used only one partition for this exercise. If you used more than one partition, you would see additional files (`part-00001`, `part-00002`, and so on). Open the file and inspect the contents.

17. Run the command from step 16 again. It should fail because the `wordcounts` directory already exists and cannot be overwritten. Simply remove or rename this directory or change the output directory for the next operation to a directory that does not exist, such as `wordcounts2`.

The complete source code for this exercise can be found in the `wordcount` folder at https://github.com/sparktraining/spark_using_python.

Join Transformations

Join operations are analogous to the `JOIN` operations you routinely see in SQL programming. Join functions combine records from two RDDs based on a common field, a key. Because join functions in Spark require a key to be defined, they operate on key/value pair RDDs.

The following is a quick refresher on joins—which you may want to skip if you have a relational database background:

- A *join* operates on two different datasets, where one field in each dataset is nominated as a key (a *join key*). The datasets are referred to in the order in which they are specified. For instance, the first dataset specified is considered the *left* entity or dataset, and the second dataset specified is considered the *right* entity or dataset.

- An *inner join*, often simply called a *join* (where the "inner" is inferred), returns all elements or records from both datasets, where the nominated key is present in both datasets.

- An *outer join* does not require keys to match in both datasets. Outer joins are implemented as either a left outer join, a right outer join, or a full outer join.

- A *left outer join* returns all records from the left (or first) dataset along with matched records only (by the specified key) from the right (or second) dataset.

- A *right outer join* returns all records from the right (or second) dataset along with matched records only (by the specified key) from the left (or first) dataset.

- A *full outer join* returns all records from both datasets whether there is a key match or not.

Joins are some of the most commonly required transformations in the Spark API, so it is imperative that you understand these functions and become comfortable using them.

To illustrate the use of the different join types in the Spark RDD API, let's consider a dataset from a fictitious retailer that includes an entity containing stores and an entity containing salespeople, loaded into RDDs, as shown in Listing 4.34.

Listing 4.34 **Datasets Used to Demonstrate Join Types in Spark**

```
stores = sc.parallelize([[(100, 'Boca Raton'),
                          (101, 'Columbia'),
                          (102, 'Cambridge'),
                          (103, 'Naperville')]])
# stores schema (store_id, store_location)
salespeople = sc.parallelize([[(1, 'Henry', 100),
                               (2, 'Karen', 100),
                               (3, 'Paul', 101),
                               (4, 'Jimmy', 102),
                               (5, 'Janice', None)]])
# salespeople schema (salesperson_id, salesperson_name, store_id)
```

The following sections look at the available join transformations in Spark, their usage, and some examples.

join()

Syntax:

```
RDD.join(<otherRDD>, numPartitions=None)
```

The join() transformation is an implementation of an inner join, matching two key/value pair RDDs by their key.

The optional numPartitions argument determines how many partitions to create in the resultant dataset. If this is not specified, the default value for the spark.default.parallelism configuration parameter is used. The numPartitions argument has the same behavior for other types of join operations in the Spark API as well.

The RDD returned is a structure containing the matched key and a value that is a tuple containing all the matched records from both RDDs as a list object. (This is where it may sound a bit foreign to you if you are used to performing INNER JOIN operations in SQL, which returns a flattened list of columns from both entities.)

Listing 4.35 demonstrates how a join() operation works in Spark.

Listing 4.35 **The join() Transformation**

```
salespeople.keyBy(lambda x: x[2]) \
          .join(stores).collect()
# returns: [(100, ((1, 'Henry', 100), 'Boca Raton')),
#           (100, ((2, 'Karen', 100), 'Boca Raton')),
#           (102, ((4, 'Jimmy', 102), 'Cambridge')),
#           (101, ((3, 'Paul', 101), 'Columbia'))]
```

This join() operation returns all salespeople assigned to stores keyed by the store ID (the join key) along with the entire store record and salesperson record. Notice that the resultant RDD contains duplicate data. You could (and should in many cases) follow the join() with a map() transformation to prune fields or project only the fields required for further processing.

> ### Optimizing Joins in Spark
>
> Joins involving RDDs that span more than one partition—and many do—require a shuffle. Spark generally plans and implements this activity to achieve the most optimal performance possible; however, a simple axiom to remember is "join large by small." This means to reference the large RDD (the one with the most elements, if this is known) first, followed by the smaller of the two RDDs. This will seem strange for users coming from relational database programming backgrounds, but unlike with relational database systems, joins in Spark are relatively inefficient. And unlike with most databases, there are no indexes or statistics to optimize the join, so the optimizations you provide are essential to maximizing performance.

leftOuterJoin()

Syntax:

```
RDD.leftOuterJoin(<otherRDD>, numPartitions=None)
```

The leftOuterJoin() transformation returns all elements or records from the first RDD referenced. If keys from the first (or left) RDD are present in the right RDD, then the right RDD record is returned along with the left RDD record. Otherwise, the right RDD record is None (empty).

The example shown in Listing 4.36 uses the leftOuterJoin() transformation to identify salespeople with no stores.

Listing 4.36 **The leftOuterJoin() Transformation**

```
salespeople.keyBy(lambda x: x[2]) \
          .leftOuterJoin(stores) \
          .filter(lambda x: x[1][1] is None) \
          .map(lambda x: "salesperson " + x[1][0][1] + " has no store") \
          .collect()
# returns ['salesperson Janice has no store']
```

rightOuterJoin()

Syntax:

RDD.rightOuterJoin(<otherRDD>, numPartitions=None)

The rightOuterJoin() transformation returns all elements or records from the second RDD referenced. If keys from the second (or right) RDD are present in the left RDD, then the left RDD record is returned along with the right RDD record. Otherwise, the left RDD record is None (empty).

Listing 4.37 shows an example of how the rightOuterJoin() transformation can be used to identify stores with no salespeople.

Listing 4.37 **The rightOuterJoin() Transformation**

```
salespeople.keyBy(lambda x: x[2]) \
          .rightOuterJoin(stores) \
          .filter(lambda x: x[1][0] is None) \
          .map(lambda x: x[1][1] + " store has no salespeople") \
          .collect()
# returns ['Naperville store has no salespeople']
```

fullOuterJoin()

Syntax:

RDD.fullOuterJoin(<otherRDD>, numPartitions=None)

The fullOuterJoin() transforms all elements from both RDDs whether there is a key matched or not. Keys not matched from either the left or right dataset are represented as None (empty).

Listing 4.38 shows an example of how the fullOuterJoin() transformation can be used to identify stores with no salespeople *as well as* salespeople with no stores.

Listing 4.38 **The fullOuterJoin() Transformation**

```
salespeople.keyBy(lambda x: x[2]) \
          .fullOuterJoin(stores) \
          .filter(lambda x: x[1][0] is None or x[1][1] is None) \
          .collect()
# returns [(,([5,'Janice',], None)),(103,(None,[103,'Naperville']))]
```

cogroup()

Syntax:

RDD.cogroup(<otherRDD>, numPartitions=None)

The cogroup() transformation groups multiple key/value pair datasets by a key. It is somewhat similar conceptually to a fullOuterJoin(), but there are a few key differences in its implementation:

- The cogroup() transformation returns an *iterable* object, similar to the object returned from the groupByKey() function you saw earlier.

- The cogroup() transformation groups multiple elements from both RDDs into *iterable* objects, whereas fullOuterJoin() creates separate output elements for the same key.

- The cogroup() transformation can group three or more RDDs using the Scala API or the groupWith() function alias.

The resultant RDD output from a cogroup() operation of two RDDs (*A*, *B*) with a key K could be summarized as:

```
[K, Iterable(K,VA, …), Iterable(K,VB, …)]
```

If an RDD does not have elements for a given key that is present in the other RDD, the corresponding *iterable* is empty. Listing 4.39 shows a cogroup() transformation using the salespeople and stores RDDs from the preceding examples.

Listing 4.39 **The cogroup() Transformation**

```
salespeople.keyBy(lambda x: x[2]) \
            .cogroup(stores).take(1)
# returns:
# [(None, (<pyspark.resultiterable.ResultIterable object at ...>,
#  <pyspark.resultiterable.ResultIterable object at ...>))]
salespeople.keyBy(lambda x: x[2]) \
            .cogroup(stores) \
            .mapValues(lambda x: [item for sublist in x for item in sublist]) \
            .collect()
# using the mapValues() to process the Iterable object returns:
# [(None, [(5, 'Janice', None)]),
#  (100, [(1, 'Henry', 100), (2, 'Karen', 100), 'Boca Raton']),
#  (102, [(4, 'Jimmy', 102), 'Cambridge']), (101, [(3, 'Paul', 101), 'Columbia']),
#  (103, ['Naperville'])]
```

cartesian()

Syntax:

```
RDD.cartesian(<otherRDD>)
```

The cartesian() transformation, sometimes referred to by its colloquial name, *cross join*, generates every possible combination of records from both RDDs. The number of records produced by this transformation is equal to the number of records in the first RDD multiplied by the number of records in the second RDD.

Listing 4.40 demonstrates the use of the cartesian() transformation.

Listing 4.40 **The `cartesian()` Transformation**

```
salespeople.keyBy(lambda x: x[2]) \
        .cartesian(stores).take(1)
# returns:
# [((100, (1, 'Henry', 100)), (100, 'Boca Raton'))]
salespeople.keyBy(lambda x: x[2]) \
        .cartesian(stores).count()
# returns 20 as there are 5 x 4 = 20 records
```

Use the `cartesian()` Transformation Cautiously

Cartesian, or cross-product, operations can yield excessively large amounts of data. Although this is a useful function for testing multiple combinations of items for machine learning, you could create a Big Data problem where one otherwise did not exist!

Joining Datasets in Spark

For this example you will use data from the Bay Area Bike Share Data Challenge. The Bay Area Bike Share program enables members to pick up bikes from designated stations and then drop off the bikes at the same station or a different one. Bay Area Bike Share has made trip data available for public use through the group's Open Data program. For more information, see these sites:

> http://www.bayareabikeshare.com/open-data

> https://www.fordgobike.com/system-data

To make your job easier, the data files for this exercise are available in this book's AWS S3 bucket:

> https://s3.amazonaws.com/sparkusingpython/bike-share/stations/stations.csv

> https://s3.amazonaws.com/sparkusingpython/bike-share/status/status.csv

> https://s3.amazonaws.com/sparkusingpython/bike-share/trips/trips.csv

> https://s3.amazonaws.com/sparkusingpython/bike-share/weather/weather.csv

You can download these files to your local Spark installation and access them locally. For this exercise, you should download the files and store them in your $SPARK_HOME/data directory as follows:

```
├── bike-share
│   ├── stations
│   │   └── stations.csv
│   ├── status
│   │   └── status.csv
│   ├── trips
│   │   └── trips.csv
│   └── weather
└       └── weather.csv
    ...
```

In this exercise, you will use this data to return the average number of bikes available by the hour for one week (February 22 to February 28) for stations located in the San Jose area only. Follow these steps:

1. Open an interactive pyspark session:

   ```
   $ pyspark --master local
   ```

2. Create an RDD named stations:

   ```
   stations = sc.textFile('/opt/spark/data/bike-share/stations')
   ```

   Table 4.2 shows the schema or structure of the files in the stations directory.

Table 4.2   **Fields in stations.csv**

Field Name	Description
station_id	Station ID number
name	Name of the station
lat	Latitude
long	Longitude
dockcount	Number of docks at the station
landmark	City
installation	Original date the station was installed

3. Create an RDD named status:

   ```
   status = sc.textFile('/opt/spark/data/bike-share/status')
   ```

   Table 4.3 shows the schema or structure of the files in the status directory.

Table 4.3   **Fields in status.csv**

Field Name	Description
station_id	Station ID number
bikes_available	Number of available bikes
docks_available	Number of available docks
time	Date and time, PST

4. Split the status data into discrete fields, projecting only the fields necessary, and decompose the date string so that you can filter records by date more easily in the next step:

   ```
   status2 = status.map(lambda x: x.split(',')) \
   .map(lambda x: (x[0], x[1], x[2], x[3].replace('"',''))) \
   .map(lambda x: (x[0], x[1], x[2], x[3].split(' '))) \
   .map(lambda x: (x[0], x[1], x[2], x[3][0].split('-'), x[3][1].split(':'))) \
   .map(lambda x: (int(x[0]), int(x[1]), int(x[3][0]), int(x[3][1]), int(x[3][2]),
       int(x[4][0])))
   ```

Inspect the status2 RDD:

```
status2.first()
```

The schema for the status2 RDD is as follows:

```
[(station_id, bikes_available, year, month, day, hour),...]
```

5. Because status.csv is the biggest of the datasets (more than 36 million records), restrict the dataset to only the dates required and then drop the date fields because they are no longer necessary:

```
status3 = status2.filter(lambda x: x[2]==2015 and \
         x[3]==2 and \
         x[4]>=22) \
         .map(lambda x: (x[0], x[1], x[5]))
```

The schema for status3 is the same as the schema for status2 because you have just removed unnecessary records.

6. Filter the stations dataset to include only stations where landmark='San Jose':

```
stations2 = stations.map(lambda x: x.split(',')) \
         .filter(lambda x: x[5] == 'San Jose') \
         .map(lambda x: (int(x[0]), x[1]))
```

Inspect the stations2 RDD:

```
stations2.first()
```

7. Convert both RDDs to key/value pair RDDs to prepare for a join() operation:

```
status_kv = status3.keyBy(lambda x: x[0])
stations_kv = stations2.keyBy(lambda x: x[0])
```

Inspect both newly created PairRDDs:

```
status_kv.first()
stations_kv.first()
```

8. Join the status_kv key/value pair RDD to the stations_kv key/value pair RDD by their keys (station_id):

```
joined = status_kv.join(stations_kv)
```

Inspect the joined RDD:

```
joined.first()
```

9. Clean the joined RDD:

```
cleaned = joined.map(lambda x: (x[0], x[1][0][1], x[1][0][2], x[1][1][1]))
```

Inspect the cleaned RDD:

```
cleaned.first()
```

The schema for the `cleaned` RDD is as follows:

```
[(station_id,bikes_available,hour,name),...]
```

10. Create a key/value pair with the key as a tuple consisting of the station name and the hour and then compute the averages by each hour for each station:

```
avgbyhour = cleaned.keyBy(lambda x: (x[3],x[2])) \
        .mapValues(lambda x: (x[1], 1)) \
        .reduceByKey(lambda x, y: (x[0] + y[0], x[1] + y[1])) \
        .mapValues(lambda x: (x[0]/x[1]))
```

Inspect the `avgbyhour` RDD:

```
avgbyhour.first()
```

The schema for the `cleaned` RDD is as follows:

```
[((name,hour),bikes_available),...]
```

11. Find the top 10 averages by station and hour by using the `sortBy()` function:

```
topavail = avgbyhour.keyBy(lambda x: x[1]) \
        .sortByKey(ascending=False) \
        .map(lambda x: (x[1][0][0], x[1][0][1], x[0]))
topavail.take(10)
```

The complete source code for this exercise can be found in the `joining-datasets` folder at https://github.com/sparktraining/spark_using_python.

Transformations on Sets

Set operations are conceptually similar to mathematical set operations. A set function operates against two RDDs and results in one RDD. Consider the Venn diagram shown in Figure 4.9, which shows a set of odd integers and a subset of Fibonacci numbers. The following sections use these two sets to demonstrate the various set transformations available in the Spark API.

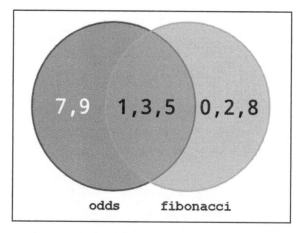

Figure 4.9 Set Venn diagram.

union()

Syntax:

```
RDD.union(<otherRDD>)
```

The union() transformation takes one RDD and appends another RDD to it, resulting in a combined output RDD. The RDDs are not required to have the same schema or structure. For instance, the first RDD can have five fields, whereas the second can have more or fewer than five fields.

The union() transformation does not filter duplicates from the output RDD in the case that two unioned RDDs have records that are identical to each other. To filter duplicates, you could follow the union() transformation with the distinct() function discussed previously.

The RDD that results from a union() operation is not sorted either, but you could sort it by following union() with a sortBy() function.

Listing 4.41 shows an example using union().

Listing 4.41 **The union() Transformation**

```
odds = sc.parallelize([1,3,5,7,9])
fibonacci = sc.parallelize([0,1,2,3,5,8])
odds.union(fibonacci).collect()
# returns [1, 3, 5, 7, 9, 0, 1, 2, 3, 5, 8]
```

intersection()

Syntax:

```
RDD.intersection(<otherRDD>)
```

The intersection() transformation returns elements that are present in both RDDs. In other words, it returns the overlap between two sets. The elements or records must be identical in both sets, with each respective record's data structure and all of its fields matching in both RDDs.

Listing 4.42 demonstrates the intersection() transformation.

Listing 4.42 **The intersection() Transformation**

```
odds = sc.parallelize([1,3,5,7,9])
fibonacci = sc.parallelize([0,1,2,3,5,8])
odds.intersection(fibonacci).collect()
# returns [1, 3, 5]
```

subtract()

Syntax:

```
RDD.subtract(<otherRDD>, numPartitions=None)
```

The subtract() transformation, as shown in Listing 4.43, returns all elements from the first RDD that are not present in the second RDD. This is an implementation of a mathematical set subtraction.

Listing 4.43 **The subtract() Transformation**

```
odds = sc.parallelize([1,3,5,7,9])
fibonacci = sc.parallelize([0,1,2,3,5,8])
odds.subtract(fibonacci).collect()
# returns [7, 9]
```

subtractByKey()

Syntax:

RDD.subtractByKey(<otherRDD>, numPartitions=None)

The subtractByKey() transformation is a set operation similar to the subtract transformation. The subtractByKey() transformation returns key/value pair elements from an RDD with keys that are not present in key/value pair elements from otherRDD.

The numPartitions argument specifies how many output partitions are to be created in the resultant RDD, and it defaults to the configured spark.default.parallelism value.

Listing 4.44 demonstrates subtractByKey() by using two RDDs containing city names as the key and a tuple containing location data for the city.

Listing 4.44 **The subtractByKey() Transformation**

```
cities1 = sc.parallelize([('Hayward',(37.668819,-122.080795)),
                          ('Baumholder',(49.6489,7.3975)),
                          ('Alexandria',(38.820450,-77.050552)),
                          ('Melbourne', (37.663712,144.844788))])
cities2 = sc.parallelize([('Boulder Creek',(64.0708333,-148.2236111)),
                          ('Hayward',(37.668819,-122.080795)),
                          ('Alexandria',(38.820450,-77.050552)),
                          ('Arlington', (38.878337,-77.100703))])
cities1.subtractByKey(cities2).collect()
# returns:
# [('Baumholder', (49.6489, 7.3975)), ('Melbourne', (37.663712, 144.844788))]
cities2.subtractByKey(cities1).collect()
# returns:
# [('Boulder Creek', (64.0708333, -148.2236111)),
#  ('Arlington', (38.878337, -77.100703))]
```

Transformations on Numeric RDDs

Numeric RDDs consist of only numeric values. They are commonly used for statistical analysis, so you will see that many of the functions available to numeric RDDs are your common statistical functions. An example of a numeric RDD is the DoubleRDD discussed earlier in this chapter. The following sections look at these functions and provide some simple examples.

min()

Syntax:

```
RDD.min(key=None)
```

The min() function is an action that returns the minimum value for a numeric RDD. The key argument is a function used to generate a key for comparing. Listing 4.45 shows the use of the min() function.

Listing 4.45 **The min() Function**

```
numbers = sc.parallelize([0,1,1,2,3,5,8,13,21,34])
numbers.min()
# returns 0
```

max()

Syntax:

```
RDD.max(key=None)
```

The max() function is an action that returns the maximum value for a numeric RDD. The key argument is a function used to generate a key for comparing. Listing 4.46 shows the use of the max() function.

Listing 4.46 **The max() Function**

```
numbers = sc.parallelize([0,1,1,2,3,5,8,13,21,34])
numbers.max()
# returns 34
```

mean()

Syntax:

```
RDD.mean()
```

The mean() function computes the arithmetic mean from a numeric RDD. Listing 4.47 demonstrates the use of the mean() function.

Listing 4.47 **The mean() Function**

```
numbers = sc.parallelize([0,1,1,2,3,5,8,13,21,34])
numbers.mean()
# returns 8.8
```

sum()

Syntax:

RDD.sum()

The sum() function returns the sum of a list of numbers from a numeric RDD. Listing 4.48 shows the use of the sum() function.

Listing 4.48   **The sum() Function**

```
numbers = sc.parallelize([0,1,1,2,3,5,8,13,21,34])
numbers.sum()
# returns 88
```

stdev()

Syntax:

RDD.stdev()

The stdev() function is an action that computes the standard deviation for a series of numbers from a numeric RDD. Listing 4.49 shows an example of stdev().

Listing 4.49   **The stdev() Function**

```
numbers = sc.parallelize([0,1,1,2,3,5,8,13,21,34])
numbers.stdev()
# returns 10.467091286503619
```

variance()

Syntax:

RDD.variance()

The variance() function computes the variance in a series of numbers in a numeric RDD. Variance is a measure of how far a set of numbers are spread out. Listing 4.50 shows an example of variance().

Listing 4.50   **The variance() Function**

```
numbers = sc.parallelize([0,1,1,2,3,5,8,13,21,34])
numbers.variance()
# returns 109.55999999999999
```

stats()

Syntax:

```
RDD.stats()
```

The stats() function returns a StatCounter object, which is a structure containing the count(), mean(), stdev(), max(), and min() in one operation. Listing 4.51 demonstrates the stats() function.

Listing 4.51 **The stats() Function**

```
numbers = sc.parallelize([0,1,1,2,3,5,8,13,21,34])
numbers.stats()
# returns (count: 10, mean: 8.8, stdev: 10.4670912865, max: 34.0, min: 0.0)
```

Summary

This chapter covers the fundamentals of Spark programming, starting with a closer look at Spark RDDs (the most fundamental atomic data object in the Spark programming model), including looking at how to load data into RDDs, how RDDs are evaluated and processed, and how RDDs achieve fault tolerance and resiliency. This chapter also discusses the concepts of transformations and actions in Spark and provides specific descriptions and examples of the most important functions in the Spark core (or RDD) API. This chapter is arguably the most important chapter in this book as it has laid the foundations for all programming in Spark, including stream processing, machine learning, and SQL. The remainder of the book regularly refers to the functions and concepts covered in this chapter.

II

Beyond the Basics

Advanced Programming Using the Spark Core API

Technology feeds on itself. Technology makes more technology possible.

Alvin Toffler, American writer and futurist

In This Chapter:

- Introduction to shared variables (broadcast variables and accumulators) in Spark
- Partitioning and repartitioning of Spark RDDs
- Storage options for RDDs
- Caching, distributed persistence, and checkpointing of RDDs

This chapter focuses on the additional programming tools at your disposal with the Spark API, including broadcast variables and accumulators as shared variables across different Workers in a Spark cluster. This chapter also dives into the important topics of Spark partitioning and RDD storage. You will learn about the various storage functions available for program optimization, durability, and process restart and recovery. You will also learn how to use external programs and scripts to process data in Spark RDDs in a Spark-managed lineage. The information in this chapter builds on the Spark API transformations you learned about in Chapter 4, "Learning Spark Programming Basics," and gives you the additional tools required to build efficient end-to-end Spark processing pipelines.

Shared Variables in Spark

The Spark API provides two mechanisms for creating and using shared variables in a Spark cluster (that is, variables that are accessible or mutable by different Workers in the Spark cluster). These mechanisms are called *broadcast variables* and *accumulators*, and we look at them both now.

Broadcast Variables

Broadcast variables are read-only variables set by the Spark Driver program that are made available to the Worker nodes in a Spark cluster, which means they are available to any tasks running on Executors on the Workers. Broadcast variables are read only after being set by the Driver. Broadcast variables are shared across Workers using an efficient peer-to-peer sharing protocol based on BitTorrent; this enables greater scalability than simply pushing variables directly to Executor processes from the Spark Driver. Figure 5.1 demonstrates how broadcast variables are initialized, disseminated among Workers, and accessed by nodes within tasks.

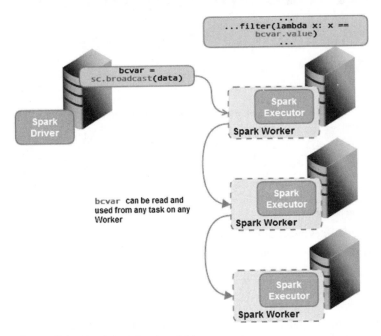

Figure 5.1   Spark broadcast variables.

The "Performance and Scalability of Broadcast in Spark" whitepaper at www.cs.berkeley.edu/~agearh/cs267.sp10/files/mosharaf-spark-bc-report-spring10.pdf documents the BitTorrent broadcast method as well as the other broadcast mechanisms considered for Spark; it's worth a read.

A broadcast variable is created under a SparkContext and is then accessible as an object in the context of the Spark application. The following sections describe the syntax for creating and accessing broadcast variables.

broadcast()

Syntax:

```
sc.broadcast(value)
```

The broadcast() method creates an instance of a Broadcast object within the specific SparkContext. The value is the object to be serialized and encapsulated in the Broadcast object; this could be any valid Python object. After they're created, these variables are available to all tasks running in the application. Listing 5.1 shows an example of the broadcast() method.

Listing 5.1   **Initializing a Broadcast Variable by Using the broadcast() Function**

```
stations = sc.broadcast({'83':'Mezes Park', '84':'Ryland Park'})
stations
# returns <pyspark.broadcast.Broadcast object at 0x…>
```

You can also create broadcast variables from the contents of a file, either on a local, network, or distributed filesystem. Consider a file named stations.csv, which contains comma-delimited data, as follows:

```
83,Mezes Park,37.491269,-122.236234,15,Redwood City,2/20/2014
84,Ryland Park,37.342725,-121.895617,15,San Jose,4/9/2014
```

Listing 5.2 shows an example of how to create a broadcast variable by using a file.

Listing 5.2   **Creating a Broadcast Variable from a File**

```
stationsfile = '/opt/spark/data/stations.csv'
stationsdata = dict(map(lambda x: (x[0],x[1]), \
                    map(lambda x: x.split(','), \
                    open(stationsfile))))
stations = sc.broadcast(stationsdata)
stations.value["83"]
# returns 'Mezes Park'
```

Listing 5.2 shows how to create a broadcast variable from a csv file (stations.csv) consisting of a dictionary of key/value pairs, including the station ID and the station name. You can now access this dictionary from within any map() or filter() RDD operations.

For initialized broadcast variable objects, a number of methods can be called within the SparkContext, as described in the following sections.

value()

Syntax:

Broadcast.value()

Listing 5.2 demonstrates the use of the value() function to return the value from the broadcast variable; in that example, the value is a dict (or map) that can access values from the map by their keys. The value() function can be used within a lambda function in a map() or filter() operation in a Spark program.

unpersist()

Syntax:

`Broadcast.unpersist(blocking=False)`

The `unpersist()` method of the `Broadcast` object is used to remove a broadcast variable from memory on all Workers in the cluster where it was present.

The Boolean `blocking` argument specifies whether this operation should block until the variable unpersists from all nodes or whether this can be an asynchronous, non-blocking operation. If you require memory to be released immediately, set this argument to `True`.

An example of the `unpersist()` method is provided in Listing 5.3.

Listing 5.3 **The unpersist() Method**

```
stations = sc.broadcast({'83':'Mezes Park', '84':'Ryland Park'})
stations.value['84']
# returns 'Ryland Park'
stations.unpersist()
# broadcast variable will eventually get evicted from cache
```

There are also several Spark configuration options related to broadcast variables, as described in Table 5.1. Typically, you can leave these at their default settings, but it is useful to know about them.

Table 5.1 **Spark Configuration Options Related to Broadcast Variables**

Configuration Option	Description
spark.broadcast.compress	Specifies whether to compress broadcast variables before transferring them to Workers. Defaults to `True` (recommended).
spark.broadcast.factory	Specifies which broadcast implementation to use. Defaults to `TorrentBroadcastFactory`.
spark.broadcast.blockSize	Specifies the size of each block of the broadcast variable (used by `TorrentBroadcastFactory`). Defaults to `4MB`.
spark.broadcast.port	Specifies the port for the Driver's HTTP broadcast server to listen on. Defaults to `random`.

What are the advantages of broadcast variables? Why are they useful or even required in some cases? As discussed in Chapter 4, it is often necessary to combine two datasets to produce a resultant dataset. This can be achieved in multiple ways.

Consider two associated datasets: `stations` (a relatively small lookup data set) and `status` (a large eventful data source). These two datasets can join on a natural key, `station_id`. You could join the two datasets as RDDs directly in your Spark application, as shown in Listing 5.4.

Listing 5.4   **Joining Lookup Data by Using an RDD `join()`**

```
status = sc.textFile('file:///opt/spark/data/bike-share/status') \
            .map(lambda x: x.split(',')) \
            .keyBy(lambda x: x[0])
stations = sc.textFile('file:///opt/spark/data/bike-share/stations') \
               .map(lambda x: x.split(',')) \
               .keyBy(lambda x: x[0])
status.join(stations) \
    .map(lambda x: (x[1][0][3],x[1][1][1],x[1][0][1],x[1][0][2])) \
    .count()
# returns 907200
```

This most likely would result in an expensive shuffle operation.

It would be better to set a table variable in the Driver for `stations`; this will then be available as a runtime variable for Spark tasks implementing `map()` operations, eliminating the requirement for a shuffle (see Listing 5.5).

Listing 5.5   **Joining Lookup Data by Using a Driver Variable**

```
stationsfile = '/opt/spark/data/bike-share/stations/stations.csv'
sdata = dict(map(lambda x: (x[0],x[1]), \
                    map(lambda x: x.split(','), \
                    open(stationsfile))))
status = sc.textFile('file:///opt/spark/data/bike-share/status') \
            .map(lambda x: x.split(',')) \
            .keyBy(lambda x: x[0])
status.map(lambda x: (x[1][3], sdata[x[0]], x[1][1], x[1][2])) \
      .count()
# returns 907200
```

This works and is better in most cases than the first option; however, it lacks scalability. In this case, the variable is part of a closure within the referencing function. This may result in unnecessary and less efficient transfer and duplication of data on the Worker nodes.

The best option would be to initialize a broadcast variable for the smaller `stations` table. This involves using peer-to-peer replication to make the variable available to all Workers, and the single copy is usable by all tasks on all Executors belonging to an application running on the Worker. Then you can use the variable in your `map()` operations, much as in the second option. An example of this is provided in Listing 5.6.

Listing 5.6   **Joining Lookup Data by Using a Broadcast Variable**

```
stationsfile = '/opt/spark/data/bike-share/stations/stations.csv'
sdata = dict(map(lambda x: (x[0],x[1]), \
                    map(lambda x: x.split(','), \
                    open(stationsfile))))
```

```
stations = sc.broadcast(sdata)
status = sc.textFile('file:///opt/spark/data/bike-share/status') \
           .map(lambda x: x.split(',')) \
           .keyBy(lambda x: x[0])
status.map(lambda x: (x[1][3], stations.value[x[0]], x[1][1], x[1][2])) \
      .count()
# returns 907200
```

As you can see in the scenario just described, using broadcast variables is an efficient method for sharing data at runtime between processes running on different nodes of a Spark cluster. Consider the following points about broadcast variables:

- Using them eliminates the need for a shuffle operation.

- They use an efficient and scalable peer-to-peer distribution mechanism.

- They replicate data once per Worker, as opposed to replicating once per task—which is important as there may be thousands of tasks in a Spark application.

- Many tasks can reuse them multiple times.

- They are serialized objects, so they are efficiently read.

Accumulators

Another type of shared variable in Spark is an *accumulator*. Unlike with broadcast variables, you can update accumulators; more specifically, they are numeric values that be incremented.

Think of accumulators as counters that you can use in a number of ways in Spark programming. Accumulators allow you to aggregate multiple values while your program is running.

Accumulators are set by the Driver and updated by Executors running tasks in the respective SparkContext. The Driver can then read back the final value from the accumulator, typically at the end of the program.

Accumulators update only once per successfully completed task in a Spark application. Worker nodes send the updates to the accumulator back to the Driver, which is the only process that can read the accumulator value. Accumulators can use integer or float values. Listing 5.7 and Figure 5.2 demonstrate how accumulators are created, updated, and read.

Listing 5.7 **Creating and Accessing Accumulators**

```
acc = sc.accumulator(0)
def addone(x):
    global acc
    acc += 1
    return x + 1
myrdd=sc.parallelize([1,2,3,4,5])
myrdd.map(lambda x: addone(x)).collect()
# returns [2, 3, 4, 5, 6]
print("records processed: " + str(acc.value))
# returns "records processed: 5"
```

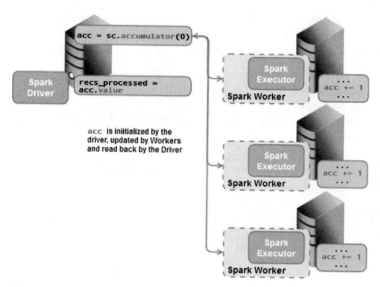

Figure 5.2   Accumulators.

From a programming standpoint, accumulators are very straightforward. The functions related to accumulators in Spark programming, used in Listing 5.7, are documented in the following sections.

accumulator()

Syntax:

```
sc.accumulator(value, accum_param=None)
```

The accumulator() method creates an instance of an Accumulator object within the specific SparkContext and initializes with a given initial value specified by the value argument. The accum_param argument is used to define custom accumulators, which we discuss next.

value()

Syntax:

```
Accumulator.value()
```

The value() method retrieves the accumulator's value. This method can be used only in the Driver program.

Custom Accumulators

Standard accumulators created in a SparkContext support primitive numeric datatypes, including int and float. Custom accumulators can perform aggregate operations on variables of types other than scalar numeric values. Custom accumulators are created using the AccumulatorParam helper object. The only requirement is that the operations performed must be associative and commutative, meaning the order and sequence of operation are irrelevant.

A common use of custom accumulators is to accumulate vectors as either lists or dictionaries. Conceptually, the same principle applies in a non-mathematical context to non-numeric operations—for instance, when you create a custom accumulator to concatenate string values.

To use custom accumulators, you need to define a custom class that extends the AccumulatorParam class. The class needs to include two specific member functions: addInPlace(), used to operate against two objects of the custom accumulators datatype and to return a new value, and zero(), which provides a "zero value" for the type—for instance, an empty map for a map type.

Listing 5.8 shows an example of a custom accumulator used to sum vectors as a Python dictionary.

Listing 5.8 **Custom Accumulators**

```
from pyspark import AccumulatorParam
class VectorAccumulatorParam(AccumulatorParam):
    def zero(self, value):
        dict1={}
        for i in range(0,len(value)):
            dict1[i]=0
        return dict1
    def addInPlace(self, val1, val2):
        for i in val1.keys():
            val1[i] += val2[i]
        return val1
rdd1=sc.parallelize([{0: 0.3, 1: 0.8, 2: 0.4}, {0: 0.2, 1: 0.4, 2: 0.2}])
vector_acc = sc.accumulator({0: 0, 1: 0, 2: 0}, VectorAccumulatorParam())
def mapping_fn(x):
    global vector_acc
    vector_acc += x
# do some other rdd processing...
rdd1.foreach(mapping_fn)
print vector_acc.value
# returns {0: 0.5, 1: 1.2000000000000002, 2: 0.6000000000000001}
```

Uses for Accumulators

Accumulators are typically used for operational purposes, such as for counting the number of records processed or tracking the number of malformed records. You can also use them for notional counts of different types of records; an example would be a count of different response codes discovered during the mapping of log events.

In some cases, as shown in the following exercise, you can use accumulators for processing within an application.

Potential for Erroneous Results in Accumulators

If accumulators are used in transformations, such as when calling accumulators to perform add-in-place operations to calculate results inside a map() operation, the results may be erroneous. Stage retries or speculative execution can cause accumulator values to be counted more than once, resulting in incorrect counts. If absolute correctness is required, you should use accumulators only within actions computed by the Spark Driver, such as the foreach() action. If you are looking only for notional or indicative counts on very large datasets, then it is okay to update accumulators in transformations. This behavior may change in future releases of Spark; for now, this is a caveat emptor.

Exercise: Using Broadcast Variables and Accumulators

This exercise shows how to calculate the average word length from the words in the works of Shakespeare text, downloaded in the section "MapReduce and Word Count Exercise" in Chapter 4. In this exercise, you will remove known stop words ("a," "and," "or," "the") by using a broadcast variable and then compute average word length by using accumulators. Follow these steps:

1. Open a PySpark shell using whatever mode is available to you (Local, YARN Client, or Standalone). Use a single-instance Spark deployment in Local mode for this example:

    ```
    $ pyspark --master local
    ```

2. Import a list of English stop words (stop-word-list.csv) from the book's S3 bucket using the built-in urllib2 Python module (Python3) and then convert the data into a Python list by using the split() function:

    ```
    import urllib.request
    stopwordsurl = "https://s3.amazonaws.com/sparkusingpython/stopwords/
    stop-word-list.csv"
    req = urllib.request.Request(stopwordsurl)
    with urllib.request.urlopen(req) as response:
        stopwordsdata = response.read().decode("utf-8")
    stopwordslist = stopwordsdata.split(",")
    ```

3. Create a broadcast variable for the stopwordslist object:

    ```
    stopwords = sc.broadcast(stopwordslist)
    ```

4. Initialize accumulators for the cumulative word count and cumulative total length of all words:

    ```
    word_count = sc.accumulator(0)
    total_len = sc.accumulator(0.0)
    ```

    Note that you have created total_len as a float because you will use it as the numerator in a division operation later, when you want to keep the precision in the result.

5. Create a function to accumulate word count and the total word length:

    ```
    def add_values(word,word_count,total_len):
    word_count += 1
    total_len += len(word)
    ```

6. Create an RDD by loading the Shakespeare text, tokenizing and normalizing all text in the document, and filtering stop words by using the `stopwords` broadcast variable:

```
words = sc.textFile('file:///opt/spark/data/shakespeare.txt') \
    .flatMap(lambda line: line.split()) \
    .map(lambda x: x.lower()) \
    .filter(lambda x: x not in stopwords.value)
```

7. Use the `foreach` action to iterate through the resultant RDD and call your `add_values` function:

```
words.foreach(lambda x: add_values(x, word_count, total_len))
```

8. Calculate the average word length from your accumulator-shared variables and display the final result:

```
avgwordlen = total_len.value/word_count.value
print("Total Number of Words: " + str(word_count.value))
print("Average Word Length: " + str(avgwordlen))
```

This should return 966958 for the total number of words and 3.608722405730135 for the average word length.

7. Now put all the code for this exercise in a file named `average_word_length.py` and execute the program using `spark-submit`. Recall that you need to add the following to the beginning of your script:

```
from pyspark import SparkConf, SparkContext
conf = SparkConf().setAppName('Broadcast Variables and Accumulators')
sc = SparkContext(conf=conf)
```

The complete source code for this exercise can be found in the `average-word-length` folder at https://github.com/sparktraining/spark_using_python.

Partitioning Data in Spark

Partitioning is integral to Spark processing in most cases. Effective partitioning can improve application performance by orders of magnitude. Conversely, inefficient partitioning can result in programs failing to complete, producing problems such as Executor-out-of-memory errors for excessively large partitions.

The following sections recap what you already know about RDD partitions and then discuss API methods that can affect partitioning behavior or that can access data within partitions more effectively.

Partitioning Overview

The number of partitions to create from an RDD transformation is usually configurable. There are some default behaviors you should be aware of, however.

Spark creates an RDD partition per block when using HDFS (typically the size of a block in HDFS is 128MB), as in this example:

```
myrdd = sc.textFile("hdfs:///dir/filescontaining10blocks")
myrdd.getNumPartitions()
# returns 10
```

Shuffle operations such as the ByKey operations—groupByKey(), reduceByKey()—and other operations in which the numPartitions value is not supplied as an argument to the method will result in a number of partitions equal to the spark.default.parallelism configuration value. Here is an example:

```
# with spark.default.parallelism=4
myrdd = sc.textFile("hdfs:///dir/filescontaining10blocks")
mynewrdd = myrdd.flatMap(lambda x: x.split()) \
  .map(lambda x:(x,1)) \
  .reduceByKey(lambda x, y: x + y)
mynewrdd.getNumPartitions()
# returns 4
```

If the spark.default.parallelism configuration parameter is not set, the number of partitions that a transformation creates will equal the highest number of partitions defined by an upstream RDD in the current RDDs lineage. Here is an example:

```
# with spark.default.parallelism not set
myrdd = sc.textFile("hdfs:///dir/filescontaining10blocks")
mynewrdd = myrdd.flatMap(lambda x: x.split()) \
  .map(lambda x:(x,1)) \
  .reduceByKey(lambda x, y: x + y)
mynewrdd.getNumPartitions()
# returns 10
```

The default partitioner class that Spark uses is HashPartitioner; it hashes all keys with a deterministic hashing function and then uses the key hash to create approximately equal buckets. The aim is to disperse data evenly across the specified number of partitions based on the key.

Some Spark transformations, such as the filter() transformation, do not allow you to change the partitioning behavior of the resultant RDD. For example, if you applied a filter() function to an RDD with four partitions, it would result in a new, filtered RDD with four partitions, using the same partitioning scheme as the original RDD (that is, hash partitioned).

Although the default behavior is normally acceptable, in some circumstances it can lead to inefficiencies. Fortunately, Spark provides several mechanisms to address these potential issues.

Controlling Partitions

How many partitions should an RDD have? There are issues at both ends of the spectrum when it comes to answering this question. Having too few, very large partitions can result in out-of-memory issues on Executors. Having too many small partitions isn't optimal because too many tasks spawn for trivial input sets. A mix of large and small partitions can result in speculative execution occurring needlessly, if this is enabled. *Speculative execution* is a mechanism that a cluster scheduler uses to preempt slow-running processes; if the root cause of the slowness of one or more processes in a Spark application is inefficient partitioning, then speculative execution won't help.

Consider the scenario in Figure 5.3.

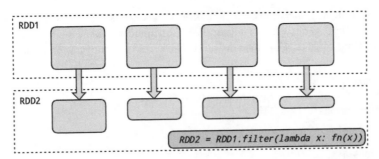

Figure 5.3   Skewed partitions.

The `filter()` operation creates a new partition for every input partition on a one-to-one basis, with only records that meet the filter condition. This can result in some partitions having significantly less data than others, which can lead to bad outcomes, such as data skewing, the potential for speculative execution, and suboptimal performance in subsequent stages.

In such cases, you can use one of the repartitioning methods in the Spark API; these include `partitionBy()`, `coalesce()`, `repartition()`, and `repartitionAndSortWithinPartitions()`, all of which are explained shortly.

These functions take a partitioned input RDD and create a new RDD with n partitions, where n could be more or fewer than the original number of partitions. Take the example from Figure 5.3. In Figure 5.4, a `repartition()` function is applied to consolidate the four unevenly distributed partitions to two "evenly" distributed partitions, using the default `HashPartitioner`.

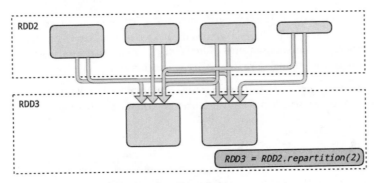

Figure 5.4   The `repartition()` function.

Determining the Optimal Number of Partitions

Often, determining the optimal number of partitions involves experimenting with different values until you find the point of diminishing returns (the point at which each additional partition starts to degrade performance). As a starting point, a simple axiom is to use two times the number of cores in your cluster—that is, two times the aggregate number of cores across all Worker nodes. In addition, as a dataset changes, it is advisable to revisit the number of partitions used.

Repartitioning Functions

The main functions used to repartition RDDs are documented in the following sections.

partitionBy()

Syntax:

```
RDD.partitionBy(numPartitions, partitionFunc=portable_hash)
```

The partitionBy() method returns a new RDD containing the same data as the input RDD but with the number of partitions specified by the numPartitions argument, using the portable_hash function (HashPartitioner) by default. An example of partitionBy() is shown in Listing 5.9.

Listing 5.9 **The partitionBy() Function**

```
kvrdd = sc.parallelize([(1,'A'),(2,'B'),(3,'C'),(4,'D')],4)
kvrdd.getNumPartitions()
# returns 4
kvrdd.partitionBy(2).getNumPartitions()
# returns 2
```

The partitionBy() function is also called by other functions, such as sortByKey(), which calls partitionBy() using rangePartitioner instead of the portable_hash function. The rangePartitioner partitions records sorted by their key into equally sized ranges; this is an alternative to hash partitioning.

The partitionBy() transformation is also a useful function for implementing a custom partitioner, such as a function to bucket web logs into monthly partitions. A custom partition function must take a key as input and return a number between zero and the numPartitions specified in the partitionBy() function and then use that return value to direct elements to their target partition.

repartition()

Syntax:

```
RDD.repartition(numPartitions)
```

The repartition() method returns a new RDD with the same data as the input RDD, consisting of exactly the number of partitions specified by the numPartitions argument. The repartition()

method may require a shuffle, and, unlike partitionBy(), it has no option to change the partitioner or partitioning function. The repartition() method also lets you create more partitions in the target RDD than existed in the input RDD. Listing 5.10 shows an example of the repartition() function.

Listing 5.10 **The repartition() Function**

```
kvrdd = sc.parallelize([(1,'A'),(2,'B'),(3,'C'),(4,'D')],4)
kvrdd.repartition(2).getNumPartitions()
# returns 2
```

coalesce()

Syntax:

```
RDD.coalesce(numPartitions, shuffle=False)
```

The coalesce() method returns a new RDD consisting of the number of partitions specified by the numPartitions argument. The coalesce() method also allows you to control whether the repartitioning triggers a shuffle, using the Boolean shuffle argument. The operation coalesce(n, shuffle=True) is functionally equivalent to repartition(n).

The coalesce() method is an optimized implementation of repartition(). Unlike repartition(), however, coalesce() gives you more control over the shuffle behavior and, in many cases, allows you to avoid data movement. Also, unlike repartition(), coalesce() only lets you decrease the number of target partitions from the number of partitions in your input RDD.

Listing 5.11 demonstrates the use of the coalesce() function with the shuffle argument set to False.

Listing 5.11 **The coalesce() Function**

```
kvrdd = sc.parallelize([(1,'A'),(2,'B'),(3,'C'),(4,'D')],4)
kvrdd.coalesce(2, shuffle=False).getNumPartitions()
# returns 2
```

repartitionAndSortWithinPartitions()

Syntax:

```
RDD.repartitionAndSortWithinPartitions(numPartitions=None,
partitionFunc=portable_hash,
ascending=True,
keyfunc=<lambda function>)
```

The repartitionAndSortWithinPartitions() method repartitions the input RDD into the number of partitions directed by the numPartitions argument and is partitioned according to the function specified by the `partitionFunc` argument. Within each resulting partition, records are sorted by their keys, as defined by the `keyfunc` argument, in the sort order determined by the `ascending` argument.

The `repartitionAndSortWithinPartitions()` method is commonly used to implement a *secondary sort*. The sorting capability for key/value pair RDDs is normally based on an arbitrary key hash or a range; this becomes more challenging with key/value pairs with composite keys, such as ((*k1, k2*), *v*). If you wanted to sort on *k1* first and then within a partition sort the *k2* values for each *k1*, this would involve a secondary sort.

Listing 5.12 demonstrates the use of the `repartitionAndSortWithinPartitions()` method to perform a secondary sort on a key/value pair RDD with a composite key. The first part of the key is grouped in separate partitions; the second part of the key is then sorted in descending order. Note the use of the `glom()` function to inspect partitions; we discuss this function shortly.

Listing 5.12 **The `repartitionAndSortWithinPartitions()` Function**

```
kvrdd = sc.parallelize([((1,99),'A'),((1,101),'B'),((2,99),'C'),((2,101),'D')],2)
kvrdd.glom().collect()
# returns:
# [[((1, 99), 'A'), ((1, 101), 'B')], [((2, 99), 'C'), ((2, 101), 'D')]]
kvrdd2 = kvrdd.repartitionAndSortWithinPartitions( \
numPartitions=2,
ascending=False,
keyfunc=lambda x: x[1])
kvrdd2.glom().collect()
# returns:
# [[((1, 101), 'B'), ((1, 99), 'A')], [((2, 101), 'D'), ((2, 99), 'C')]]
```

Partition-Specific or Partition-Aware API Methods

Many of Spark's methods are designed to interact with partitions as atomic units; these include both actions and transformations. Some of the methods are described in the following sections.

foreachPartition()

Syntax:

```
RDD.foreachPartition(func)
```

The `foreachPartition()` method is an action similar to the `foreach()` action, applying a function specified by the `func` argument to each partition of an RDD. Listing 5.13 shows an example of the `foreachPartition()` method.

Listing 5.13 **The foreachPartition() Action**

```
def f(x):
    for rec in x:
        print(rec)
kvrdd = sc.parallelize([((1,99),'A'),((1,101),'B'),((2,99),'C'),((2,101),'D')],2)
kvrdd.foreachPartition(f)
# returns:
# ((1, 99), 'A')
# ((1, 101), 'B')
# ((2, 99), 'C')
# ((2, 101), 'D')
```

Keep in mind that foreachPartition() is an action, not a transformation, and it therefore triggers evaluation of the input RDD and its entire lineage. Furthermore, the function results in data going to the Driver, so be mindful of the final RDD data volumes when running this function.

glom()

Syntax:

```
RDD.glom()
```

The glom() method returns an RDD created by coalescing all the elements within each partition into a list. This is useful for inspecting RDD partitions as collated lists; you saw an example of this function in Listing 5.12.

lookup()

Syntax:

```
RDD.lookup(key)
```

The lookup() method returns the list of values in an RDD for the key referenced by the key argument. If used against an RDD partitioned with a known partitioner, lookup() uses the partitioner to narrow its search to only the partitions where the key would be present.

Listing 5.14 shows an example of the lookup() method.

Listing 5.14 **The lookup() Method**

```
kvrdd = sc.parallelize([(1,'A'),(1,'B'),(2,'C'),(2,'D')],2)
kvrdd.lookup(1)
# returns ['A', 'B']
```

mapPartitions()

Syntax:

```
RDD.mapPartitions(func, preservesPartitioning=False)
```

The mapPartitions() method returns a new RDD by applying a function (the func argument) to each partition of this RDD. Listing 5.15 demonstrates using the mapPartitions() method to invert the key and value within each partition.

Listing 5.15 **The mapPartitions() Function**

```
kvrdd = sc.parallelize([(1,'A'),(1,'B'),(2,'C'),(2,'D')],2)
def f(iterator): yield [(b, a) for (a, b) in iterator]
kvrdd.mapPartitions(f).collect()
# returns [[('A', 1), ('B', 1)], [('C', 2), ('D', 2)]]
```

One of the biggest advantages of the mapPartitions() method is that the function referenced is called once per partition as opposed to once per element; this can be particularly beneficial if the function has notable overhead for creation.

Many of Spark's other transformations use the mapPartitions() function internally. There is also a related transformation called mapPartitionsWithIndex(), which returns functions similarly but tracks the index of the original partition.

RDD Storage Options

Thus far, we have discussed RDDs as distributed immutable collections of objects that reside in memory on cluster Worker nodes. There are, however, other storage options for RDDs that are beneficial for a number of reasons. Before we discuss the various RDD storage levels and then caching and persistence, let's review the concept of RDD lineage.

RDD Lineage Revisited

Recall that Spark plans the execution of a program as a DAG (directed acyclic graph), which is a set of operations separated into stages with stage dependencies. Some operations, such as map() operations, can be completely parallelized, and some operations, such as reduceByKey(), require a shuffle. This naturally introduces a stage dependency.

The Spark Driver keeps track of every RDD's lineage—that is, the series of transformations performed to yield an RDD or a partition thereof. This enables every RDD at every stage to be reevaluated in the event of a failure, which provides the resiliency in Resilient Distributed Datasets.

Consider the simple example involving only one stage shown in Figure 5.5.

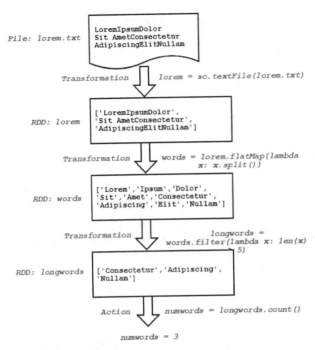

Figure 5.5   RDD lineage.

Listing 5.16 shows a summary of a physical execution plan created by Spark using the toDebugString() function.

Listing 5.16 **The toDebugString() Function**

```
>>> print(longwords.toDebugString())
(1) PythonRDD[6] at collect at <stdin>:1 []
 | MapPartitionsRDD[1] at textFile at ..[]
 | file://lorem.txt HadoopRDD[0] at textFile at ..[]
```

The action longwords.count() forces evaluation of each of the parent RDDs to longwords. If this or any other action, such as longwords.take(1) or longwords.collect(), is called a subsequent time, the entire lineage is reevaluated. In simple cases, with small amounts of data with one or two stages, these reevaluations are not an issue, but in many circumstances, they can be inefficient and impact recovery times in the event of failure.

RDD Storage Options

RDDs are stored in their partitions on various worker nodes in a Spark YARN, Standalone, or Mesos cluster. RDDs have six basic storage levels available, as summarized in Table 5.2.

Table 5.2 **RDD Storage Levels**

Storage Level	Description
MEMORY_ONLY	RDD partitions are stored in memory only. This is the default.
MEMORY_AND_DISK	RDD partitions that do not fit in memory are stored on disk.
MEMORY_ONLY_SER*	RDD partitions are stored as serialized objects in memory. Use this option to save memory, as serialized objects may consume less space than the deserialized equivalent.
MEMORY_AND_DISK_SER*	RDD partitions are stored as serialized objects in memory. Objects that do not fit into memory spill to disk.
DISK_ONLY	RDD partitions are stored on disk only.
OFF_HEAP	RDD partitions are stored as serialized objects in memory. This requires that off-heap memory be enabled. Note that this storage option is for experimental use only.

* These options are relevant for Java or Scala use only. Using the Spark Python API, objects are always serialized using the Pickle library, so it is not necessary to specify serialization.

In addition, there are replicated storage options available with each of the basic storage levels listed in Table 5.2. These replicate each partition to more than one cluster node. Replication of RDDs consumes more space across the cluster but enables tasks to continue to run in the event of a failure without having to wait for lost partitions to reprocess. Although fault tolerance is provided for all Spark RDDs, regardless of their storage level, replicated storage levels provide much faster fault recovery.

Storage-Level Flags

A storage level is implemented as a set of flags that control the RDD storage. There are flags that determine whether to use memory, whether to spill data to disk if it does not fit in memory, whether to store objects in serialized format, and whether to replicate the RDD partitions to multiple nodes. Flags are implemented in the StorageClass constructor, as shown in Listing 5.17.

Listing 5.17 **StorageClass Constructor**

```
StorageLevel(useDisk,
    useMemory,
    useOffHeap,
    deserialized,
    replication=1)
```

The useDisk, useMemory, useOffHeap, and deserialized arguments are Boolean values, whereas the replication argument is an integer value that defaults to 1. The RDD storage levels listed in Table 5.2 are actually static constants that you can use for common storage levels. Table 5.3 shows these static constants with their respective flags.

Table 5.3 **StorageLevel Constants and Flags**

Constant	useDisk	useMemory	useOffHeap	deserialized	replication
MEMORY_ONLY	False	True	False	True	1
MEMORY_AND_DISK	True	True	False	True	1
MEMORY_ONLY_SER	False	True	False	False	1
MEMORY_AND_DISK_SER	True	True	False	False	1
DISK_ONLY	True	False	False	False	1
MEMORY_ONLY_2	False	True	False	True	2
MEMORY_AND_DISK_2	True	True	False	True	2
MEMORY_ONLY_SER_2	False	True	False	False	2
MEMORY_AND_DISK_SER_2	True	True	False	False	2
DISK_ONLY_2	True	False	False	False	2
OFF_HEAP	False	False	True	False	1

getStorageLevel()

Syntax:

```
RDD.getStorageLevel()
```

The Spark API includes a function called getStorageLevel() that you can use to inspect the storage level for an RDD. The getStorageLevel() function returns the different storage option flags set for an RDD. The return value in the case of PySpark is an instance of the class pyspark.StorageLevel. Listing 5.18 shows how to use the getStorageLevel() function.

Listing 5.18 **The getStorageLevel() Function**

```
>>> lorem = sc.textFile('file://lorem.txt')
>>> lorem.getStorageLevel()
StorageLevel(False, False, False, False, 1)
# get individual flags
>>> lorem_sl = lorem.getStorageLevel()
>>> lorem_sl.useDisk
False
>>> lorem_sl.useMemory
False
>>> lorem_sl.useOffHeap
False
>>> lorem_sl.deserialized
False
>>> lorem_sl.replication
1
```

Choosing a Storage Level

RDD storage levels enable you to tune Spark jobs and to accommodate large-scale operations that would otherwise not fit into the aggregate memory available across the cluster. In addition, replication options for the available storage levels can reduce recovery times in the event of a task or node failure.

Generally speaking, if an RDD fits into the available memory across the cluster, the default memory-only storage level is sufficient and will provide the best performance.

RDD Caching

A Spark RDD, including all of its parent RDDs, is normally recomputed for each action called in the same session or application. Caching an RDD persists the data in memory; the same routine can then reuse it multiple times when subsequent actions are called, without requiring reevaluation.

Caching does not trigger execution or computation; rather, it is a suggestion. If there is not enough memory available to cache the RDD, it is reevaluated for each lineage triggered by an action. Caching never spills to disk because it only uses memory. The cached RDD persists using the MEMORY_ONLY storage level.

Under the appropriate circumstances, caching is a useful tool to increase application performance. Listing 5.19 shows an example of caching with RDDs.

Listing 5.19   **Caching RDDs**

```
doc = sc.textFile("file:///opt/spark/data/shakespeare.txt")
words = doc.flatMap(lambda x: x.split()) \
    .map(lambda x: (x,1)) \
    .reduceByKey(lambda x, y: x + y)
words.cache()
words.count() # triggers computation
# returns: 33505
words.take(3) # no computation required
# returns: [('Quince', 8), ('Begin', 9), ('Just', 12)]
words.count() # no computation required
# returns: 33505
```

Persisting RDDs

Cached partitions, partitions of an RDD where the cache() method ran, are stored in memory on Executor JVMs on Spark Worker nodes. If one of the Worker nodes were to fail or become unavailable, Spark would need to re-create the cached partition from its lineage.

The persist() method, introduced in Chapter 4, offers additional storage options, including MEMORY_AND_DISK, DISK_ONLY, MEMORY_ONLY_SER, MEMORY_AND_DISK_SER, and MEMORY_ONLY, which is the same as the cache() method. When using persistence with one of the disk storage options, the persisted partitions are stored as local files on the Worker nodes running Spark Executors for the application. You can use the persisted data on disk to reconstitute partitions lost due to Executor or memory failure.

In addition, persist() can use replication to persist the same partition on more than one node. Replication makes reevaluation less likely because more than one node would need to fail or be unavailable to trigger recomputation.

Persistence offers additional durability over caching, while still offering increased performance. It is worth reiterating that Spark RDDs are fault tolerant regardless of persistence and can always be re-created in the event of a failure. Persistence simply expedites this process.

Persistence, like caching, is only a suggestion, and it takes place only after an action is called to trigger evaluation of an RDD. If sufficient resources are not available—for instance, if there is not enough memory available—persistence is not implemented.

You can inspect the persistence state and current storage levels from any RDD at any stage by using the getStorageLevel() method, discussed earlier in this chapter.

The methods available for persisting and unpersisting RDDs are documented in the following sections.

persist()

Syntax:

```
RDD.persist(storageLevel=StorageLevel.MEMORY_ONLY_SER)
```

The persist() method specifies the desired storage level and storage attributes for an RDD. The desired storage options are implemented the first time the RDD is evaluated. If this is not possible—for example, if there is insufficient memory to persist the RDD in memory—Spark reverts to its normal behavior of retaining only required partitions in memory.

The storageLevel argument is expressed as either a static constant or a set of storage flags (see the section "RDD Storage Options," earlier in this chapter). For example, to set a storage level of MEMORY_AND_DISK_SER_2, you could use either of the following:

```
myrdd.persist(StorageLevel.MEMORY_AND_DISK_SER_2)
myrdd.persist(StorageLevel(True, True, False, False, 2))
```

The default storage level is MEMORY_ONLY.

unpersist()

Syntax:

```
RDD.unpersist()
```

The unpersist() method "unpersists" the RDD. Use it if you no longer need the RDD to persist. Also, if you want to change the storage options for a persisted RDD, you must unpersist the RDD first. If you attempt to change the storage level of an RDD marked for persistence, you get the exception "Cannot change storage level of an RDD after it was already assigned a level."

Listing 5.20 shows several examples of persistence.

Listing 5.20   **Persisting an RDD**

```
doc = sc.textFile("file:///opt/spark/data/shakespeare.txt")
words = doc.flatMap(lambda x: x.split()) \
    .map(lambda x: (x,1)) \
    .reduceByKey(lambda x, y: x + y)
words.persist()
words.count()
# returns: 33505
words.take(3)
# returns: [('Quince', 8), ('Begin', 9), ('Just', 12)]
print(words.toDebugString().decode("utf-8"))
# returns:
# (1) PythonRDD[46] at RDD at PythonRDD.scala:48 [Memory Serialized 1x Replicated]
#  |       CachedPartitions: 1; MemorySize: 644.8 KB; ExternalBlockStoreSize: ...
#  |  MapPartitionsRDD[45] at mapPartitions at PythonRDD.scala:427 [...]
#  |  ShuffledRDD[44] at partitionBy at NativeMethodAccessorImpl.java:0 [...]
# +-(1) PairwiseRDD[43] at reduceByKey at <stdin>:3 [Memory Serialized 1x ...]
#      |  PythonRDD[42] at reduceByKey at <stdin>:3 [Memory Serialized 1x Replicated]
#      |  file:///opt/spark/data/shakespeare.txt MapPartitionsRDD[41] at textFile ...
#      |  file:///opt/spark/data/shakespeare.txt HadoopRDD[40] at textFile at ...
```

Note that the unpersist() method can also be used to remove an RDD that was cached using the cache() method.

Persisted RDDs are also viewable in the Spark application UI via the Storage tab, as shown in Figures 5.6 and 5.7.

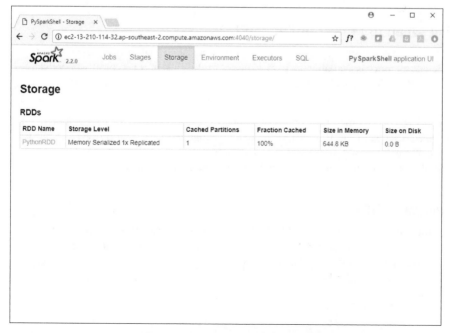

Figure 5.6   Viewing persisted RDDs in the Spark application UI.

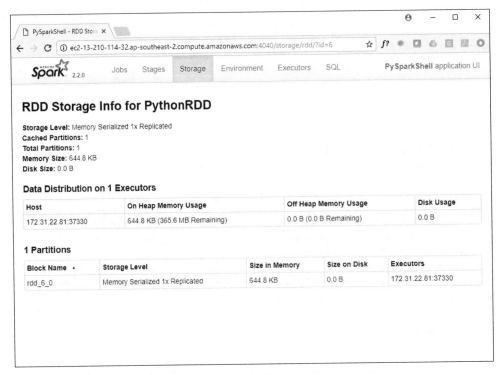

Figure 5.7 Viewing details of a persisted RDD in the Spark application UI.

Choosing When to Persist or Cache RDDs

Caching can improve performance or reduce recovery times. If an RDD is likely to be reused and if sufficient memory is available on Worker nodes in the cluster, it is typically beneficial to cache these RDDs. Iterative algorithms such as those used in machine learning routines are often good candidates for caching.

Caching reduces recovery times in the event of failure because RDDs need to be recomputed only starting from the cached RDDs. However, if you require a higher degree of in-process durability, consider one of the disk-based persistence options or a higher replication level, which increases the likelihood that a persisted replica of an RDD exists somewhere in the Spark cluster.

Checkpointing RDDs

Checkpointing involves saving data to a file. Unlike the disk-based persistence option just discussed, which deletes the persisted RDD data when the Spark Driver program finishes, checkpointed data persists beyond the application.

Checkpointing eliminates the need for Spark to maintain RDD lineage, which can be problematic when the lineage gets long, such as with streaming or iterative processing applications. Long lineage typically leads to long recovery times and the possibility of a stack overflow.

Checkpointing data to a distributed filesystem such as HDFS provides additional storage fault tolerance as well. Checkpointing is expensive, so implement it with some consideration about when you should checkpoint an RDD.

As with the caching and persistence options, checkpointing happens only after an action is called against an RDD to force computation, such as count(). Note that checkpointing must be requested before any action is requested against an RDD.

The methods associated with checkpointing are documented in the following sections.

setCheckpointDir()

Syntax:

```
sc.setCheckpointDir(dirName)
```

The setCheckpointDir() method sets the directory under which RDDs will be checkpointed. If you are running Spark on a Hadoop cluster, the directory specified by the dirName argument must be an HDFS path.

checkpoint()

Syntax:

```
RDD.checkpoint()
```

The checkpoint() method marks the RDD for checkpointing. It will be checkpointed upon the first action executed against the RDD, and the files saved to the directory will be configured using the setCheckpointDir() method. The checkpoint() method must be called before any action is requested against the RDD.

When checkpointing is complete, the complete RDD lineage, including all references to the RDDs and parent RDDs, are removed.

> ### Specifying the Checkpoint Directory Prior to Running checkpoint()
>
> You must specify the checkpoint directory by using the setCheckpointDir() method before attempting to checkpoint an RDD; otherwise, you will receive the following error:
>
> ```
> org.apache.spark.SparkException:
> Checkpoint directory has not been set in the SparkContext
> ```

The checkpoint directory is valid only for the current SparkContext, so you need to execute setCheckpointDir() for each separate Spark application. In addition, the checkpoint directory cannot be shared across different Spark applications.

isCheckpointed()

Syntax:

```
RDD.isCheckpointed()
```

The isCheckpointed() function returns a Boolean response about whether the RDD was checkpointed.

getCheckpointFile()

Syntax:

```
RDD.getCheckpointFile()
```

The getCheckpointFile() function returns the name of the file to which the RDD was checkpointed.

Listing 5.21 demonstrates the use of checkpointing.

Listing 5.21 **Checkpointing RDDs**

```
sc.setCheckpointDir('file:///opt/spark/data/checkpoint')
doc = sc.textFile("file:///opt/spark/data/shakespeare.txt")
words = doc.flatMap(lambda x: x.split()) \
    .map(lambda x: (x,1)) \
    .reduceByKey(lambda x, y: x + y)
words.checkpoint()
words.count()
# returns: 33505
words.isCheckpointed()
# returns: True
words.getCheckpointFile()
# returns:
# 'file:/opt/spark/data/checkpoint/df6370eb-7b5f-4611-99a8-bacb576c2ea1/rdd-15'
```

Exercise: Checkpointing RDDs

This exercise shows the impact that checkpointing can have on an iterative routine. Use any installation of Spark for this exercise and follow these steps:

1. For this exercise, you will run a script in non-interactive mode and need to suppress informational log messages, so perform the following steps:

   a. Make a copy of the default log4j.properties template file, as follows:
   ```
   cd /opt/spark/conf
   cp log4j.properties.template log4j.properties.erroronly
   ```

   b. Use a text editor (such as Vi or Nano) to open the newly created log4j.properties. erroronly file and locate the following line:
   ```
   log4j.rootCategory=INFO, console
   ```

c. Change the line to the following:

```
log4j.rootCategory=ERROR, console
```

Save the file.

2. Create a new script called `looping_test.py`, and copy and paste the code below into the file:

```
import sys
from pyspark import SparkConf, SparkContext
sc = SparkContext()
sc.setCheckpointDir("file:///tmp/checkpointdir")
rddofints = sc.parallelize([1,2,3,4,5,6,7,8,9,10])
try:
    # this will create a very long lineage for rddofints
    for i in range(1000):
        rddofints = rddofints.map(lambda x: x+1)
        if i % 10 == 0:
            print("Looped " + str(i) + " times")
            #rddofints.checkpoint()
            rddofints.count()
except Exception as e:
    print("Exception : " + str(e))
    print("RDD Debug String : ")
    print(rddofints.toDebugString())
    sys.exit()
print("RDD Debug String : ")
print(rddofints.toDebugString())
```

3. Execute the `looping_test.py` script by using `spark-submit` and your custom `log4j.properties` file, as follows:

```
$ spark-submit \
--master local \
--driver-java-options \
"-Dlog4j.configuration=log4j.properties.erroronly" \
looping_test.py
```

After a certain number of iterations, you should see an exception like this:

```
PicklingError: Could not pickle object as excessively deep recursion required.
```

4. Open the `looping_test.py` file again with a text editor and uncomment the following line:

```
#rddofints.checkpoint()
So the file should now read:
...
print("Looped " + str(i) + " times")
rddofints.checkpoint()
rddofints.count()
...
```

5. Execute the script again, using `spark-submit`, as shown in step 3. You should now see that all 1,000 iterations have completed, thanks to the periodic checkpointing of the RDD. Furthermore, note the debug string printed after the routine:

```
(1) PythonRDD[301] at RDD at PythonRDD.scala:43 []
 | PythonRDD[298] at RDD at PythonRDD.scala:43 []
 | ReliableCheckpointRDD[300] at count at ...
```

Checkpointing, caching, and persistence are useful functions in Spark programming. They can not only improve performance but, in some cases, as you have just seen, can mean the difference between a program completing successfully or not.

Find the complete source code for this exercise in the `checkpointing` folder at https://github.com/sparktraining/spark_using_python.

Processing RDDs with External Programs

Spark provides a mechanism to run functions (transformations) using languages other than those native to Spark (Scala, Python, and Java). You can also use Ruby, Perl, or Bash, among others. The languages do not need to be scripting languages, either; you can use Spark with C or FORTRAN, for example.

There are different reasons for wanting to do use languages other than those native to Spark, such as wanting to use in your Spark programs some existing code libraries that are not in Python, Scala, or Java without having to rewrite them in a native Spark language.

Using external programs with Spark is achieved through the `pipe()` function.

Possible Issues with External Processes in Spark

Use the `pipe()` function carefully because piped commands may fork excessive amounts of RAM. Because the forked subprocesses created by the `pipe()` function are out of Spark's resource management scope, they may also cause performance degradation for other tasks running on Worker nodes.

`pipe()`

Syntax:

```
RDD.pipe(command, env=None, checkCode=False)
```

The `pipe()` method returns an RDD created by "piping" elements through a forked external process specified by the command argument. The env argument is a `dict` of environment variables that defaults to None. The checkCode parameter specifies whether to check the return value of the shell command.

The script or program you supply as the command argument needs to read from STDIN and write its output to STDOUT.

Consider the Perl script saved as `parsefixedwidth.pl` in Listing 5.22; it is used to parse fixed-width output data, a common file format with extracts from mainframes and legacy systems. To make this script executable, you need to use the following:

```
chmod +x parsefixedwidth.pl.
```

Listing 5.22   **Sample External Transformation Program (`parsefixedwidth.pl`)**

```perl
#!/usr/bin/env perl
my $format = 'A6 A8 A20 A2 A5';
while (<>) {
        chomp;
        my( $custid, $orderid, $date,
         $city, $state, $zip) =
        unpack( $format, $_ );
        print "$custid\t$orderid\t$date\t$city\t$state\t$zip";
}
```

Listing 5.23 demonstrates the use of the `pipe()` command to run the `parsefixedwidth.pl` script from Listing 5.22.

Listing 5.23   **The `pipe()` Function**

```python
sc.addFile("/home/ubuntu/parsefixedwidth.pl")
fixed_width = sc.parallelize(['3840961028752220160317Hayward       CA94541'])
piped = fixed_width.pipe("parsefixedwidth.pl") \
.map(lambda x: x.split('\t'))
piped.collect()
# returns [['384096', '10287522', '20160317', 'Hayward', 'CA', '94541']]
```

The `addFile()` operation is required because you need to distribute the `parsefixedwidth.pl` Perl script to all Worker nodes participating in the cluster prior to running the `pipe()` transformation.

Note that you also need to ensure that the interpreter or host program (in this case, Perl) exists in the path of all Worker nodes. The complete source code for this example is in the using-external-programs folder at https://github.com/sparktraining/spark_using_python.

Data Sampling with Spark

When using Spark for development and discovery, you may need to sample data in RDDs before running a process across the entirety of an input dataset or datasets. The Spark API includes several functions to sample RDDs and produce new RDDs from the sampled data. These sample functions include transformations that return new RDDs and actions that return data to the Spark Driver program. The following sections look at a couple sampling transformations and actions that Spark provides.

sample()

Syntax:

```
RDD.sample(withReplacement, fraction, seed=None)
```

The sample() transformation creates a sampled subset RDD from an original RDD, based on a percentage of the overall dataset.

The withReplacement argument is a Boolean value that specifies whether elements in an RDD can be sampled multiple times.

The fraction argument is a double value between 0 and 1 that represents the probability an element will be chosen. Effectively, this represents the approximate percentage of the dataset you wish to return to the resultant sampled RDD. Note that if you specify a value larger than 1 for this argument, it defaults to 1 anyway.

The optional seed argument is an integer representing a seed for the random number generator used to determine whether to include an element in the return RDD.

Listing 5.24 shows an example of the sample() transformation used to create approximately a 10% subset of web log events from a corpus of web logs.

Listing 5.24 **Sampling Data Using the sample() Function**

```
doc = sc.textFile("file:///opt/spark/data/shakespeare.txt")
doc.count()
# returns: 129107
sampled_doc = doc.sample(False, 0.1, seed=None)
sampled_doc.count()
# returns: 12879 (approximately 10% of the original RDD)
```

There is also a similar sampleByKey() function that operates on a key/value pair RDD.

takeSample()

Syntax:

```
RDD.takeSample(withReplacement, num, seed=None)
```

The takeSample() action returns a random list of values (elements or records) from the sampled RDD.

The num argument is the number of randomly selected records to be returned.

The withReplacement and seed arguments behave similarly to the sample() function just described.

Listing 5.25 shows an example of the takeSample() action.

Listing 5.25 **Using the `takeSample()` Function**

```
dataset = sc.parallelize([1,2,3,4,5,6,7,8,9,10])
dataset.takeSample(False, 3)
# returns [6, 7, 5] (your results may vary!)
```

Understanding Spark Application and Cluster Configuration

Practically everything in Spark is configurable, and everything that is configurable typically has a default setting. This section takes a closer look at configuration for Spark applications and clusters, focusing specifically on the settings and concepts you need to be aware of as a Spark engineer or developer.

Spark Environment Variables

Spark environment variables are set by the `spark-env.sh` script located in the `$SPARK_HOME/conf` directory. The variables set Spark daemon behavior and configuration, and they set environment-level application configuration settings, such as which Spark Master an application should use. The `spark-env.sh` script is read by the following:

- Spark Standalone Master and Worker daemons upon startup

- Spark applications, using `spark-submit`

Listing 5.26 provides some examples of settings for some common environment variables; these could be set in your `spark-env.sh` file or as environment variables in your shell prior to running an interactive Spark process such as `pyspark` or `spark-shell`.

Listing 5.26 **Spark Environment Variables**

```
export SPARK_HOME=${SPARK_HOME:-/usr/lib/spark}
export SPARK_LOG_DIR=${SPARK_LOG_DIR:-/var/log/spark}
export HADOOP_HOME=${HADOOP_HOME:-/usr/lib/hadoop}
export HADOOP_CONF_DIR=${HADOOP_CONF_DIR:-/etc/hadoop/conf}
export HIVE_CONF_DIR=${HIVE_CONF_DIR:-/etc/hive/conf}
export STANDALONE_SPARK_MASTER_HOST=sparkmaster.local
export SPARK_MASTER_PORT=7077
export SPARK_MASTER_IP=$STANDALONE_SPARK_MASTER_HOST
export SPARK_MASTER_WEBUI_PORT=8080
export SPARK_WORKER_DIR=${SPARK_WORKER_DIR:-/var/run/spark/work}
export SPARK_WORKER_PORT=7078
export SPARK_WORKER_WEBUI_PORT=8081
export SPARK_DAEMON_JAVA_OPTS="-XX:OnOutOfMemoryError='kill -9 %p'"
```

The following sections take a look at some of the most common Spark environment variables and their use.

Cluster Manager Independent Variables

Some of the environment variables that are independent of the cluster manager used are described in Table 5.4.

Table 5.4   **Cluster Manager Independent Variables**

Environment Variable	Description
SPARK_HOME	The root of the Spark installation directory (for example, /opt/spark or /usr/lib/spark). You should always set this variable, especially if you have multiple versions of Spark installed on a system. Failing to set this variable is a common cause of issues when running Spark applications.
JAVA_HOME	The location where Java is installed.
PYSPARK_PYTHON	The Python binary executable to use for PySpark in both the Driver and Workers. If not specified, the default Python installation is used (resolved by the which python command). This should definitely be set if you have more than one version of Python on any Driver or Worker instances.
PYSPARK_DRIVER_PYTHON	The Python binary executable to use for PySpark in the Driver only; defaults to the value defined for PYSPARK_PYTHON.
SPARKR_DRIVER_R	The R binary executable to use for the SparkR shell; the default is R.

Hadoop-Related Environment Variables

The variables described in Table 5.5 are required for Spark applications that need access to HDFS from any deployment mode, YARN if running in YARN Client or YARN Cluster mode, and objects in HCatalog or Hive.

Table 5.5   **Hadoop-Related Environment Variables**

Environment Variable	Description
HADOOP_CONF_DIR or YARN_CONF_DIR	The location of the Hadoop configuration files (typically /etc/hadoop/conf). Spark uses this to locate the default filesystem, usually the URI of the HDFS NameNode, and the address of the YARN ResourceManager. Either of these environment variables can be set, but typically, HADOOP_CONF_DIR is preferred.
HADOOP_HOME	The location where Hadoop is installed. Spark uses this to locate the Hadoop configuration files.

Environment Variable	Description
HIVE_CONF_DIR	The location of the Hive configuration files. Spark uses this to locate the Hive metastore and other Hive properties when instantiating a HiveContext object. There are also environment variables specific to HiveServer2, such as HIVE_SERVER2_THRIFT_BIND_HOST and HIVE_SERVER2_THRIFT_PORT. Typically, just setting HADOOP_CONF_DIR is sufficient because Spark can infer the other properties relative to this.

YARN-Specific Environment Variables

The environment variables described in Table 5.6 are specific to Spark applications running on a YARN cluster, either in Cluster or Client deployment mode.

Table 5.6   **YARN-Specific Environment Variables**

Environment Variable	Description
SPARK_EXECUTOR_INSTANCES	The number of Executor processes to start in the YARN cluster; defaults to 2.
SPARK_EXECUTOR_CORES	The number of CPU cores allocated to each Executor; defaults to 1.
SPARK_EXECUTOR_MEMORY	The amount of memory allocated to each Executor; defaults to 1GB.
SPARK_DRIVER_MEMORY	The amount of memory allocated to Driver processes when running in Cluster deployment mode; defaults to 1GB.
SPARK_YARN_APP_NAME	The name of your application. This displays in the YARN ResourceManager UI; defaults to Spark.
SPARK_YARN_QUEUE	The named YARN queue to which applications are submitted by default; defaults to default. Can also be set by a spark-submit argument. This determines allocation of resources and scheduling priority.
SPARK_YARN_DIST_FILES or SPARK_YARN_DIST_ARCHIVES	A comma-separated list of files of archives to be distributed with the job. Executors can then reference these files at runtime.

As previously mentioned, you must set the HADOOP_CONF_DIR environment variable when deploying a Spark application on YARN.

Cluster Application Deployment Mode Environment Variables

The variables listed in Table 5.7 are used for applications submitted in Cluster mode—that is, applications using the Standalone or YARN cluster managers submitted with the --deploy-mode cluster option to spark-submit. In the case of YARN, this property can combine with the master argument as --master yarn-cluster. These variables are read by Executor and Driver processes running on Workers in the cluster (Spark Workers or YARN NodeManagers).

Table 5.7 **Cluster Application Deployment Mode Environment Variables**

Environment Variable	Description
SPARK_LOCAL_IP	The IP address of the machine for binding Spark processes.
SPARK_PUBLIC_DNS	The hostname the Spark Driver uses to advertise to other hosts.
SPARK_CLASSPATH	The default classpath for Spark. This is important if you are importing additional classes not packaged with Spark that you will refer to at runtime.
SPARK_LOCAL_DIRS	The directories to use on the system for RDD storage and shuffled data.

When running an interactive Spark session (using pyspark or spark-shell), the spark-env.sh file is not read, and the environment variables in the current user environment (if set) are used.

Many Spark environment variables have equivalent configuration properties that you can set in a number of additional ways; we discuss this shortly.

Spark Standalone Daemon Environment Variables

The environment variables shown in Table 5.8 are read by daemons—Masters and Workers—in a Spark Standalone cluster.

Table 5.8 **Spark Standalone Daemon Environment Variables**

Environment Variable	Description
SPARK_MASTER_IP	The hostname or IP address of the host running the Spark Master process. This should be set on all nodes of the Spark cluster and on any client hosts that will be submitting applications.
SPARK_MASTER_PORT and SPARK_MASTER_ WEBUI_PORT	The ports used for IPC communication and the Master web UI, respectively. If not specified, the defaults 7077 and 8080 are used.
SPARK_MASTER_OPTS and SPARK_WORKER_OPTS	Additional Java options supplied to the JVM hosting the Spark Master or Spark Worker processes. If used, the value should be in the standard form -Dx=y. Alternatively, you can set the SPARK_DAEMON_JAVA_OPTS environment variable, which applies to all Spark daemons running on the system.
SPARK_DAEMON_MEMORY	The amount of memory to allocate to the Master, Worker, and HistoryServer processes; defaults to 1GB.
SPARK_WORKER_INSTANCES	The number of Worker processes per slave node; defaults to 1.
SPARK_WORKER_CORES	The number of CPU cores for the Spark Worker process used by Executors on the system.
SPARK_WORKER_MEMORY	The amount of total memory Workers have to grant to Executors.
SPARK_WORKER_PORT and SPARK_WORKER_ WEBUI_PORT	The ports used for IPC communication and the Worker web UI, respectively. If not specified, the defaults of 8081 for the web UI and a random port for the Worker port are used.
SPARK_WORKER_DIR	Sets the working directory for Worker processes.

Spark Configuration Properties

Spark configuration properties are typically set on a node, such as a Master or Worker node, or an application by the Driver host submitting the application. They often have a more restricted scope—such as for the life of an application—than their equivalent environment variables, and they take higher precedence than environment variables.

There are numerous Spark configuration properties related to different operational aspects; some of the most common ones are described in Table 5.9.

Table 5.9 **Common Spark Configuration Properties**

Property	Description
spark.master	The address of the Spark Master (for example, spark:// <masterhost>:7077 for a Standalone cluster). If the value is yarn, the Hadoop configuration files are read to locate the YARN ResourceManager. There is no default value for this property.
spark.driver.memory	The amount of memory allocated to the Driver; defaults to 1GB.
spark.executor.memory	The amount of memory to use per Executor process; defaults to 1GB.
spark.executor.cores	The number of cores to use on each Executor. In Standalone mode, this property defaults to using all available cores on the Worker node. Setting this property to a value less than the available number of cores enables multiple concurrent Executor processes to spawn. In YARN mode, this property defaults to 1 core per Executor.
spark.driver.extraJavaOptions and spark.executor.extraJavaOptions	Additional Java options supplied to the JVM hosting the Spark Driver or Executor processes. If used, the value should be in the standard form -Dx=y.
spark.driver.extraClassPath and spark.executor.extraClassPath	Additional classpath entries for the Driver and Executor processes if you require additional classes that are not packaged with Spark to be imported.
spark.dynamicAllocation.enabled and spark.shuffle.service.enabled	Properties that are used together to modify the default scheduling behavior in Spark. (Dynamic allocation is discussed later in this chapter.)

Setting Spark Configuration Properties

Spark configuration properties are set through the $SPARK_HOME/conf/spark-defaults.conf file, read by Spark applications and daemons upon startup. Listing 5.27 shows an excerpt from a typical spark-defaults.conf file.

Listing 5.27   **Spark Configuration Properties in the `spark-defaults.conf` File**

```
spark.master                    yarn
spark.eventLog.enabled          true
spark.eventLog.dir              hdfs:///var/log/spark/apps
spark.history.fs.logDirectory   hdfs:///var/log/spark/apps
spark.executor.memory           2176M
spark.executor.cores            4
```

Spark configuration properties can also be set programmatically in your Driver code by using the SparkConf object, as shown in Listing 5.28.

Listing 5.28   **Setting Spark Configuration Properties Programmatically**

```
from pyspark.context import SparkContext
from pyspark.conf import SparkConf
conf = SparkConf()
conf.set("spark.executor.memory","3g")
sc = SparkContext(conf=conf)
```

There are also several SparkConf methods for setting specific common properties. These methods appear in Listing 5.29.

Listing 5.29   **Spark Configuration Object Methods**

```
from pyspark.context import SparkContext
from pyspark.conf import SparkConf
conf = SparkConf()
conf.setAppName("MySparkApp")
conf.setMaster("yarn")
conf.setSparkHome("/usr/lib/spark")
sc = SparkContext(conf=conf)
```

In most cases, setting Spark configuration properties using arguments to spark-shell, pyspark, and spark-submit is recommended, as setting configuration properties programmatically requires code changes or rebuilding in the case of Scala or Java applications.

Setting configuration properties as arguments to spark-shell, pyspark, and spark-submit is done using specific named arguments for common properties, such as --executor-memory. Properties not exposed as named arguments are provided using --conf PROP=VALUE to set an arbitrary Spark configuration property or --properties-file FILE to load additional arguments from a configuration file. Listing 5.30 provides examples of both methods.

Listing 5.30   **Passing Spark Configuration Properties to `spark-submit`**

```
# setting config properties using arguments
$SPARK_HOME/bin/spark-submit --executor-memory 1g \
  --conf spark.dynamicAllocation.enabled=true \
  myapp.py
```

```
# setting config properties using a conf file
$SPARK_HOME/bin/spark-submit \
 --properties-file test.conf \
 myapp.py
```

You can use the SparkConf.toDebugString() method to print out the current configuration for a Spark application, as demonstrated in Listing 5.31.

Listing 5.31 **Showing the Current Spark Configuration**

```
from pyspark.context import SparkContext
from pyspark.conf import SparkConf
conf = SparkConf()
print(conf.toDebugString())
...
spark.app.name=PySparkShell
spark.master=yarn-client
spark.submit.deployMode=client
spark.yarn.isPython=true ...
```

As you can see, there are several ways to pass the same configuration parameter, including as an environment variable, as a Spark default configuration property, or as a command line argument. Table 5.10 shows just a few of the various ways to set the same property in Spark. Many other properties have analogous settings.

Table 5.10 **Spark Configuration Options**

Argument	Configuration Property	Environment Variable
--master	spark.master	SPARK_MASTER_IP/ SPARK_MASTER_PORT
--name	spark.app.name	SPARK_YARN_APP_NAME
--queue	spark.yarn.queue	SPARK_YARN_QUEUE
--executor-memory	spark.executor.memory	SPARK_EXECUTOR_MEMORY
--executor-cores	spark.executor.cores	SPARK_EXECUTOR_CORES

Defaults for Environment Variables and Configuration Properties

Looking at the conf directory of a fresh Spark deployment, you may notice that by default the spark-defaults.conf and spark-env.sh files are not implemented. Instead, templates are provided (spark-defaults.conf.template and spark-env.sh.template). You are encouraged to copy these templates and rename them without the .template extension and make the appropriate modifications for your environment.

Spark Configuration Precedence

Configuration properties set directly within an application using a `SparkConf` object take the highest precedence, followed by arguments passed to `spark-submit`, `pyspark`, or `spark-shell`, followed by options set in the `spark-defaults.conf` file. Many configuration properties have system default values used in the absence of properties explicitly set through the other means discussed. Figure 5.8 shows the order of precedence for Spark configuration properties.

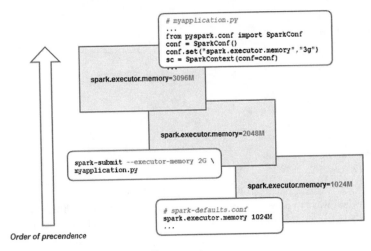

Figure 5.8 Spark configuration precedence.

Configuration Management

Managing configuration is one of the biggest challenges involved in administering a Spark cluster—or any other cluster, for that matter. Often, configuration settings need to be consistent across different hosts, such as different Worker nodes in a Spark cluster. Configuration management and deployment tools such as Puppet and Chef can be useful for managing Spark deployments and their configurations. If you are rolling out and managing Spark as part of a Hadoop deployment using a commercial Hadoop distribution, you can manage Spark configuration by using the Hadoop vendor's management interface, such as Cloudera Manager for Cloudera installations or Ambari for Hortonworks installations.

In addition, there are other options for configuration management, such as Apache Amaterasu (http://amaterasu.incubator.apache.org/), which uses pipelines to build, run, and manage environments as code.

Optimizing Spark

The Spark runtime framework generally does its best to optimize stages and tasks in a Spark application. However, as a developer, you can make many optimizations for notable performance improvements. We discuss some of them in the following sections.

Filter Early, Filter Often

It sounds obvious, but filtering nonrequired records or fields early in your application can have a significant impact on performance. Big Data (particularly event data, log data, or sensor data) is often characterized by a low signal-to-noise ratio. Filtering out noise early saves processing cycles, I/O, and storage in subsequent stages. Use `filter()` transformations to remove unneeded records and `map()` transformations to project only required fields in an RDD. Perform these operations before operations that may invoke a shuffle, such as `reduceByKey()` or `groupByKey()`. Also use them before and after a `join()` operation. These small changes can make the difference between hours and minutes or minutes and seconds.

Optimizing Associative Operations

Associative operations such as `sum()` and `count()` are common requirements when programming in Spark, and you have seen numerous examples of these operations throughout this book. Often on distributed, partitioned datasets, these associative key/value operations may involve shuffling. Typically, `join()`, `cogroup()`, and transformations that have By or ByKey in their name, such as `groupByKey()` or `reduceByKey()`, can involve shuffling. This is not necessarily a bad thing because it is often required.

However, if you need to perform a shuffle with the ultimate objective of performing an associative operation—counting occurrences of a key, for instance—different approaches that can provide very different performance outcomes. The best example of this is the difference between using `groupByKey()` and using `reduceByKey()` to perform a `sum()` or `count()` operation. Both operations can achieve the same result. However, if you group by a key on a partitioned or distributed dataset solely for the purposes of aggregating values for each key, using `reduceByKey()` is generally a better approach.

`reduceByKey()`combines values for each key prior to any required shuffle operation, thereby reducing the amount of data sent over the network and also reducing the computation and memory requirements for tasks in the next stage. Consider the two code examples in Listing 5.32. Both provide the same result.

Listing 5.32 **Associative Operations in Spark**

```
rdd.map(lambda x: (x[0],1)) \
  .groupByKey() \
  .mapValues(lambda x: sum(x)) \
  .collect()
# preferred method
rdd.map(lambda x: (x[0],1)) \
  .reduceByKey(lambda x, y: x + y) \
  .collect()
```

Now consider Figure 5.9, which depicts the `groupByKey()` implementation.

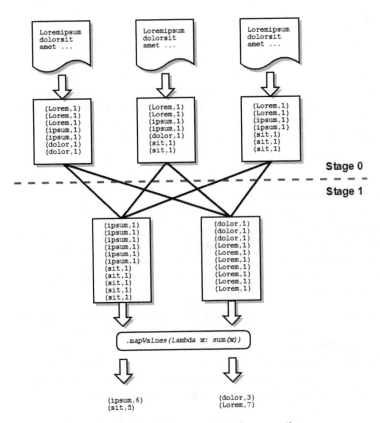

Figure 5.9   groupByKey() for an associative operation.

Contrast what you have just seen with Figure 5.10, which shows the functionally equivalent reduceByKey() implementation.

As you can see from the preceding figures, reduceByKey() combines records locally by key before shuffling the data; this is often referred to as a *combiner* in MapReduce terminology. Combining can result in a dramatic decrease in the amount of data shuffled and thus a corresponding increase in application performance.

Some other alternatives to groupByKey() are combineByKey(), which you can use if the inputs and outputs to your reduce function are different, and foldByKey(), which performs an associative operation providing a zero value. Additional functions to consider include treeReduce(), treeAggregate(), and aggregateByKey().

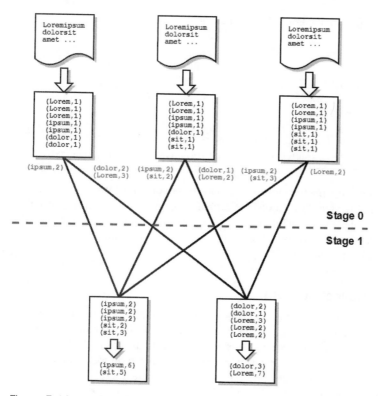

Figure 5.10   reduceByKey() for an associative operation.

Understanding the Impact of Functions and Closures

Recall the discussions of functions and closures in Chapter 1, "Introducing Big Data, Hadoop, and Spark." Functions are sent to Executors in a Spark cluster, enclosing all bound and free variables. This process enables efficient, shared-nothing distributed processing. It can also be a potential issue that impacts performance and stability at the same time. It's important to understand this.

A key example of an issue that could arise is passing too much data to a function in a Spark application. This would cause excessive data to be sent to the application Executors at runtime, resulting in excess network I/O, and it could result in memory issues on Spark Workers.

Listing 5.33 shows a fictitious example of declaring a function that encloses a large object and then passing that function to a Spark map() transformation.

Listing 5.33 **Passing Large Amounts of Data to a Function**

```
...
massive_list = [...]
def big_fn(x):
# function enclosing massive_list
...
...
rdd.map(lambda x: big_fn(x)).saveAsTextFile...
# parallelize data which would have otherwise been enclosed
massive_list_rdd = sc.parallelize(massive_list) rdd.join(massive_list_rdd).saveAsTextFile...
```

A better approach might be to use the broadcast method to create a broadcast variable, as discussed earlier in this chapter; recall that broadcast variables are distributed using an efficient peer-to-peer sharing protocol based on BitTorrent. You could also consider parallelizing larger objects, if possible. This is not meant to discourage you from passing data in functions, but you do need to be aware of how closures operate.

Considerations for Collecting Data

Two useful functions in Spark are collect() and take(). Recall that these actions trigger evaluation of an RDD, including its entire lineage. When executing collect(), all resultant records from the RDD return to the Driver from the Executors on which the final tasks in the lineage are executed. For large datasets, this can be in gigabytes or terabytes of magnitude. It can create unnecessary network I/O and, in many cases, result in exceptions if there is insufficient memory on the Driver host to store the collected objects.

If you just need to inspect the output data, take(n) and takeSample() are better options. If the transformation is part of an ETL routine, the best practice is to save the dataset to a filesystem such as HDFS or a database.

The key point here is not to bring too much data back to the Driver if it's not required.

Configuration Parameters for Tuning and Optimizing Applications

In addition to application development optimizations, there are also some systemwide or platform changes that can provide substantial increases to performance and throughput. The following sections look at some of the many configuration settings that can influence performance.

Optimizing Parallelism

A specific configuration parameter that could be beneficial to set at an application level or using spark-defaults.conf is the spark.default.parallelism setting. This setting specifies the default number of RDD partitions returned by transformations such as reduceByKey(), join(), and parallelize() where the numPartitions argument is not supplied. You saw the effect of this configuration parameter earlier in this chapter.

It is often recommended to make the value for this setting *equal to* or *double* the number of cores on each Worker. As with many other settings, you may need to experiment with different values to find the optimal setting for your environment.

Dynamic Allocation

Spark's default runtime behavior is that the Executors requested or provisioned for an application are retained for the life of the application. If an application is long lived, such as a pyspark session or Spark Streaming application, this may not be optimal, particularly if the Executors are idle for long periods of time and other applications are unable to get the resources they require.

With *dynamic allocation*, Executors can be released back to the cluster resource pool if they are idle for a specified period of time. Dynamic allocation is typically implemented as a system setting to help maximize use of system resources.

Listing 5.34 shows the configuration parameters used to enable dynamic allocation.

Listing 5.34   **Enabling Spark Dynamic Allocation**

```
# enable Dynamic Allocation, which is disabled by default
spark.dynamicAllocation.enabled=True
spark.dynamicAllocation.minExecutors=n
# lower bound for the number of Executors
spark.dynamicAllocation.maxExecutors=n
# upper bound for the number of Executors spark.dynamicAllocation.executorIdleTimeout=ns
# the time at which an Executor will be removed if it has been idle, defaults to 60s
```

Avoiding Inefficient Partitioning

Inefficient partitioning is one of the major contributors to suboptimal performance in a distributed Spark processing environment. The following sections take a closer look at some of the common causes for inefficient partitioning.

Small Files Resulting in Too Many Small Partitions

Small partitions, or partitions containing a small amount of data, are inefficient, as they result in many small tasks. Often, the overhead of spawning these tasks is greater than the processing required to execute the tasks.

A filter() operation on a partitioned RDD may result in some partitions being much smaller than others. The solution to this problem is to follow the filter() operation with a repartition() or coalesce() function and specify a number less than the input RDD; this combines small partitions into fewer more appropriately sized partitions.

Recall that the difference between `repartition()` and `coalesce()` is that `repartition()` always shuffles records if required, whereas `coalesce()` accepts a `shuffle` argument that can be set to `False`, avoiding a shuffle. Therefore, `coalesce()` can only reduce the number of partitions, whereas `repartition()` can increase or reduce the number of partitions.

Working with small files in a distributed filesystem results in small, inefficient partitions as well. This is especially true for filesystems such as HDFS, where blocks form the natural boundary for Spark RDD partitions created from a `textFile()` operation, for example. In such cases, a block can only associate with one file object, so a small file results in a small block, which in turn results in a small RDD partition. One option for addressing this issue is to specify the `numPartitions` argument of the `textFile()` function, which specifies how many RDD partitions to create from the input data (see Figure 5.11).

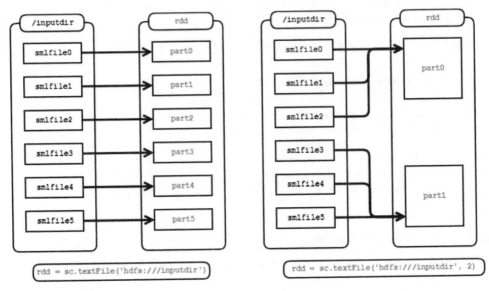

Figure 5.11 Optimizing partitions loaded from small files.

The `spark.default.parallelism` configuration property mentioned in the previous section can also be used to designate the desired number of partitions for an RDD.

Avoiding Exceptionally Large Partitions

Exceptionally large partitions can cause performance issues. A common reason for large partitions is loading an RDD from one or more large files compressed using an unsplittable compression format such as Gzip.

Because unsplittable compressed files are not indexed and cannot be split (by definition), the entire file must be processed by one Executor. If the uncompressed data size exceeds the memory available to the Executor, the partition may spill to disk, causing performance issues.

Solutions to this problem include the following:

- Avoid using unsplittable compression, if possible.

- Uncompress each file locally (for example, to /tmp) before loading the file into an RDD.

- Repartition immediately after the first transformation against the RDD.

Moreover, large partitions can also result from a shuffle operation using a custom partitioner, such as a month partitioner for a corpus of log data where one month is disproportionately larger than the others. In this case, the solution is to use `repartition()` or `coalesce()` after the reduce operation, using a hash partitioner.

Another good practice is to repartition before a large shuffle operation as this can provide a significant performance benefit.

Determining the Right Number or Size of Partitions

Generally, if you have fewer partitions than Executors, some of the Executors will be idle. However, the optimal, or "Goldilocks," number or size for partitions is often found only by trial and error. A good practice is to make this an input parameter (or parameters) to your program so you can easily experiment with different values and see what works best for your system or your application.

Diagnosing Application Performance Issues

You have seen many application development practices and programming techniques in this chapter and throughout the book that can provide significant performance improvement. This section provides a simple introduction to identifying potential performance bottlenecks in your application so you can address them.

Using the Application UI to Diagnose Performance Issues

The Spark application UI that you have seen throughout this book is probably the most valuable source of information about application performance. The application UI contains detailed information and metrics about tasks, stages, scheduling, storage, and more to help you diagnose performance issues. Recall from our discussions that the application UI is served on port 4040 (or successive ports if more than one application is running) of the host running the Driver for the application. For YARN clusters, the application UI is available via the ApplicationMaster link in the YARN ResourceManager UI. The following sections take a further look at how you can identify various performance issues using the application UI.

Shuffle and Task Execution Performance

Recall that an application consists of one or more jobs, as a result of an action such as saveAsTextFile(), collect(), or count(). A job consists of one or more stages that consist of one or more tasks. Tasks operate against an RDD partition. The first place to look when diagnosing performance issues is the stage summary from the Stages tab of the application UI. On this tab, you can see the duration of each stage as well as the amount of data shuffled, as shown in Figure 5.12.

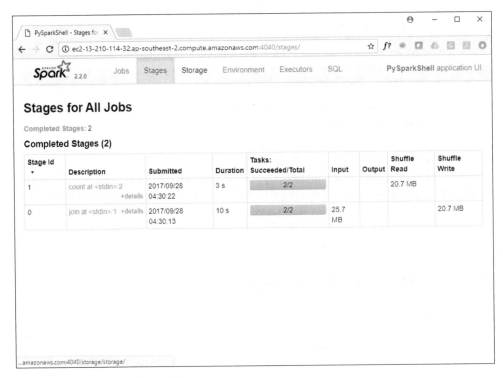

Figure 5.12   Spark application UI stage summary.

By clicking on a stage in the Description column of the Completed Stages table, you can see details for that stage, including the duration and write time for each task in the stage. This is where you may see disparity in the values of different tasks, as shown in Figure 5.13.

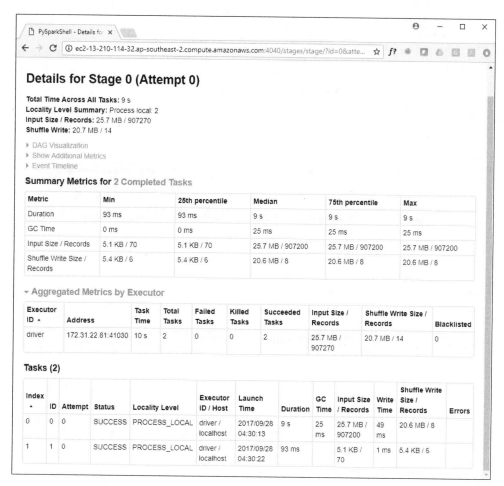

Figure 5.13   Spark application UI stage detail.

The difference in task durations or write times may be an indication of inefficient partitioning, as discussed in the previous section.

Collection Performance

If your program has a collection stage, you can get summary and detailed performance information from the Spark application UI. From the Details page, you can see metrics related to the collection process, including the data size collected, as well as the duration of collection tasks; this is shown in Figure 5.14.

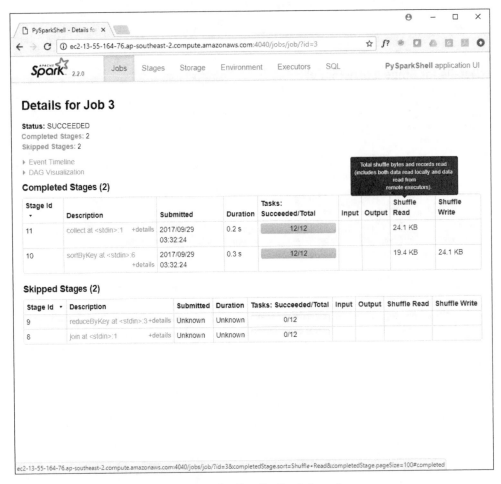

Figure 5.14   Spark application UI stage detail: collection information.

Using the Spark History UI to Diagnose Performance Issues

The application UI (served on port 404*x*) is available only during an application's lifetime, which makes it handy for diagnosing issues with running applications. It's useful and sometimes necessary to profile the performance of completed applications, successful or otherwise, as well. The *Spark History Server* provides the same information as the application UI for completed applications. Moreover, you can often use completed application information in the Spark History Server as an indicative benchmark for the same applications that are currently running. Figure 5.15 shows an example of the Spark History Server UI, typically served on port 18080 of the host running this process.

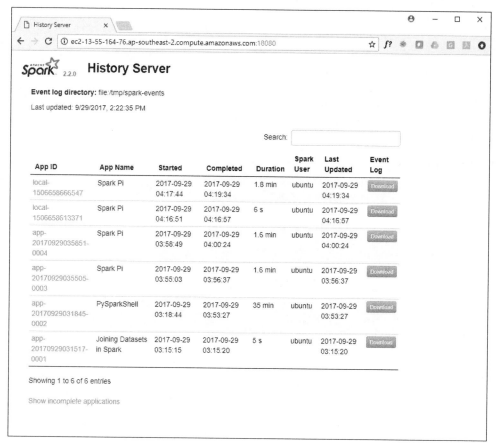

Figure 5.15   Spark History Server.

Summary

This chapter completes our coverage of the Spark core (or RDD) API using Python. This chapter introduces the different shared variables available in the Spark API, including broadcast variables and accumulators, along with their purpose and usage. Broadcast variables are useful for distributing reference information, such as lookup tables, to Workers to avoid expensive "reduce side" joins. Accumulators are useful as general-purpose counters in Spark applications and also can be used to optimize processing. This chapter also discusses RDD partitioning in much more detail, as well as the methods available for repartitioning RDDs, including `repartition()` and `coalesce()`, as well as functions designed to work on partitions atomically, such as `mapPartitions()`. This chapter also looks at the behavior of partitioning and its influence on performance as well as RDD storage options. You have learned about the effects of checkpointing RDDs, which is especially useful for periodic saving of state for iterative algorithms, where elongated lineage can make recovery very expensive. In addition, you have learned about the `pipe()` function, which you can use with external programs with Spark. Finally, you got a look at how to sample data in Spark and explored some considerations for optimizing Spark programs.

6

SQL and NoSQL Programming with Spark

> *Data is a precious thing and will last longer than the systems themselves.*
>
> Tim Berners-Lee, father of the World Wide Web

In This Chapter:

- Introduction to Hive and Spark SQL
- Introduction to the `SparkSession` object and DataFrame API
- Creating and accessing Spark DataFrames
- Using Spark SQL with external applications
- Introduction to NoSQL concepts and systems
- Using Spark with HBase, Cassandra, and DynamoDB

Moore's law and the birth and explosion of mobile ubiquitous computing have permanently altered the data, computing, and database landscape. This chapter focuses on how Spark can be used in SQL applications using well-known semantics, as well as how Spark can be used in NoSQL applications where a SQL approach is not practical.

Introduction to Spark SQL

Structured Query Language (SQL) is the language most commonly and widely used to define and express questions about data. The vast majority of operational data that exists today is stored in tabular format in relational database systems. Many data analysts innately deconstruct complex problems into a series of SQL Data Manipulation Language (DML) or `SELECT` statements. A discussion of Spark SQL requires a basic understanding of the Hive project, which was born from the Hadoop ecosystem.

Introduction to Hive

Many of the SQL abstractions to Big Data processing platforms, such as Spark, are based on the Hive project. Hive and the Hive metastore remain integral components to projects such as Spark SQL.

The Apache Hive project started at Facebook in 2010 to provide a high-level SQL-like abstraction on top of Hadoop MapReduce. Hive introduced a new language called Hive Query Language (HiveQL), which implements a subset of SQL-92, an internationally accepted standard specification for the SQL language, with some extensions.

The creation of Hive was motivated by the fact that, at the time, few analysts had Java MapReduce programming skills, but most analysts were proficient in SQL. Furthermore, SQL is the common language for BI and visualization and reporting tools, which commonly use ODBC/JDBC as a standard interface.

In Hive's original implementation, HiveQL was parsed by the Hive client and mapped to a sequence of Java MapReduce operations, which were then submitted as jobs on the Hadoop cluster. The progress was monitored, and results were returned to the client or written to the desired location in HDFS. Figure 6.1 provides a high-level depiction of how Hive processes data on HDFS.

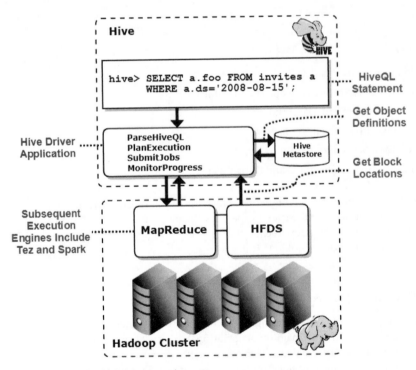

Figure 6.1   Hive high-level overview.

Hive Objects and the Hive Metastore

Hive implements a tabular abstraction to objects in HDFS, presenting directories and all files they contain as tables in its programming model. Just as in a conventional relational database, tables have predefined columns with designated datatypes. The data in HDFS is accessible via SQL DML statements, as with a normal database management system. This is where the similarity ends, however, as Hive is a "schema-on-read" platform, backed by an immutable filesystem, HDFS. As Hive simply implements SQL tabular abstractions over raw files in HDFS, the following key differences exist between Hive and a conventional relational database platform:

- UPDATE is not really supported. Although UPDATE was introduced into the HiveQL dialect, HDFS is still an immutable filesystem, so this abstraction involves applying coarse-grained transformations, whereas a true UPDATE in an RDBMS is a fine-grained operation.

- There are no transactions, journaling, rollbacks, or real transaction isolation levels.

- There is no declarative referential integrity (DRI), which means there are no definitions for primary keys or foreign keys.

- Incorrectly formatted data, such as mistyped data or malformed records, are simply represented to the client as null values.

The mapping of tables to their directory locations in HDFS and the columns and their definitions is maintained in the *Hive metastore*. The metastore is a relational database written to and read by the Hive client. The object definitions also include the input and output formats for the files represented by the table objects (CSVInputFormat and so on) and SerDes (Serialization/ Deserialization), which instruct Hive on how to extract records and fields from the files. Figure 6.2 shows a high-level example of interactions between Hive and the metastore.

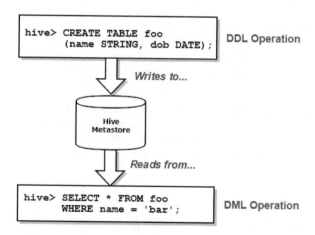

Figure 6.2   Hive metastore interaction.

The metastore can be an embedded Derby database (the default) or a local or remote database, such as MySQL or Postgres. In most cases, you want to implement a shared database, which enables developers and analysts to share object definitions.

There is also a Hive subproject called *HCatalog*, an initiative to extend objects created in Hive to other projects with a common interface, such as Apache Pig. Spark SQL leverages the Hive metastore, as we soon discuss.

Accessing Hive

Hive provides a client command line interface (CLI) that accepts and parses HiveQL input commands. This is a common method for performing ad hoc queries. Figure 6.3 shows the Hive CLI.

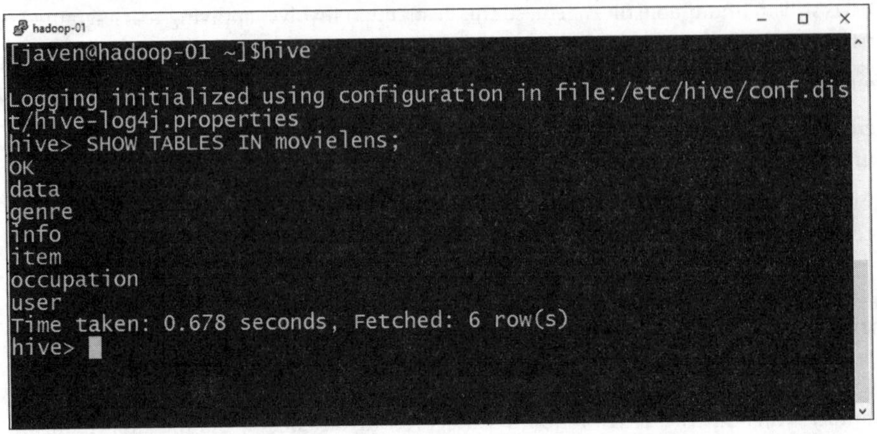

```
hadoop-01                                              —   □   ×
[javen@hadoop-01 ~]$hive

Logging initialized using configuration in file:/etc/hive/conf.dis
t/hive-log4j.properties
hive> SHOW TABLES IN movielens;
OK
data
genre
info
item
occupation
user
Time taken: 0.678 seconds, Fetched: 6 row(s)
hive>
```

Figure 6.3   The Hive command line interface.

The Hive CLI is used when the Hive client or driver application deploys to the local machine, including the connection to the metastore. For large-scale implementations, a client/server approach is often more appropriate because the details about the connection to the metastore stay in one place on the server, and access can be controlled to the cluster. This approach uses a server component called *HiveServer2*.

HiveServer2 can now act as a multi-session driver application for multiple clients. HiveServer2 provides a JDBC interface that is usable by external clients, such as visualization tools, as well as a lightweight CLI called Beeline. Beeline is included and usable directly with Spark SQL. In addition, a web-based interface called *Beeswax* is used within the Hadoop User Experience (HUE) project.

Hive Datatypes and Data Definition Language (DDL)

Hive supports most common primitive datatypes, similar to those found in most database systems, as well as several complex datatypes. These types, used as the underlying types for Spark SQL, are listed in Table 6.1.

Table 6.1 **Hive Datatypes**

Datatype	Category	Description
TINYINT	Primitive	1-btye signed integer
SMALLINT	Primitive	2-byte signed integer
INT	Primitive	4-byte signed integer
BIGINT	Primitive	8-byte signed integer
FLOAT	Primitive	4-byte single precision floating-point number
DOUBLE	Primitive	8-byte double precision floating-point number
BOOLEAN	Primitive	True/false value
STRING	Primitive	Character string
BINARY	Primitive	Byte array
TIMESTAMP	Primitive	Timestamp with nanosecond precision
DATE	Primitive	Year/month/day, in the form YYYYMMDD
ARRAY	Complex	Ordered collection of fields of the same type
MAP	Complex	Unordered collection of key value pairs
STRUCT	Complex	Collection of named fields of varying types

Listing 6.1 provides an example of a typical Hive DDL statement used to create a table in Hive.

Listing 6.1 **Hive CREATE TABLE Statement**

```
CREATE EXTERNAL TABLE stations (
station_id INT,
name STRING,
lat DOUBLE,
long DOUBLE,
dockcount INT,
landmark STRING,
installation STRING )
ROW FORMAT DELIMITED FIELDS TERMINATED BY ','
STORED AS TEXTFILE
LOCATION 'hdfs:///data/bike-share/stations';
```

Internal Tables Versus External Tables in Hive

When you create tables in Hive, the default option is to create a Hive "internal" table. Hive manages directories for internal tables, and a DROP TABLE statement for an internal table deletes the corresponding files from HDFS. It is recommended to use external tables by specifying the keyword EXTERNAL in the CREATE TABLE statement. This provides the schema and location for the object in HDFS, but a DROP TABLE operation does not delete the directory and files.

Spark SQL Architecture

Spark SQL provides a mainly HiveQL-compatible SQL abstraction to its RDD-based storage, scheduling, and execution model. Many of the key characteristics of the core Spark project are in Spark SQL, including lazy evaluation and mid-query fault tolerance. Moreover, Spark SQL is usable with the Spark core API within a single application.

Spark SQL includes some key extensions to the core API that are designed to optimize typical relational access patterns. These include the following:

- **Partial DAG execution (PDE):** PDE enables DAGs to be changed and optimized on the fly as information about the data is discovered during processing. The DAG modifications include optimization for performing joins, handling skew in the data, and altering the degree of parallelism that Spark uses.

- **Partition statistics:** Spark SQL maintains statistics about data within partitions, which can be leveraged in PDE, and provides the capability to do map pruning (pruning or filtering of partitions based on columnar statistics) and optimize normally expensive join operations.

- **The DataFrame API:** We discuss this in detail later in this chapter, in the section "Getting Started with DataFrames."

- **Columnar storage:** Spark SQL stores objects in memory using columnar storage, which organizes data by columns instead of by rows. This has a significant performance impact on SQL access patterns. Figure 6.4 shows the difference between columnar and row-oriented data storage.

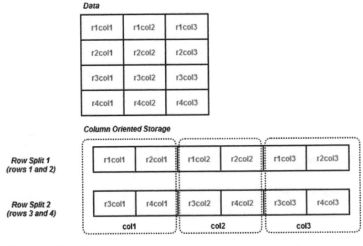

Figure 6.4   Column-oriented storage.

Spark SQL also includes native support for files in Parquet format, which is a columnar file-based storage format optimized for relational access.

Spark SQL is designed for use with environments already using Hive, with a Hive metastore and Hive (or HCatalog) object definitions for data stored in HDFS, S3, or other sources. The SQL dialect that Spark SQL supports is a subset of HiveQL and supports many HiveQL built-in functions and user-defined functions (UDFs). Spark SQL can also be used without Hive or a Hive metastore. Figure 6.5 shows a high-level overview of the Spark SQL architecture, along with the interfaces exposed by Spark SQL.

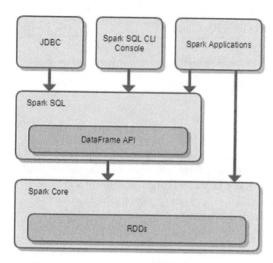

Figure 6.5   Spark SQL high-level architecture.

For more information on the Spark SQL architecture, see the whitepaper "Spark SQL: Relational Data Processing in Spark," which is available at http://people.csail.mit.edu/matei/papers/2015/sigmod_spark_sql.pdf.

The SparkSession Entry Point

Just as the SparkContext is the main entry point for an application using the Spark core API, the SparkSession object is the main entry point for Spark SQL applications. Prior to release 2 of Spark, special contexts called the SQLContext and HiveContext were the main entry points for Spark SQL applications. The SparkSession object encapsulates these contexts into one succinct entry point.

A SparkSession entry point, instantiated as spark in the interactive shells, contains a reference to a metastore to hold object (table) definitions. If Hive is available and configured, its metastore is used; otherwise, it uses its own local metastore.

Configure Hive for use with Spark can be achieved by placing your hive-site.xml, core-site.xml (for security configuration), and hdfs-site.xml (for HDFS configuration) files in the conf/ directory of your $SPARK_HOME. The primary Hive configuration file, hive-site.xml, includes location and connection details for the Hive metastore.

Listing 6.2 shows instantiation of a SparkSession for a batch application. Note that this instantiation is not necessary when using the shells pyspark and spark-shell.

SparkSession and SQLContext

You may still find references to the SQLContext object in various examples, typically instantiated as sqlContext. This object is available in the interactive Spark shells and can be used interchangeably with the spark object. It is generally preferable to use an instantiation of the SparkSession object, as the SQLContext may be deprecated in a future release.

Listing 6.2   **Creating a SparkSession Object with Hive Support**

```
from pyspark.sql import SparkSession
spark = SparkSession \
    .builder \
    .appName("My Spark SQL Application") \
    .enableHiveSupport() \
    .getOrCreate()
...
```

The SparkSession object exposes the DataFrame API, which we discuss in the next section, and enables you to create and query table objects using SQL statements and operators. If you have Hive available and configured as shown in Listing 6.2, you can query objects referenced in the Hive metastore using HiveQL statements as shown in Listing 6.3.

Listing 6.3   **Hive Queries Using Spark SQL**

```
# SparkSession available as 'spark'
sql_cmd = """SELECT name, lat, long FROM stations WHERE landmark = 'San Jose'"""
spark.sql(sql_cmd).show()
# returns:
# +--------------------+---------+----------+
# |                name|      lat|      long|
# +--------------------+---------+----------+
# |San Jose Diridon ...|37.329732|-121.901782|
# |San Jose Civic Ce...|37.330698|-121.888979|
# |Santa Clara at Al...|37.333988|-121.894902|
# |    Adobe on Almaden|37.331415|  -121.8932|
# |    San Pedro Square|37.336721|-121.894074|
# +--------------------+---------+----------+
# only showing top 5 rows
```

Getting Started with DataFrames

Spark SQL *DataFrames* are distributed collections of records, all with the same defined schema, conceptually analogous to a sharded table from a relational database. Spark SQL DataFrames were first introduced as SchemaRDD objects; they are loosely based on the DataFrame object constructs in R, discussed in Chapter 8, "Introduction to Data Science and Machine Learning Using Spark," and Pandas (the Python library for data manipulation and analysis).

DataFrames are an abstraction for Spark RDDs. However, unlike primitive RDDs, DataFrames track their schema and provide native support for many common SQL functions and relational operators. DataFrames, like RDDs, are evaluated as DAGs, using lazy evaluation and providing lineage and fault tolerance. Also like RDDs, DataFrames support caching and persistence using methods similar to those discussed in the previous chapter.

DataFrames can be created in many different ways, including from the following:

- An existing RDD
- A JSON file
- A text file, a Parquet file, or an ORC file
- A table in Hive
- A table in an external database
- A temporary table in Spark

The following sections look at some of the common methods of constructing DataFrames if there is an existing `SparkSession` object.

Creating a DataFrame from an Existing RDD

The main function used to create DataFrames from RDDs is the `createDataFrame()` method, described next.

createDataFrame()

Syntax:

```
SparkSession.createDataFrame(data, schema=None, samplingRatio=None)
```

The `createDataFrame()` method creates a DataFrame object from an existing RDD. The `data` argument is a reference to a named RDD object consisting of tuples or list elements. The `schema` argument refers to the schema to be projected to the DataFrame object. The `samplingRatio` argument is for sampling the data if the schema is inferred. (You'll learn more about defining or inferring schemas for DataFrame objects shortly.) Listing 6.4 shows an example of loading a DataFrame from an existing RDD.

Listing 6.4 **Creating a DataFrame from an RDD**

```
myrdd = sc.parallelize([('Jeff', 48),('Kellie', 45)])
spark.createDataFrame(myrdd).collect()
# returns:
# [Row(_1=u'Jeff', _2=48), Row(_1=u'Kellie', _2=45)]
```

Notice that the return value from the `collect` action is a list of Row (`pyspark.sql.Row`) objects. In this case, because the schema, including the field names, is unspecified, the fields are referenced by `_<fieldnumber>`, where the field number starts at one.

Creating a DataFrame from a Hive Table

To load data from a Hive table into a Spark SQL DataFrame, you need to create a `HiveContext`. Recall that the `HiveContext` reads the Hive client configuration (`hive-site.xml`) to obtain connection details for the Hive metastore. This enables seamless access to Hive tables from a Spark application. You can do this in a couple different ways, including using the `sql()` method or the `table()` method, as described in the following sections.

sql()

Syntax:

```
SparkSession.sql(sqlQuery)
```

The `sql()` method creates a DataFrame object from a table in Hive by supplying a `sqlQuery` argument and performing a DML operation from a table in Hive. If the table is in a database other than the Hive default database, it needs to be referenced using the `<databasename>.<tablename>` format. The `sqlQuery` can be any valid HiveQL statement, including `SELECT *` or a `SELECT` statement with a `WHERE` clause or a `JOIN` predicate. Listing 6.5 shows an example of creating a DataFrame using a HiveQL query against a table in the Hive default database.

Listing 6.5 **Creating a DataFrame from a Table in Hive**

```
sql_cmd = """SELECT name, lat, long
             FROM stations
             WHERE landmark = 'San Jose'"""
df = spark.sql(sql_cmd)
df.count()
# returns: 16
df.show(5)
# returns:
# +--------------------+--------+----------+
# |                name|     lat|      long|
# +--------------------+--------+----------+
# |San Jose Diridon ...|37.329732|-121.901782|
# |San Jose Civic Ce...|37.330698|-121.888979|
# |Santa Clara at Al...|37.333988|-121.894902|
# |    Adobe on Almaden|37.331415|  -121.8932|
# |    San Pedro Square|37.336721|-121.894074|
# +--------------------+--------+----------+
# only showing top 5 rows
```

table()

Syntax:

```
SparkSession.table(tableName)
```

The `table()` method creates a DataFrame object from a table in Hive. Unlike with the `sql()` method, there is no opportunity to prune columns with a column list or filter rows with a `WHERE` clause. The entire table loads into the DataFrame. Listing 6.6 demonstrates the `table()` method.

Listing 6.6   **`table()` Method for Creating a DataFrame from a Table in Hive**

```
df = spark.table('stations')
df.columns
# returns:
# ['station_id', 'name', 'lat', 'long', 'dockcount', 'landmark', 'installation']
df.count()
# returns: 70
```

There are other useful methods for interrogating the Hive system and database catalogs, such as the `tables()` method, which returns a DataFrame containing names of tables in a given database, and the `tableNames()` method, which returns a list of names of tables in a given Hive database.

Creating DataFrames from JSON Objects

JSON is a common, standard, human-readable serialization or wire transfer format often used in web service responses. Because JSON is a semi-structured source with a schema, support for JSON is included in Spark SQL.

read.json()

Syntax:

```
DataFrameReader.read.json(path,
                          schema=None,
                          primitivesAsString=None,
                          prefersDecimal=None,
                          allowComments=None,
                          allowUnquotedFieldNames=None,
                          allowSingleQuotes=None,
                          allowNumericLeadingZero=None,
                          allowBackslashEscapingAnyCharacter=None,
                          mode=None,
                          columnNameOfCorruptRecord=None,
                          dateFormat=None,
                          timestampFormat=None,
                          multiLine=None)
```

The `json()` method of the `DataFrameReader` creates a DataFrame object from a JSON file. Listing 6.7 demonstrates the `read.json()` method; notice that the `DataFrameReader` is accessible from the `SparkSession` object. The `path` argument refers to the fully qualified path (in a local or remote filesystem such as HDFS) of the JSON file. The `schema` argument can explicitly define a target schema for the resultant DataFrame, which we look at later in this chapter. Many additional arguments are used to specify formatting options, and the full description of them is in the Spark SQL Python API documentation at https://spark.apache.org/docs/latest/api/python/pyspark.sql.html#pyspark.sql.DataFrameReader.

Listing 6.7 `read.json()` Method for Creating a DataFrame from a JSON File

```
people_json_file = '/opt/spark/examples/src/main/resources/people.json'
people_df = spark.read.json(people_json_file)
people_df.show()
# returns:
# +----+-------+
# | age|   name|
# +----+-------+
# |null|Michael|
# |  30|   Andy|
# |  19| Justin|
# +----+-------+
```

Note that each line in a JSON file must be a valid JSON object. The schemas, or keys, do not need to be uniform across all JSON objects in a file. Keys that are not present in a given JSON object are represented as `null` in the resultant DataFrame.

In addition, the `read.json()` method allows you to create a DataFrame from an existing RDD consisting of a list of one or more discrete JSON objects as strings (see Listing 6.8).

Listing 6.8 Creating a DataFrame from a JSON RDD

```
rdd= sc.parallelize( \
 ['{"name":"Adobe on Almaden", "lat":37.331415, "long":-121.8932}', \
  '{"name":"Japantown", "lat":37.348742, "long":-121.894715}'])
json_df = spark.read.json(rdd)
json_df.show()
# returns:
# +---------+-----------+----------------+
# |      lat|       long|            name|
# +---------+-----------+----------------+
# |37.331415|  -121.8932|Adobe on Almaden|
# |37.348742|-121.894715|       Japantown|
# +---------+-----------+----------------+
```

Creating DataFrames from Flat Files

The `DataFrameReader` can also be used to load DataFrames from other types of files, such as CSV files, as well as external SQL and NoSQL data sources. The following sections look at some examples of creating DataFrames from plaintext files and columnar storage files, including Parquet and ORC.

text()

Syntax:

```
DataFrameReader.read.text(path)
```

The text() method of the DataFrameReader is used to load DataFrames from text files in an external filesystem (local, NFS, HDFS, S3, or others). Its behavior is similar to its RDD equivalent, sc.textFile(). The path argument refers to a path that could be a file, directory, or file glob. ("Globbing" expressions are similar to regular expressions used to return a list of files satisfying the glob pattern.)

Listing 6.9 demonstrates the read.text() function.

Listing 6.9 **Creating a DataFrame from a Plaintext File or Files**

```
# read an individual file
df = spark.read.text('file:///opt/spark/data/bike-share/stations/stations.csv')
df.take(1)
# returns:
# [Row(value=u'9,Japantown,37.348742,-121.894715,15,San Jose,8/5/2013')]
# you can also read all files from a directory...
df = spark.read.text('file:///opt/spark/data/bike-share/stations/')
df.count()
# returns: 83
```

Note that the Row object returned for each line in the text file or files contains one string, which is the entire line of the file.

> **Columnar Storage and Parquet Files**
>
> Columnar storage concepts, introduced earlier in this chapter, extend beyond in-memory structures to persistent file formats such as Parquet and ORC (Optimized Row Columnar) files. *Apache Parquet* is a popular, generalized columnar storage format designed for integration with any Hadoop ecosystem project. Parquet is a "first-class citizen" in the Spark project and is the preferred storage format for Spark SQL processing. ORC is a successor to RCFile, a columnar storage format built to improve Hive read performance. If you need to share data structures with Hive and accommodate non-Spark access patterns, such as Tez, ORC may be an appropriate format. Parquet support is available through the Hive project as well.

parquet()

Syntax:

```
DataFrameReader.read.parquet(paths)
```

The parquet() method of the DataFrameReader is for loading files stored with the Parquet columnar storage format. These files are often the output of another process, such as output from a previous Spark process. The paths argument refers to a Parquet file or files, or a directory containing Parquet files.

The Parquet format encapsulates the schema and data in one structure, so the schema is applied and available to the resultant DataFrame.

Given an existing file in Parquet format, Listing 6.10 demonstrates the use of the `DataFrameReader.read.parquet()` method.

Listing 6.10   **Creating a DataFrame from a Parquet File or Files**

```
df = spark.read.parquet('hdfs:///user/hadoop/stations.parquet')
df.printSchema()
# returns:
# root
#  |-- station_id: integer (nullable = true)
#  |-- name: string (nullable = true)
#  |-- lat: double (nullable = true)
#  |-- long: double (nullable = true)
#  |-- dockcount: integer (nullable = true)
#  |-- landmark: string (nullable = true)
#  |-- installation: string (nullable = true)
df.take(1)
# returns:
# [Row(station_id=2, name=u'San Jose Diridon Caltrain Station', lat=37.329732...)]
```

Parquet and Compression

By default, Spark uses the Gzip codec to compress Parquet files. If you require an alternative codec (such as Snappy) to read or write compressed Parquet files, supply the following config:

```
sqlContext.setConf("spark.sql.parquet.compression.codec.", "snappy")
```

orc()

Syntax:

`DataFrameReader.read.orc(path)`

The `orc()` method of the `DataFrameReader` is used to load a DataFrame from a file or directory consisting of ORC format files. ORC is a format native to the Hive project. The `path` argument refers to a directory containing ORC files, typically associated with a table in ORC format in a Hive warehouse. Listing 6.11 shows the use of the `orc()` method to load the ORC files associated with a Hive table stored as ORC.

Listing 6.11   **Creating a DataFrame from Hive ORC Files**

```
df = spark.read.orc('hdfs:///user/hadoop/stations_orc/')
df.printSchema()
# returns:
# root
#  |-- station_id: integer (nullable = true)
```

```
# |-- name: string (nullable = true)
# |-- lat: double (nullable = true)
# |-- long: double (nullable = true)
# |-- dockcount: integer (nullable = true)
# |-- landmark: string (nullable = true)
# |-- installation: string (nullable = true)
df.take(1)
# returns:
# [Row(station_id=2, name=u'San Jose Diridon Caltrain Station', lat=37.329732 ...)]
```

You can also use the `DataFrameReader` and the `spark.read.jdbc()` method to load data from external data sources such as MySQL, Oracle, or others.

Converting DataFrames to RDDs

You can easily convert DataFrames to native RDDs by using the `rdd()` method, as shown in Listing 6.12. The resultant RDD consists of `pyspark.sql.Row` objects.

Listing 6.12   **Converting a DataFrame to an RDD**

```
stationsdf = spark.read.parquet('hdfs:///user/hadoop/stations.parquet')
stationsrdd = stationsdf.rdd
stationsrdd
# returns:
# MapPartitionsRDD[4] at javaToPython at ...
stationsrdd.take(1)
# returns:
# [Row(station_id=2, name=u'San Jose Diridon Caltrain Station', lat=37.329732 ...)]
```

DataFrame Data Model: Primitive Types

The data model for the DataFrame API is based on the Hive data model. Datatypes used with DataFrames map directly to their equivalents in Hive. This includes all common primitive types as well as complex, nested types such as the equivalents to lists, dictionaries, and tuples.

Table 6.2 lists the primitive types encapsulated by PySpark types derived from the base class `pyspark.sql.types.DataType`.

Table 6.2   **Spark SQL Primitive Types (`pyspark.sql.types`)**

Type	Hive Equivalent	Python Equivalent
ByteType	TINYINT	int
ShortType	SMALLINT	int
IntegerType	INT	int
LongType	BIGINT	long

Type	Hive Equivalent	Python Equivalent
FloatType	FLOAT	float
DoubleType	DOUBLE	float
BooleanType	BOOLEAN	bool
StringType	STRING	string
BinaryType	BINARY	bytearray
TimestampType	TIMESTAMP	datetime.datetime
DateType	DATE	datetime.date

DataFrame Data Model: Complex Types

Complex, nested structures are accessible in Spark SQL using native HiveQL-based operators. Table 6.3 lists the complex types in the DataFrame API, along with their Hive and Python equivalents.

Table 6.3 **Spark SQL Complex Types (`pyspark.sql.types`)**

Type	Hive Equivalent	Python Equivalent
ArrayType	ARRAY	list, tuple, or array
MapType	MAP	dict
StructType	STRUCT	list or tuple

Inferring DataFrame Schemas

The schema for a Spark SQL DataFrame can be explicitly defined or inferred. In previous examples, the schema was not explicit, so in each case, it was *inferred*. Inferring the schema is the simplest method. However, it is generally better practice to define the schema in your code.

Spark SQL uses *reflection*, a process of examining an object to determine its composition, to infer the schema of a DataFrame object. Reflection can interpret a schema for an RDD converted to a DataFrame. In this case, the process involves creating a Row object from each record in the RDD and assigning a datatype from each field in the RDD. The datatypes are inferred from the first record, so it is important for the first record to be representative of the dataset and to have no missing values.

Listing 6.13 shows an example of schema inference for a DataFrame created from an RDD. Note the use of the printSchema() DataFrame method to print the schema to the console in a tree format.

Listing 6.13 **Schema Inference for a DataFrame Created from an RDD**

```
rdd = sc.textFile('file:///home/hadoop/stations.csv') \
        .map(lambda x: x.split(',')) \
        .map(lambda x: (int(x[0]), str(x[1]),
                        float(x[2]), float(x[3]),
                        int(x[4]), str(x[5]), str(x[6])))
```

```
rdd.take(1)
# returns:
# [(2, 'San Jose Diridon Caltrain Station', 37.329732, -121.901782, 27, 'San Jose',
# '8/6/2013')]
df = spark.createDataFrame(rdd)
df.printSchema()
# returns:
# root
#  |-- _1: long (nullable = true)
#  |-- _2: string (nullable = true)
#  |-- _3: double (nullable = true)
#  |-- _4: double (nullable = true)
#  |-- _5: long (nullable = true)
#  |-- _6: string (nullable = true)
#  |-- _7: string (nullable = true)
```

Note that the fields use the _<fieldnumber> convention for their identifiers and have a
nullable property value set to True, meaning these values are not required. Also notice that
the larger type variants are assumed. For instance, the lat and long fields in this RDD are cast
as float values, yet the inferred schema in the resultant DataFrame uses double (actually,
an instance of the DoubleType) for the same fields. Likewise, long values are inferred from
int values.

Schema inference is performed automatically for DataFrames created from JSON documents, as
shown in Listing 6.14.

Listing 6.14   **Schema Inference for DataFrames Created from JSON Objects**

```
rdd = sc.parallelize( \
    ['{"name":"Adobe on Almaden", "lat":37.331415, "long":-121.8932}', \
     '{"name":"Japantown", "lat":37.348742, "long":-121.894715}'])
df = spark.read.json(rdd)
df.printSchema()
# returns:
# root
#  |-- lat: double (nullable = true)
#  |-- long: double (nullable = true)
#  |-- name: string (nullable = true)
```

The schema for a DataFrame created from a Hive table is automatically inherited from its Hive
definition, as shown in Listing 6.15.

Listing 6.15   **Schema for a DataFrame Created from a Hive Table**

```
df = spark.table("stations")
df.printSchema()
# returns:
# root
```

```
# |-- station_id: integer (nullable = true)
# |-- name: string (nullable = true)
# |-- lat: double (nullable = true)
# |-- long: double (nullable = true)
# |-- dockcount: integer (nullable = true)
# |-- landmark: string (nullable = true)
# |-- installation: string (nullable = true)
```

Defining DataFrame Schemas

The preferred method of defining a schema for DataFrame objects is to explicitly supply it in your code. To create a schema, you need to create a `StructType` object containing a collection of `StructField` objects. You then apply this schema to your DataFrame when it is created. Listing 6.16 shows an example of explicitly defining a schema using a previous example. Notice the difference in behavior between the inferred and defined schemas.

Listing 6.16 **Defining the Schema for a DataFrame Explicitly**

```
from pyspark.sql.types import *
myschema = StructType([ \
          StructField("station_id", IntegerType(), True), \
          StructField("name", StringType(), True), \
          StructField("lat", FloatType(), True), \
          StructField("long", FloatType(), True), \
          StructField("dockcount", IntegerType(), True), \
          StructField("landmark", StringType(), True), \
          StructField("installation", StringType(), True) \
          ])
rdd = sc.textFile('file:///home/hadoop/stations.csv') \
        .map(lambda x: x.split(',')) \
        .map(lambda x: (int(x[0]), str(x[1]),
                        float(x[2]), float(x[3]),
                        int(x[4]), str(x[5]), str(x[6])))
df = spark.createDataFrame(rdd, myschema)
df.printSchema()
# returns:
# root
#  |-- station_id: integer (nullable = true)
#  |-- name: string (nullable = true)
#  |-- lat: float (nullable = true)
#  |-- long: float (nullable = true)
#  |-- dockcount: integer (nullable = true)
#  |-- landmark: string (nullable = true)
#  |-- installation: string (nullable = true)
```

Using DataFrames

The DataFrame API is currently one of the fastest-moving areas in the Spark project. New and significant features and functions appear with every minor release. Extensions to the Spark SQL DataFrame model, such as the Datasets API, are moving equally quickly. In fact, Spark SQL, including its core component, the DataFrame API, could warrant its own book. The following sections cover the basics of the DataFrame API using Python, providing enough information to get you up and running with DataFrames. The rest is up to you!

DataFrame Metadata Operations

Several metadata functions are available with the DataFrame API. These are functions that return information about the data structure, not the data itself. You have already seen one of the available functions, `printSchema()`, which returns the schema defined for a DataFrame object in a tree format. The following sections explore some of the additional metadata functions.

columns()

Syntax:

```
DataFrame.columns()
```

The `columns()` method returns a list of column names for the given DataFrame. An example is provided in Listing 6.17.

Listing 6.17   **Returning a List of Columns from a DataFrame**

```
df = spark.read.parquet('hdfs:///user/hadoop/stations.parquet')
df.columns
# returns:
# ['station_id', 'name', 'lat', 'long', 'dockcount', 'landmark', 'installation']
```

dtypes()

Syntax:

```
DataFrame.dtypes()
```

The `dtypes()` method returns a list of tuples, with each tuple consisting of the column names and the datatypes for a column for a given DataFrame object. This may be more useful than the previously discussed `printSchema()` method because you can access it programmatically. Listing 6.18 demonstrates the `dtypes()` method.

Listing 6.18   **Returning Column Names and Datatypes from a DataFrame**

```
df = spark.read.parquet('hdfs:///user/hadoop/stations.parquet')
df.dtypes
# returns:
# [('station_id', 'int'), ('name', 'string'), ('lat', 'double'), ('long', 'double'),
# ('dockcount', 'int'), ('landmark', 'string'), ('installation', 'string')]
```

Basic DataFrame Operations

Because DataFrames are columnar abstractions of RDDs, you see many similar functions, such as transformations and actions, that are direct descendants of RDD methods, with some additional relational methods such as select(), drop(), and where(). Core functions such as count(), collect(), take(), and foreach() are functionally and syntactically analogous to the functions with the same names in the RDD API. As with the RDD API, each of these methods, as an action, triggers evaluation of the DataFrame and its lineage.

Much as with the collect() and take() actions, you may have noticed an alternative method, show(), used in previous examples. show() is an action that triggers evaluation of a DataFrame if the DataFrame does not exist in cache.

The select(), drop(), filter(), where(), and distinct() methods can prune columns or filter rows from a DataFrame. In each case, the results of these operations create a new DataFrame object.

show()

Syntax:

```
DataFrame.show(n=20, truncate=True)
```

The show() method prints the first n rows of a DataFrame to the console. Unlike collect() or take(n), show() cannot return to a variable. It is solely intended for viewing the contents or a subset of the contents in the console or notebook. The truncate argument specifies whether to truncate long strings and align cells to the right.

The output of the show() command is "pretty printed," meaning it is formatted as a grid result set, including column headings for readability.

select()

Syntax:

```
DataFrame.select(*cols)
```

The select() method returns a new DataFrame object from the list of columns specified by the cols argument. You can use an asterisk (*) to select all columns from the DataFrame with no manipulation. Listing 6.19 shows an example of the select() function.

Listing 6.19 **select()** Method in Spark SQL

```
df = spark.read.parquet('hdfs:///user/hadoop/stations.parquet')
newdf = df.select((df.name).alias("Station Name"))
newdf.show(2)
# returns:
# +--------------------+
# |        Station Name|
# +--------------------+
# |San Jose Diridon ...|
# |San Jose Civic Ce...|
# +--------------------+
# only showing top 2 rows
```

As you can see from Listing 6.19, you can also apply column aliases with `select()` by using the `alias` operator; `select()` is also the primary method for applying column-level functions in DataFrame transformation operations. You will see an example of this shortly.

drop()

Syntax:

`DataFrame.drop(col)`

The `drop()` method returns a new DataFrame with the column specified by the `col` argument removed. Listing 6.20 demonstrates the use of the `drop()` method.

Listing 6.20   **Dropping a Column from a DataFrame**

```
df = spark.read.parquet('hdfs:///user/hadoop/stations.parquet')
df.columns
# returns:
# ['station_id', 'name', 'lat', 'long', 'dockcount', 'landmark', 'installation']
newdf = df.drop(df.installation)
newdf.columns
# returns:
# ['station_id', 'name', 'lat', 'long', 'dockcount', 'landmark']
```

filter()

Syntax:

`DataFrame.filter(condition)`

The `filter()` method returns a new DataFrame that contains only rows that satisfy the given condition, an expression provided by the `condition` argument that evaluates to `True` or `False`. Listing 6.21 demonstrates the use of `filter()`.

Listing 6.21   **Filtering Rows from a DataFrame**

```
df = spark.read.parquet('hdfs:///user/hadoop/stations.parquet')
df.filter(df.name == 'St James Park') \
  .select(df.name,df.lat,df.long) \
  .show()
# returns:
# +-------------+---------+-----------+
# |         name|      lat|       long|
# +-------------+---------+-----------+
# |St James Park|37.339301|-121.889937|
# +-------------+---------+-----------+
```

The `where()` method is an alias for `filter()`, and the two can be used interchangeably.

distinct()

Syntax:

```
DataFrame.distinct()
```

The `distinct()` method returns a new DataFrame that contains the distinct rows in the input DataFrame, essentially filtering out duplicate rows. A duplicate row is a row where all values for all columns are the same as for another row in the same DataFrame. Listing 6.22 shows an example of the `distinct()` method.

Listing 6.22 **Filtering Duplicate Rows from a DataFrame**

```
rdd = sc.parallelize([('Jeff', 48),('Kellie', 45),('Jeff', 48)])
df = spark.createDataFrame(rdd)
df.show()
# returns:
# +------+---+
# |    _1| _2|
# +------+---+
# |  Jeff| 48|
# |Kellie| 45|
# |  Jeff| 48|
# +------+---+
df.distinct().show()
# returns:
# +------+---+
# |    _1| _2|
# +------+---+
# |Kellie| 45|
# |  Jeff| 48|
# +------+---+
```

Note that `drop_duplicates()` is a similar method that also lets you optionally consider certain columns to filter for duplicates.

In addition, `map()` and `flatMap()` are available, using `DataFrame.rdd.map()` and `DataFrame.rdd.flatMap()`, respectively. Prior to Spark's 2.0 release, you could run the `map()` and `flatMap()` methods directly on a DataFrame object; however, these were simply aliases for the `rdd.map()` and `rdd.flatMap()` methods.

Along with the `select()` method, you can use the `rdd.map()` and `rdd.flatMap()` methods to apply column-level functions to rows in Spark SQL DataFrames, as well as project-specific columns, including computed columns. However, `select()` operates on a DataFrame and returns a new DataFrame, whereas the `rdd.map()` and `rdd.flatMap()` methods operate on a DataFrame and return an RDD.

Conceptually, these methods function like their named equivalents in the RDD API. However, when dealing with DataFrames with named columns, the `lambda` functions are slightly different. Listing 6.23 uses the `rdd.map()` method to project a column from a DataFrame into a new RDD named `rdd`.

Listing 6.23 **map()** Functions with Spark SQL DataFrames

```
df = spark.read.parquet('hdfs:///user/hadoop/stations.parquet')
rdd = df.rdd.map(lambda r: r.name)
rdd
# returns:
# PythonRDD[62] at RDD at PythonRDD.scala:48
rdd.take(1)
# returns:
# [u'San Jose Diridon Caltrain Station']
```

If you want the result of a mapping operation to return a new DataFrame instead of an RDD, select() is a better option.

Some other operations in the Spark SQL DataFrame API are worth mentioning. The methods sample() and sampleBy() work similarly to their RDD equivalents, and the limit() function creates a new DataFrame with a specific number of arbitrary rows from the originating DataFrame. All these methods are helpful for working with data at scale, limiting the working set during development.

Another useful method during development is explain(). The explain() method returns a query plan, including a logical and physical plan for evaluating the DataFrame. This can be helpful in troubleshooting or optimizing Spark SQL programs.

You are encouraged to explore the documentation to learn more about all the functions available in the DataFrame API. Notably, Python *docstrings* are included with all functions in the Python Spark SQL API. You can use them to explore the syntax and usage of any function in Spark SQL, as well as any other functions in the Spark Python API. Python docstrings are accessible using the __doc__ method of a function with the fully qualified class path, as shown in Listing 6.24.

Listing 6.24 **Getting Help for Spark SQL Functions**

```
from pyspark.sql import DataFrame
print(DataFrame.sample.__doc__)
# returns:
# Returns a sampled subset of this :class:`DataFrame`.
#.. note:: This is not guaranteed to provide exactly the fraction specified of the
# total
#  count of the given :class:`DataFrame`.
# >>> df.sample(False, 0.5, 42).count()
# 2
#.. versionadded:: 1.3
```

DataFrame Built-in Functions

Numerous functions available in Spark SQL are present in most other common DBMS implementations of SQL. Using the Python Spark API, these built-in functions are available through the pyspark.sql.functions module. Functions include scalar and aggregate functions and can operate on fields, columns, or rows, depending on the function. Table 6.4 shows a sampling of the functions available in the pyspark.sql.functions library.

Table 6.4   **Examples of Built-in Functions Available in Spark SQL**

Type	Available Functions
String functions	`startswith, substr, concat, lower, upper, regexp_extract, regexp_replace`
Math functions	`abs, ceil, floor, log, round, sqrt`
Statistical functions	`avg, max, min, mean, stddev`
Date functions	`date_add, datediff, from_utc_timestamp`
Hashing functions	`md5, sha1, sha2`
Algorithmic functions	`soundex, levenshtein`
Windowing functions	`over, rank, dense_rank, lead, lag, ntile`

Implementing User-Defined Functions in the DataFrame API

If you can't find a function for what you want to do, you can create a user-defined function (UDF) in Spark SQL. You can create column-level UDFs to incorporate into Spark programs by using the udf() method described next.

udf()

Syntax:

`pyspark.sql.functions.udf(func, returnType=StringType)`

The udf method creates a column expression representing a user-defined function; func is a named or anonymous function, using the lambda syntax, that operates on a column within a DataFrame row. The returnType argument specifies the datatype of the object returned from the function. This type is a member of pyspark.sql.types or a subtype of the pyspark.sql.types.DataType class.

Suppose you want to define functions to convert decimal latitudinal and longitudinal coordinates to their geopositional direction with respect to the equator and the prime meridian. Listing 6.25 demonstrates creating two UDFs to take the decimal latitude and longitude coordinates and return N, S, E, or W, as appropriate.

Listing 6.25   **User-Defined Functions in Spark SQL**

```
from pyspark.sql.functions import *
from pyspark.sql.types import *
df = spark.read.parquet('hdfs:///user/hadoop/stations.parquet')
lat2dir = udf(lambda x: 'N' if x > 0 else 'S', StringType())
lon2dir = udf(lambda x: 'E' if x > 0 else 'W', StringType())
df.select(df.lat, lat2dir(df.lat).alias('latdir'),
          df.long, lon2dir(df.lat).alias('longdir')) \
          .show(5)
# returns:
```

```
# +---------+------+-----------+-------+
# |     lat|latdir|       long|longdir|
# +---------+------+-----------+-------+
# |37.329732|    N|-121.901782|      E|
# |37.330698|    N|-121.888979|      E|
# |37.333988|    N|-121.894902|      E|
# |37.331415|    N|  -121.8932|      E|
# |37.336721|    N|-121.894074|      E|
# +---------+------+-----------+-------+
# only showing top 5 rows
```

Operations on Multiple DataFrames

Set operations, such as join() and union(), are common requirements for DataFrames because they are integral operations in relational SQL programming.

Joining DataFrames support all join operations supported in the RDD API and in HiveQL, including inner joins, outer joins, and left semi-joins.

join()

Syntax:

DataFrame.join(other, on=None, how=None)

The join() method creates a new DataFrame from the results of a join operation against the DataFrame referenced in the other argument (the right side of the argument). The on argument specifies a column, a list of columns, or an expression to evaluate the join operation. The how argument specifies the type of join to be performed. Valid values include inner (default), outer, left_outer, right_outer, and leftsemi.

Consider a new entity from the bike-share dataset called trips, which includes two fields, start_terminal and end_terminal, that correspond to station_id in the stations entity. Listing 6.26 demonstrates an inner join between these two entities, using the join() method.

Listing 6.26   **Joining DataFrames in Spark SQL**

```
trips = spark.table("trips")
stations = spark.table("stations")
joined = trips.join(stations, trips.startterminal == stations.station_id)
joined.printSchema()
# returns:
# root
#  |-- tripid: integer (nullable = true)
#  |-- duration: integer (nullable = true)
#  |-- startdate: string (nullable = true)
#  |-- startstation: string (nullable = true)
#  |-- startterminal: integer (nullable = true)
#  |-- enddate: string (nullable = true)
#  |-- endstation: string (nullable = true)
```

```
#  |-- endterminal: integer (nullable = true)
#  |-- bikeno: integer (nullable = true)
#  |-- subscribertype: string (nullable = true)
#  |-- zipcode: string (nullable = true)
#  |-- station_id: integer (nullable = true)
#  |-- name: string (nullable = true)
#  |-- lat: double (nullable = true)
#  |-- long: double (nullable = true)
#  |-- dockcount: integer (nullable = true)
#  |-- landmark: string (nullable = true)
#  |-- installation: string (nullable = true)
joined.select(joined.startstation, joined.duration) \
     .show(2)
# returns:
# +--------------------+--------+
# |        startstation|duration|
# +--------------------+--------+
# |Harry Bridges Pla...|     765|
# |San Antonio Shopp...|    1036|
# +--------------------+--------+
# only showing top 2 rows
```

Other set operations such as `intersect()` and `subtract()` are available functions for Spark SQL DataFrames and function like the equivalent RDD functions described previously in this book. In addition, a `unionAll()` method is available for DataFrames instead of `union()`, also described previously. Note that if you need to remove duplicates, you can do so after the `unionAll()` operation by using the aforementioned `distinct()` or `drop_ duplicates()` functions.

The DataFrame API also includes several standard methods for sorting or ordering, as described in the following sections.

orderBy()

Syntax:

`DataFrame.orderBy(cols, ascending)`

The `orderBy()` method creates a new DataFrame ordered by the columns specified in the `cols` argument; `ascending` is a Boolean argument that defaults to `True`, which determines the sort order for the column. Listing 6.27 shows an example of the `orderBy()` function.

Listing 6.27 **Ordering a DataFrame**

```
stations = spark.read.parquet('hdfs:///user/hadoop/stations.parquet')
stations.orderBy([stations.name], ascending=False) \
    .select(stations.name) \
    .show(2)
# returns:
```

```
# +-------------------+
# |               name|
# +-------------------+
# |Yerba Buena Cente...|
# |Washington at Kea...|
# +-------------------+
# only showing top 2 rows
```

Note that sort() is a function synonymous with orderBy() in the DataFrame API.

Grouping is a common precursor to performing aggregations on a column or columns in a DataFrame. The DataFrame API includes the groupBy() method (also aliased by groupby()), which groups the DataFrame on specific columns. This function returns a pyspark.sql. GroupedData object, a special type of DataFrame that contains grouped data exposing common aggregate functions, such as sum() and count().

groupBy()

Syntax:

DataFrame.groupBy(cols)

The groupBy() method creates a new DataFrame containing the input DataFrame grouped by the column or columns specified in the cols argument. Listing 6.28 demonstrates the use of groupBy() to average trip durations from the trips entity in the bike-share dataset.

Listing 6.28 **Grouping and Aggregating Data in DataFrames**

```
trips = spark.table("trips")
averaged = trips.groupBy([trips.startterminal]).avg('duration') \
                .show(2)
# returns:
# +-------------+------------------+
# |startterminal|     avg(duration)|
# +-------------+------------------+
# |           31|2747.6333021515434|
# |           65| 626.1329988365329|
# +-------------+------------------+
# only showing top 2 rows
```

Caching, Persisting, and Repartitioning DataFrames

The DataFrame API supports methods for caching, persisting, and repartitioning that are similar to those in the Spark RDD API for these operations.

Methods for caching and persisting DataFrames include cache(), persist(), and unpersist(), which behave like the RDD functions with the same names. In addition, Spark SQL adds the cacheTable() method, which caches a table from Spark SQL or Hive in memory. The clearCache() method removes a cached table from memory. DataFrames also support the coalesce() and repartition() methods for repartitioning DataFrames.

Saving DataFrame Output

The DataFrameWriter is the interface used to write a DataFrame to external storage systems such as a file system or a database. The DataFrameWriter is accessible using DataFrame.write(). The following sections provide some examples.

Writing Data to a Hive Table

Earlier in this chapter, you saw how to load data into a DataFrame from a Hive table. Similarly, you may often need to write data from a DataFrame to a Hive table; you can do this by using the saveAsTable() function.

saveAsTable()

Syntax:

DataFrame.write.saveAsTable(name, format=None, mode=None, partitionBy=None)

The saveAsTable() method writes the data from a DataFrame into the Hive table specified in the name argument. The format argument specifies the output format for the target table; the default is Parquet format. Likewise, mode is the behavior with respect to an existing object, and valid values are append, overwrite, error, and ignore. Listing 6.29 shows an example of the saveAsTable() method.

Listing 6.29 **Saving a DataFrame to a Hive Table**

```
stations = spark.table("stations")
stations.select([stations.station_id,stations.name]).write \
        .saveAsTable("station_names")
# load new table
station_names = spark.table("station_names")
station_names.show(2)
# returns:
# +----------+--------------------+
# |station_id|                name|
# +----------+--------------------+
# |         2|San Jose Diridon ...|
# |         3|San Jose Civic Ce...|
# +----------+--------------------+
# only showing top 2 rows
```

There is also a similar method in the DataFrame API named insertInto().

Writing Data to Files

Data from DataFrames can write to files in any supported filesystem: local, network, or distributed. Output is written as a directory with files emitted for each partition, much as with the RDD output examples shown earlier in this chapter.

Comma-separated values (CSV) is a common file export format. DataFrames can export to CSV files by using the `DataFrameWriter.write.csv()` method.

Parquet is a popular columnar format that is optimized for Spark SQL. You have seen several examples so far from Parquet format files. DataFrames can write to Parquet format files by using the `DataFrameWriter.write.parquet()` method.

write.csv()

Syntax:

```
DataFrameWriter.write.csv(path,
                          mode=None,
                          compression=None,
                          sep=None,
                          quote=None,
                          escape=None,
                          header=None,
                          nullValue=None,
                          escapeQuotes=None,
                          quoteAll=None,
                          dateFormat=None,
                          timestampFormat=None,
                          ignoreLeadingWhiteSpace=None,
                          ignoreTrailingWhiteSpace=None)
```

The `write.csv()` method of the `DataFrameWriter` class, accessed through the `DataFrame.write.csv()` interface, writes the content of a DataFrame to CSV files in the path specified by the `path` argument. The `mode` argument defines the behavior if a target directory already exists for the operation; valid values include `append`, `overwrite`, `ignore`, and `error` (the default). The `mode` argument is available on all `DataFrame.write()` method. Additional arguments define the desired formatting for the output CSV files. For example, the `quoteAll` argument indicates whether all values should always be enclosed in quotes. Specific information on all arguments available for the `write.csv()` method is available at https://spark.apache.org/docs/latest/api/python/pyspark.sql.html#pyspark.sql.DataFrameWriter. Listing 6.30 demonstrates the use of the `write.csv()` method.

Listing 6.30 **Writing a DataFrame to a CSV File or Files**

```
spark.table("stations") \
    .write.csv("stations_csv")
```

The target for a `write.csv()` operation could be a local filesystem (using the `file://` scheme), HDFS, S3, or any other filesystem available to you and configured for access from your Spark environment. In Listing 6.30, the filesystem defaults to the home directory in HDFS of the user running the command; `stations_csv` is a directory in HDFS, the contents of which are shown in Figure 6.6.

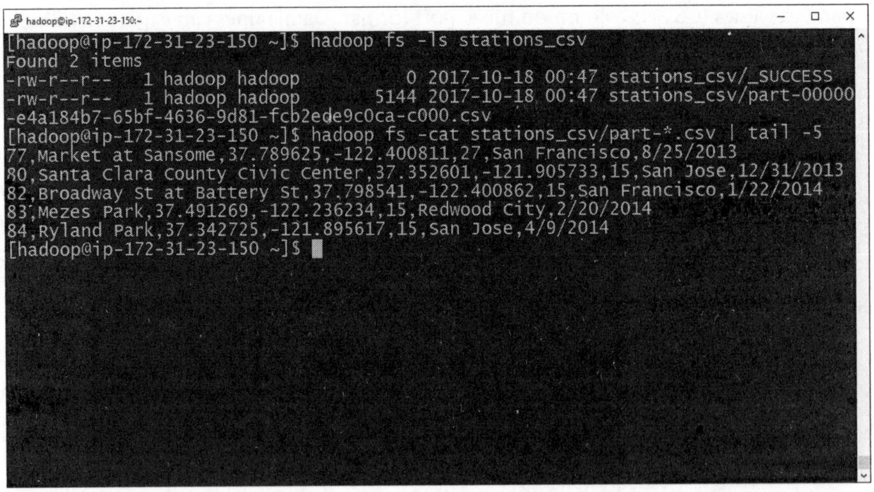

Figure 6.6   HDFS directory contents from a `write.csv()` DataFrame operation.

parquet()

Syntax:

```
DataFrameWriter.write.parquet(path, mode=None, partitionBy=None)
```

The `write.parquet()` method writes out the data from a DataFrame to a directory containing Parquet format files. Files compress according to the compression configuration settings in the current SparkContext. The mode argument specifies the behavior if the directory or files exist. Valid values for mode are append, overwrite, ignore, and error (the default); partitionBy specifies the names of columns by which to partition the output files (using the hash partitioner). Listing 6.31 demonstrates using parquet() to save a DataFrame to a Parquet file using Snappy compression.

Listing 6.31   **Saving a DataFrame to a Parquet File or Files**

```
spark = SparkSession.builder \
    .config("spark.sql.parquet.compression.codec.", "snappy") \
    .getOrCreate()
stations = spark.table("stations")
stations.select([stations.station_id,stations.name]).write \
        .parquet("file:///home/hadoop/stations.parquet", mode='overwrite')
```

Figure 6.7 shows a listing of the local directory containing the Snappy-compressed Parquet-formatted output file from the operation performed in Listing 6.31.

Figure 6.7   Output files created from a `write.parquet()` operation.

ORC files can be written using the `orc()` method, which is similar in usage to `parquet()`. JSON files can also be written using the `json()` method.

You can save DataFrames to external JDBC-compliant databases by using the `DataFrameWriter.write.jdbc()` method.

Accessing Spark SQL

So far in this chapter, the examples of Spark SQL have been within the Python (PySpark) interface. However, PySpark may not be the appropriate interface for users who are not programmers. A SQL shell or access to the Spark SQL engine from a visualization tool such as Tableau or Excel via ODBC may be more applicable.

Accessing Spark SQL Using the `spark-sql` Shell

Spark includes a SQL shell utility called `spark-sql` in the `bin` directory of your Spark installation. The `spark-sql` shell program is a lightweight REPL (read-evaluate-print loop) shell that can access Spark SQL and Hive using your local configuration and Spark Driver binaries. The shell accepts HiveQL statements, including metadata operations such as SHOW TABLES and DESCRIBE. Figure 6.8 shows an example of the `spark-sql` shell.

Note that `spark-sql` is useful for testing SQL commands locally as a developer, but it is limited because it's not a SQL engine that is accessible by other users and remote applications. This is where the Thrift JDBC/ODBC server comes into play.

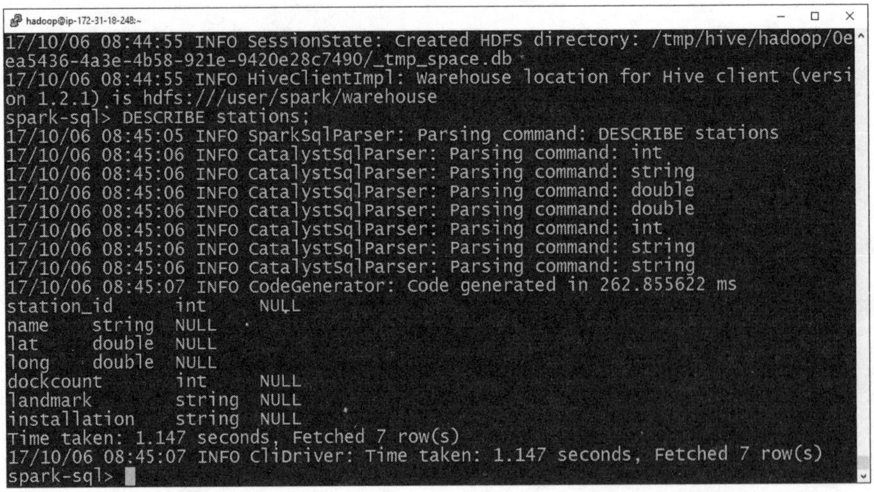

Figure 6.8   The `spark-sql` shell.

Running the Thrift JDBC/ODBC Server

Spark SQL is useful as a distributed query engine with a JDBC/ODBC interface. As with the `spark-sql` shell, the JDBC/ODBC server enables users to run SQL queries without writing Python or Scala Spark code. External applications, such as visualization tools, can connect to the server and interact directly with Spark SQL.

The JDBC/ODBC interface is implemented through a Thrift JDBC/ODBC server. *Thrift* is an Apache project used for cross-language service development. The Spark SQL Thrift JDBC/ODBC server is based on the HiveServer2 project, a server interface that enables remote clients to execute queries against Hive and retrieve the results.

The Thrift JDBC/ODBC server is included with the Spark release. To run the server, execute the following command:

`$SPARK_HOME/sbin/start-thriftserver.sh`

All valid `spark-submit` command line arguments, such as `--master`, are accepted by the `start-thriftserver.sh` script. In addition, you can supply Hive-specific properties by using the `--hiveconf` option. The Thrift JDBC/OBDC server listens on port 10000, but you can change this by using a special environment variable, as shown here:

`export HIVE_SERVER2_THRIFT_PORT=<customport>`

You can use `beeline`, discussed next, to test the JDBC/ODBC server. To stop the Thrift server, simply execute the following:

`$SPARK_HOME/sbin/stop-thriftserver.sh`

Using `beeline`

You can use `beeline`, a command line shell, to connect to HiveServer2 or the Spark SQL Thrift JDBC/ODBC server. `beeline` is a lightweight JDBC client application that is based on the SQLLine CLI project (http://sqlline.sourceforge.net/).

Like SQLLine, `beeline` is a Java console–based utility for connecting to relational databases and executing SQL commands. It is designed to function similarly to other command line database access utilities, such as `sqlplus` for Oracle, `mysql` for MySQL, and `isql` or `osql` for Sybase/SQL Server.

Because `beeline` is a JDBC client, you can use it to test the Spark SQL JDBC Thrift server when you start it. Use the `beeline` CLI utility included with the Spark release as follows:

`$SPARK_HOME/bin/beeline`

At the `beeline` prompt, you need to connect to a JDBC server—the Spark SQL Thrift server you started previously. Do this as follows:

`beeline> !connect jdbc:hive2://localhost:10000`

You are prompted for a username and password to connect to the server. Figure 6.9 shows an example of a `beeline` CLI session connecting to the Spark SQL Thrift server.

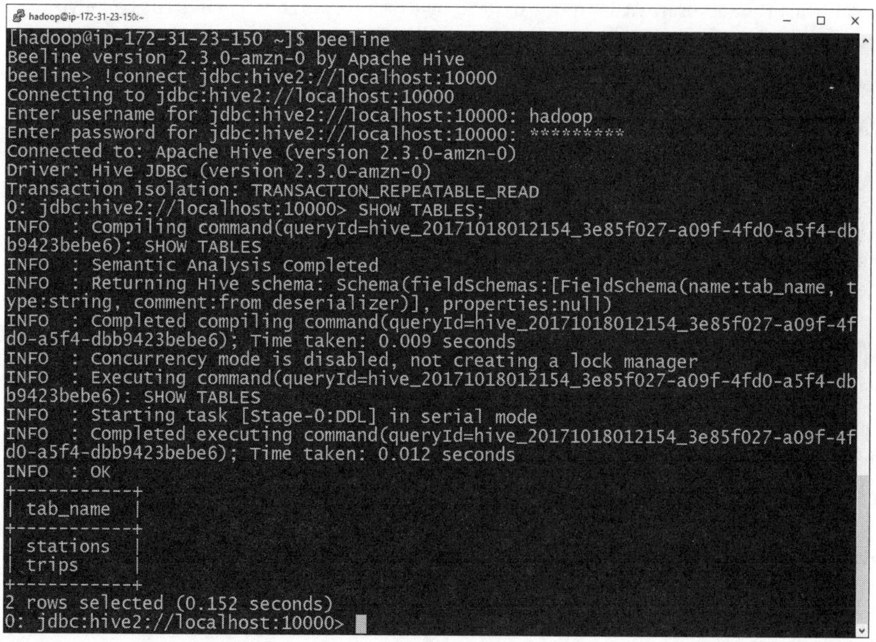

Figure 6.9   The `beeline` Spark SQL JDBC client.

Using External Applications via JDBC/ODBC

The Spark JDBC/ODBC Thrift server can also connect to other JDBC/ODBC client applications, such as Tableau or Excel. This usually requires that you install the relevant JDBC/ODBC drivers on your client. You can then create a data source and connect to Spark SQL to access and process data in Hive. Consult your visualization tool vendor for more information or to obtain the specific drivers required.

Exercise: Using Spark SQL

This exercise shows how to start a Spark SQL Thrift server and use the beeline client utility to connect to the server. You will create Hive tables based on sample data and use beeline and Thrift to run a SQL query against the data, executed by Spark SQL. You will use the bike-share dataset used for exercises in the previous chapter. Follow these steps:

1. Start the JDBC/ODBC Thrift server:

    ```
    $ sudo $SPARK_HOME/sbin/start-thriftserver.sh \
    --master local \
    --hiveconf hive.server2.thrift.port=10001 \
    --hiveconf hive.server2.thrift.bind.host=10001
    ```

    You can start the server in YARN mode instead by using --master yarn-cluster if you have a YARN cluster available to you.

2. Open a beeline session:

    ```
    $SPARK_HOME/bin/beeline
    ```

3. At the beeline> prompt, create a connection to your Thrift server:

    ```
    beeline> !connect jdbc:hive2://localhost:10001
    Enter username for jdbc:hive2://localhost:10001: hadoop
    Enter password for jdbc:hive2://localhost:10001: *********
    ```

    You are prompted for a username and password, as shown above. The username provided must exist on the Thrift server and have the appropriate permissions on the filesystem.

4. After you connect to the server, create the trips table from the bike-share demo by entering the following HiveQL DDL command:

    ```
    CREATE EXTERNAL TABLE trips (
    TripID int,
    Duration int,
    StartDate string,
    StartStation string,
    StartTerminal int,
    EndDate string,
    EndStation string,
    EndTerminal int,
    BikeNo int,
    SubscriberType string,
    ```

```
ZipCode string )
ROW FORMAT DELIMITED
FIELDS TERMINATED BY ','
LOCATION 'file:///opt/spark/data/bike-share/trips/';
```

5. Execute the following SQL query against the table you just created:

```
SELECT StartTerminal, StartStation, COUNT(1) AS count
FROM trips
GROUP BY StartTerminal, StartStation
ORDER BY count DESC
LIMIT 10;
```

6. View your Spark application web UI to confirm that your query executed using Spark SQL. Recall that this is accessible using port 4040 of your localhost if you are running Spark locally or the application master host if you are using YARN (accessible from the Resource Manager UI). Figure 6.10 shows the SQL tab in the application UI as well.

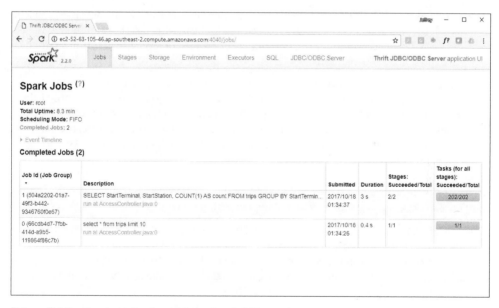

Figure 6.10   Spark application UI for a Spark SQL session.

Using Spark with NoSQL Systems

Increasingly aggressive non-functional and non-relational requirements necessitate alternative approaches to data storage, management, and processing. Enter NoSQL, a new data paradigm that allows you to look at data in terms of cells rather than just the relational paradigm of tables, rows, and columns. This is not to say that the relational database is dead—far from it—but the NoSQL approach provides a new set of capabilities to solve today's—and tomorrow's—problems.

This section introduces NoSQL systems and methodologies and looks at their integration with Spark-processing workflows. First, let's look at some of the core concepts of NoSQL systems.

Introduction to NoSQL

There is some friendly disagreement about what NoSQL means; some say it means "not SQL," others say "not only SQL," and others have other interpretations or definitions. Regardless of the disagreement around the nomenclature, NoSQL systems have specific defining characteristics and come in different variants.

NoSQL System Characteristics

All NoSQL variants share some common properties, including the following:

- **They are schemaless at design time and "schema-on-read" at runtime:** This means they do not have predefined columns, but columns are created with each PUT (INSERT) operation, and each record, document, or data instance can have a different schema than the previous instance.

- **Data has no predefined relationship to any other object:** This means there is no concept of foreign keys or referential integrity, declarative or otherwise. Relationships may exist between data objects or instances, but they are discovered or leveraged at runtime rather than prescribed at design time.

- **Joins are typically avoided:** In most NoSQL implementations, joins are kept to an absolute minimum or avoided altogether. This is typically accomplished by denormalizing data, often with the trade-off of storing duplicate data. However, with most NoSQL implementations leveraging cost-efficient commodity or cloud infrastructure, the material cost is offset by the computation cost reduction of not having to perform excessive joins when the data is accessed.

In all cases, there is no logical or physical model that dictates how data is structured, unlike with a third normal form data warehouse or an online transaction processing system.

Moreover, NoSQL systems are typically distributed (for example, Apache Cassandra, HBase) and structured for fast lookups. Write operations are typically faster and more scalable as well, as many of the processes of traditional relational database systems that lead to overhead are not used, such as datatype or domain checks, atomic/blocking transactions, and management of transaction isolation levels.

In the majority of cases, NoSQL systems are built for scale and scalability (from petabytes of storage to queries bounded in terabytes), performance, and low friction (or having the ability to adapt to changes). NoSQL systems are often comparatively analytically friendly, as they provide a denormalized structure, which is conducive to feature extraction, machine learning, and scoring.

Types of NoSQL Systems

As mentioned earlier in this chapter, NoSQL systems come in several variants or categories: key/value stores, document stores, and graph stores (see Table 6.5).

Table 6.5   **Types of NoSQL Systems**

Type	Description	Examples
Key/value stores/ column family stores	A key/value store contains a set or sets of indexed keys and associated values. Values are typically uninterpreted byte arrays but can represent complex objects such as nested maps, structs, or lists. The schema is not defined at design time; however, some storage properties such as column families, which are effectively storage containers for values, and compression attributes can be defined at table design time.	HBase, Cassandra, and DynamoDB
Document stores	Document stores, or document databases, store complex objects, documents such as JSON or BSON objects, or other complex nested objects. Each document is assigned a key or document ID, and the contents are the semi-structured document data.	MongoDB and CouchDB
Graph stores	Graph stores are based on graph theory and used to describe relationships between objects or entities.	Neo4J and GraphBase

Using Spark with HBase

HBase is a Hadoop ecosystem project designed to deliver a distributed, massively scalable key/value store on top of HDFS. Before we discuss the use of Spark with HBase, it is important that you understand some basic HBase concepts.

Introduction to HBase

HBase stores data as a sparse, multidimensional, sorted map. The map is indexed by its key (the row key), and values are stored in cells, each consisting of a column key and a column value. The row key and column keys are strings, and the column value is an uninterpreted byte array that could represent any primitive or complex datatype. HBase is multidimensional; that is, each cell is versioned with a timestamp.

At table design time, one or more column families is defined. Column families are used as physical storage groups for columns. Different column families may have different physical storage characteristics, such as block size, compression settings, or the number of cell versions to retain.

Although there are projects such as Hive and Phoenix to provide SQL-like access to data in HBase, the natural methods for accessing and updating data in HBase are essentially get, put, scan, and delete. HBase includes a shell program as well as programmatic interfaces for multiple languages. The HBase shell is an interactive Ruby REPL shell with access to HBase API functions to create and modify tables and read and write data. The shell application is accessible only by entering hbase shell on a system with the HBase client binaries and configuration available (see Figure 6.11).

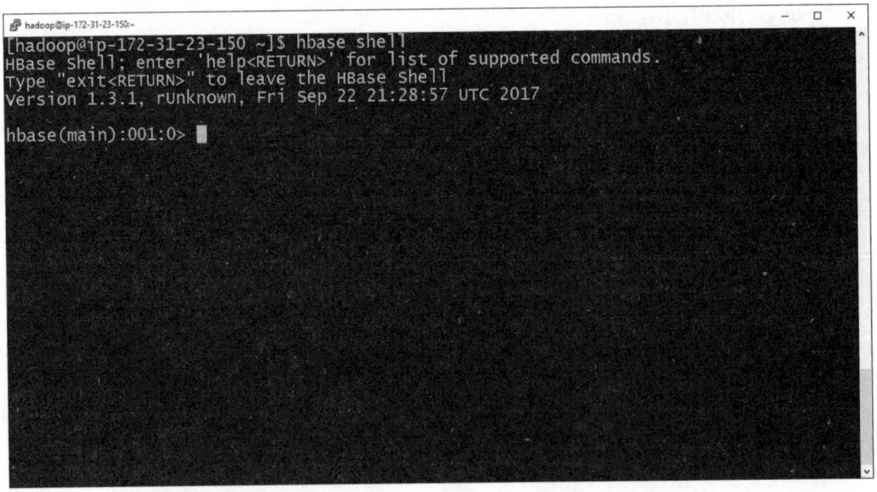

Figure 6.11   HBase shell.

Listing 6.32 demonstrates the use of hbase shell to create a table and insert data into the table.

Listing 6.32   **Creating a Table and Inserting Data in HBase**

```
hbase> create 'my-hbase-table', \
hbase* {NAME => 'cf1', COMPRESSION => 'SNAPPY', VERSIONS => 20}, \
hbase* {NAME => 'cf2'}
hbase> put 'my-hbase-table', 'rowkey1', 'cf1:fname', 'John'
hbase> put 'my-hbase-table', 'rowkey1', 'cf1:lname', 'Doe'
hbase> put 'my-hbase-table', 'rowkey2', 'cf1:fname', 'Jeffrey'
hbase> put 'my-hbase-table', 'rowkey2', 'cf1:lname', 'Aven'
hbase> put 'my-hbase-table', 'rowkey2', 'cf1:city', 'Hayward'
hbase> put 'my-hbase-table', 'rowkey2', 'cf2:password', 'c9cb7dc02b3c0083eb70898e549'
```

The create statement creates a new HBase table with two column families: cf1 and cf2. One column family is configured to use compression, and the other is not. The subsequent put statements insert data into a cell as defined by the row key (rowkey1 or rowkey2, in this case) and a column specified in the format <column_family>:<column_name>. Unlike with a traditional database, the columns are not defined at table design time and are not typed. (Recall that all data is an uninterpreted array of bytes.) A scan command of the new table is shown in Listing 6.33.

Listing 6.33   **Scanning the HBase Table**

```
hbase> scan 'my-hbase-table'
ROW                      COLUMN+CELL
 rowkey1                 column=cf1:fname, timestamp=1508291546300, value=John
 rowkey1                 column=cf1:lname, timestamp=1508291560041, value=Doe
 rowkey2                 column=cf1:city, timestamp=1508291579756, value=Hayward
```

```
rowkey2                 column=cf1:fname, timestamp=1508291566663, value=Jeffrey
rowkey2                 column=cf1:lname, timestamp=1508291572939, value=Aven
rowkey2                   column=cf2:password, timestamp=1508291585467, value=
                c9cb7dc02b3c0083eb70898e549
2 row(s) in 0.0390 seconds
```

Figure 6.12 shows a conceptual view of the data inserted in this example.

Row Key	Column Family "cf1"	Column Family "cf2"
rowkey1	fname: John, lname: Doe	
rowkey2	fname: Jeffrey, lname: Aven, city: Hayward	password: c9cb7dc...

Figure 6.12   HBase data.

As you can see in Figure 6.12, HBase supports *sparsity*. That is, not every column needs to exist in each row in a table, and nulls are not stored.

Although HBase data is stored on HDFS, an immutable file system, HBase allows in-place updates to cells in HBase tables. It does this by creating a new version of the cell with a new timestamp if the column key already exists, and then a background compaction process collapses multiple files into a smaller number of larger files.

Listing 6.34 demonstrates an update to an existing cell and the resultant new version.

Listing 6.34   **Updating a Cell in HBase**

```
hbase> put 'my-hbase-table', 'rowkey2', 'cf1:city', 'Melbourne'
hbase> get 'my-hbase-table', 'rowkey2', {COLUMNS => ['cf1:city']}
COLUMN                  CELL
 cf1:city                timestamp=1508292292811, value=Melbourne
1 row(s) in 0.0390 seconds
hbase> get 'my-hbase-table', 'rowkey2', {COLUMNS => ['cf1:city'], VERSIONS => 2}
COLUMN                  CELL
 cf1:city                timestamp=1508292546999, value=Melbourne
 cf1:city                timestamp=1508292538926, value=Hayward
1 row(s) in 0.0110 seconds
```

Notice in Listing 6.34 that HBase supports cell versioning. The number of versions retained is defined by the column family upon table creation.

HBase data is stored in *HFile* objects in HDFS. An HFile object is the intersection of a column family (storage group) and a sorted range of row keys. Ranges of sorted row keys are referred to as *regions* and are also known as *tablets* in other implementations. Regions are assigned to a *region server* by HBase; see Figure 6.13. Regions are used to provide fast row key lookups, as the regions and row keys they contain are known by HBase. HBase splits and compacts regions as necessary as part of its normal operation. Non-row key–based lookups, such as looking for a column key and value satisfying a criterion, are slower. However, HBase uses *bloom filters* to help expedite the search.

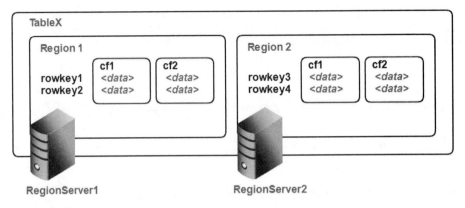

Figure 6.13   HBase regions.

HBase and Spark

The most failsafe method of reading and writing to HBase from Spark using the Python API is to use the HappyBase Python package (https://happybase.readthedocs.io/en/latest/). HappyBase is a Python library built for accessing and manipulating data in an HBase cluster. To use HappyBase, you must first install the Python package by using pip or easy_install, as shown here:

```
$ sudo pip install happybase
```

If you require more scalability, consider using either the Scala API for Spark or various third-party HBase connectors for Spark, available as Spark packages (https://spark-packages.org/).

Exercise: Using Spark with HBase

Setting up HBase is beyond the scope of this book. However, HBase is a normal component of many Hadoop vendor distributions, such as Cloudera and Hortonworks, including the sandbox VM environments provided by these vendors. You can provision HBase as an additional application in the AWS EMR-managed Hadoop service offering. For this exercise, you need a system with Hadoop, HBase, and Spark installed and running. Follow these steps:

1. Open the HBase shell:

   ```
   $ hbase shell
   ```

2. From the hbase shell prompt, create a table named people with a single-column family cf1 (using the default storage options):

   ```
   hbase> create 'people', 'cf1'
   ```

3. Create several cells in two records in the table by using the put method:

   ```
   hbase> put 'people', 'userid1', 'cf1:fname', 'John'
   hbase> put 'people', 'userid1', 'cf1:lname', 'Doe'
   hbase> put 'people', 'userid1', 'cf1:age', '41'
   ```

```
hbase> put 'people', 'userid2', 'cf1:fname', 'Jeffrey'
hbase> put 'people', 'userid2', 'cf1:lname', 'Aven'
hbase> put 'people', 'userid2', 'cf1:age', '48'
hbase> put 'people', 'userid2', 'cf1:city', 'Hayward'
```

4. View the data in the table by using the scan method, as follows:

```
hbase> scan 'people'
ROW COLUMN+CELL userid1  column=cf1:age, timestamp=1461296454933, value=41
...
```

5. Open another terminal session and launch pyspark by using the arguments shown here:

```
$ pyspark --master local
```

You can instead use YARN Client mode if you have a YARN cluster available to you.

6. Read the data from the people table by using happybase and create a Spark RDD:

```
import happybase
connection = happybase.Connection('localhost')
table = connection.table('people')
hbaserdd = sc.parallelize(table.scan())
hbaserdd.collect()
```

The output should resemble the following:

```
[('userid1', {'cf1:age': '41', 'cf1:lname': 'Doe', 'cf1:fname': 'John'}),
('userid2', {'cf1:age': '48', 'cf1:lname': 'Aven', 'cf1:fname': 'Jeffrey',
'cf1:city': 'Hayward'})]
```

7. Within your pyspark shell, create a new parallelized collection of users and save the contents of the Spark RDD to the people table in HBase:

```
newpeople = sc.parallelize([('userid3', 'cf1:fname', 'NewUser')])
for person in newpeople.collect():
    table.put(person[0], {person[1] : person[2]})
```

8. In your hbase shell, run the scan method again to confirm that the new user from the Spark RDD in step 7 exists in the HBase people table:

```
hbase> scan 'people' ROW COLUMN+CELL userid1 column=cf1:age,
timestamp=1461296454933, value=41 ... userid3 column=cf1:fname,
timestamp=146..., value=NewUser
```

Although this book is based on Python, there are other Spark HBase connector projects designed for the Scala API, such as spark-hbase-connector, at https://github.com/nerdammer/spark-hbase-connector. If you are using Spark with HBase, be sure to look at the available projects for Spark HBase connectivity.

Using Spark with Cassandra

Another notable NoSQL project is Apache Cassandra, initially developed at Facebook and later released as an open source project under the Apache software licensing scheme.

Introduction to Cassandra

Cassandra is similar to HBase in its application of the core NoSQL principles, such as not requiring a predefined schema (although Cassandra lets you define one) and not having referential integrity. However, there are differences in its physical implementation, predominantly in the fact that HBase has many Hadoop ecosystem dependencies, such as HDFS, ZooKeeper, and more, whereas Cassandra is more monolithic in its implementation, having fewer external dependencies. They also have differences in their cluster architecture: Whereas HBase is a master/slave architecture, Cassandra is a symmetric architecture that uses a "gossip" protocol to pass messages and govern cluster processes. There are many other differences, including the way the systems manage consistency, but they are beyond the scope of this discussion.

Much like HBase, Cassandra is a multidimensional, distributed map. Cassandra tables, called *keyspaces*, contain row keys and column families referred to as *tables*. Columns exist within column families but are not defined at table design time. Data is located at the intersection of a row key, column family, and column key.

In addition to row keys, Cassandra also supports *primary keys*, which can also contain a *partition key* and a *clustering key* in the case of composite primary keys. These directives are for storage and distribution of data and allow fast lookups by key.

Unlike HBase, Cassandra enables, and even encourages, you to define structure (a schema) for your data and assign datatypes. Cassandra supports *collections* within a table, which are used to store nested or complex data structures such as sets, lists, and maps. Furthermore, Cassandra enables defining *secondary indexes* to expedite lookups based on non-key values.

The *Cassandra Query Language* (CQL) is a SQL-like language for interacting with Cassandra. CQL supports the full set of DDL and DML operations for creating, reading, updating, and deleting objects in Cassandra. Because CQL is a SQL-like language, it supports ODBC and JDBC interfaces, enabling access from common SQL and visualization utilities. CQL is also available from an interactive shell environment, cqlsh.

Listing 6.35 demonstrates creating a keyspace and table in Cassandra by using the cqlsh utility.

Listing 6.35　**Creating a Keyspace and Table in Cassandra**

```
cqlsh> CREATE KEYSPACE mykeyspace WITH REPLICATION = { 'class' : 'SimpleStrategy',
        'replication_factor' : 1 };
cqlsh> USE mykeyspace;
cqlsh:mykeyspace> CREATE TABLE users (
            user_id int PRIMARY KEY,
        fname text,
        lname text
        );
cqlsh:mykeyspace> INSERT INTO users (user_id,  fname, lname)
        VALUES (1745, 'john', 'smith');
```

```
cqlsh:mykeyspace> INSERT INTO users (user_id,  fname, lname)
          VALUES (1744, 'john', 'doe');
cqlsh:mykeyspace> INSERT INTO users (user_id,  fname, lname)
          VALUES (1746, 'jane', 'smith');
cqlsh:mykeyspace> SELECT * FROM users;
 user_id | fname | lname
---------+-------+-------
    1745 |  john | smith
    1744 |  john |   doe
    1746 |  jane | smith
```

This should look very familiar to you if your background includes relational databases such as SQL Server, Oracle, or Teradata.

Cassandra and Spark

Because the Cassandra and Spark movements are closely linked in their ties back to the Big Data/open source software community, there are several projects and libraries available to enable read/write access to Cassandra from Spark programs. The following are some of the projects providing this support:

https://github.com/datastax/spark-cassandra-connector

http://tuplejump.github.io/calliope/pyspark.html

https://github.com/TargetHolding/pyspark-cassandra

https://github.com/anguenot/pyspark-cassandra

Many of the available projects have been built and provisioned as Spark packages, available at https://spark-packages.org/.

DataStax Enterprise, which is a commercial Cassandra offering by DataStax, also ships with Spark and YARN as well.

This section uses the pyspark-cassandra package here, but you are encouraged to investigate all the connectivity options available—or write your own!

With many projects, classes, scripts, examples, or artifacts in the open source world, you will often find system, library, or class dependencies that you need to satisfy. Resourcefulness is a necessity when working with open source software.

For the following examples, run the pyspark command provided in Listing 6.36 first and note the conf option required to configure the Cassandra connection.

Listing 6.36 **Using the pyspark-cassandra Package**

```
pyspark --master local \
--packages anguenot:pyspark-cassandra:0.6.0 \
--conf spark.cassandra.connection.host=127.0.0.1
```

Listing 6.37 shows how to load the contents of the `users` table created in Listing 6.35 into an RDD.

Listing 6.37 **Reading Cassandra Data into a Spark RDD**

```
import pyspark_cassandra
spark.createDataFrame(sc.cassandraTable("mykeyspace", "users") \
    .collect()).show()
# returns:
# +-----+-------+-----+
# |lname|user_id|fname|
# +-----+-------+-----+
# |smith|   1746|  jane|
# |smith|   1745|  john|
# |  doe|   1744|  john|
# +-----+-------+-----+
# (3 rows)
```

Listing 6.38 demonstrates writing Spark data out to a Cassandra table.

Listing 6.38 **Updating Data in a Cassandra Table Using Spark**

```
import pyspark_cassandra
rdd = sc.parallelize([{ "user_id": 1747, "fname": "Jeffrey", "lname": "Aven" }])
rdd.saveToCassandra( "mykeyspace", "users", )
```

Running a `SELECT * FROM users` command in `cqlsh`, you can see the results of the `INSERT` from Listing 6.38 in Listing 6.39.

Listing 6.39 **Cassandra INSERT Results**

```
cqlsh> USE mykeyspace;
cqlsh:mykeyspace> SELECT * FROM users;
 user_id | fname    | lname
---------+---------+-------
    1745 |    john | smith
    1747 | Jeffrey |  Aven
    1744 |    john |   doe
    1746 |    jane | smith
(4 rows)
```

Using Spark with DynamoDB

DynamoDB is the AWS NoSQL PaaS offering. DynamoDB's data model comprises *tables* containing *items*, each of which contains one or more *attributes*. Like a Cassandra table, a DynamoDB table has a primary key used for storage and fast retrieval. DynamoDB also supports secondary indexes. DynamoDB is a key/value store and a document store, as objects can be treated as documents.

Because DynamoDB originated as a web service, it has rich integration with many other language bindings and software development kits. You can implement DDL and DML statements by using Dynamo's API endpoints and JSON-based DSL.

As with HBase, there are several ways to read and write data to and from DynamoDB using Spark. The simplest and most failsafe method for accessing DynamoDB from Spark using the Python API is to use the `boto3` Python library, which is designed to interact with AWS services. To use `boto3`, you need to install the package using `pip` or `easy_install`, as shown here:

```
$ sudo pip install boto3
```

You also need your AWS API credentials to connect to AWS.

Although other approaches using Spark packages or the Scala API may provide greater scalability, `boto3` always works for connecting to AWS services using Python.

Consider the DynamoDB table shown in Figure 6.14, which contains information about stocks.

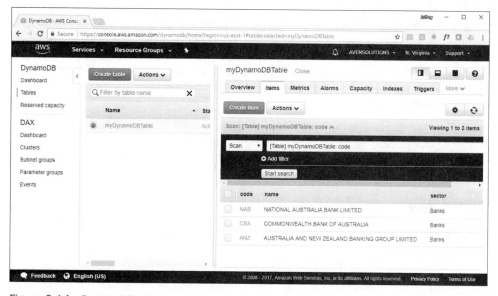

Figure 6.14   DynamoDB table.

Listing 6.40 demonstrates how to load the items from this DynamoDB table into a Spark RDD.

Listing 6.40   **Accessing Amazon DynamoDB from Spark**

```
import boto3
from pyspark.sql.types import *
myschema = StructType([ \
            StructField("code", StringType(), True), \
            StructField("name", StringType(), True), \
            StructField("sector", StringType(), True) \
            ])
```

```
client = boto3.client('dynamodb','us-east-1')
dynamodata = sc.parallelize(client.scan(TableName='myDynamoDBTable')['Items'])
dynamordd = dynamodata.map(lambda x: (x['code']['S'], x['name']['S'],
x['sector']['S'])).collect()
spark.createDataFrame(dynamordd, myschema).show()
# returns:
# +----+--------------------+------+
# |code|                name|sector|
# +----+--------------------+------+
# | NAB|NATIONAL AUSTRALI...| Banks|
# | CBA|COMMONWEALTH BANK...| Banks|
# | ANZ|AUSTRALIA AND NEW...| Banks|
# +----+--------------------+------+
```

Other NoSQL Platforms

In addition to the HBase, Cassandra, and DynamoDB projects, there are countless other NoSQL platforms, including document stores such as MongoDB and CouchDB, key/value stores such as Couchbase and Riak, and memory-centric key/value stores such as Memcached and Redis. There are also full text search and indexing platforms adapted to become general-purpose NoSQL platforms. These include Apache Solr and Elasticsearch, which are both based on the Lucene search engine processing project.

Many of the NoSQL platforms have available connectors or libraries that enable them to read and write RDD data in Spark. Check the project or vendor's website or GitHub for your selected NoSQL platform's integration. If an integration does not exist, you can always develop your own.

Summary

This chapter focuses on some of the important extensions to Spark for data manipulation and access: SQL and NoSQL.

Spark SQL is one of the most popular extensions to Spark. Spark SQL enables interactive queries, supporting business intelligence and visualization tools and making Spark accessible to a much wider audience of analysts. Spark SQL provides access to the powerful Spark runtime distributed processing framework, using SQL interfaces and a relational database-like programming approach. Spark SQL introduces many optimizations aimed specifically at relational-type access patterns using SQL. These optimizations include columnar storage, maintaining column- and partition-level statistics, and Partial DAG execution, which allows DAGs to change during processing based on statistics and skew observed in the data. Spark SQL also introduces the DataFrame, a structured, columnar abstraction of the Spark RDD. The DataFrame API enables many features and functions familiar to most SQL developers, analysts, enthusiasts, and general users. Spark SQL is evolving rapidly, and new and interesting functions and capabilities are added with every minor release. With its familiar programming interface, Spark SQL opens up a world of possibilities for a much wider community of analysts.

NoSQL databases have become a viable complement and alternative to traditional SQL systems, offering Internet-scale storage capabilities and query boundaries, as well as fast read and write access to support distributed device and mobile application interactions. NoSQL concepts and implementations have emerged in parallel with Spark, as these concepts both emanated from early Google and Yahoo! work. This chapter covers some fundamental NoSQL concepts and looks at some practical applications of key/value and document stores—Apache HBase, Apache Cassandra, and Amazon DynamoDB—to demonstrate how Spark can interact with NoSQL platforms as both a consumer and provider of data.

Stream Processing and Messaging Using Spark

Never confuse motion with action.

Benjamin Franklin, American founding father

In This Chapter:

- Introduction to Spark Streaming, the `StreamingContext`, and DStreams
- Operations on DStreams
- Sliding window and state operations on DStreams
- Introduction to Structured Streaming in Spark
- Spark with Apache Kafka
- Spark Streaming with Amazon Kinesis Streams

Real-time event processing has become a defining feature of Big Data systems. From sensors and network data processing to fraud detection to website monitoring and much more, the capability to consume, process, and derive insights from streaming data sources has never been more relevant. To this point in the book, the processing covered for the Spark core API and with Spark SQL has been batch oriented. This chapter focuses on stream processing and another key extension to Spark: Spark Streaming.

Introducing Spark Streaming

Event processing, also called *stream processing*, is a key component of Big Data platforms. The Spark project includes a subproject that enables low latency processing with fault tolerance and data guarantees: *Spark Streaming*.

Spark Streaming delivers an event-processing system integrated with its RDD-based batch framework, and it delivers a guarantee that each event will processed exactly once, even if a node failure or similar fault occurs.

The design goals for Spark Streaming include the following:

- Low (second-scale) latency
- One-time (and only one-time) event processing
- Linear scalability
- Integration with the Spark core and DataFrame APIs

Perhaps the biggest advantage of Spark Streaming (and its overriding design goal) is that it provides a unified programming model for both stream and batch operations.

Spark Streaming Architecture

Spark Streaming introduces the concept of discretized streams, or *DStreams*. DStreams are essentially batches of data stored in multiple RDDs, each batch representing a time window, typically in seconds. The resultant RDDs can then be processed using the core Spark RDD API and all the available transformations discussed so far in this book. (The section "Introduction to DStreams," later in this chapter, discusses DStreams in more detail.) Figure 7.1 shows a high-level overview of Spark Streaming.

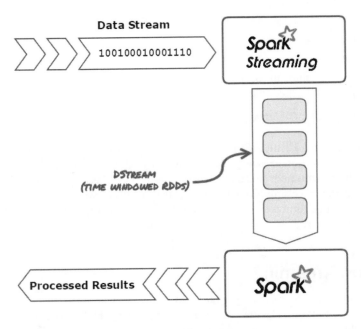

Figure 7.1 High-level overview of Spark Streaming.

As with the SparkContext and SparkSession program entry points discussed earlier in this book, Spark Streaming applications have an entry point called the StreamingContext. The StreamingContext represents a connection to a Spark platform or cluster using an existing SparkContext. You can use the StreamingContext to create DStreams from streaming input sources and govern streaming computation and DStream transformations.

The StreamingContext also specifies the batchDuration argument, which is a time interval, in seconds, by which streaming data is split into batches. After instantiating a StreamingContext, you create a connection to a data stream and define a series of transformations to be performed. You can use the start() method (or ssc.start()) to trigger evaluation of the incoming data after establishing a StreamingContext. You can stop the StreamingContext programmatically by using ssc.stop() or ssc.awaitTermination(), as shown in Listing 7.1.

Listing 7.1   Creating a **StreamingContext**

```
from pyspark.streaming import StreamingContext
ssc = StreamingContext(sc, 1)
...
# Initialize Data Stream
# DStream transformations
...
ssc.start()
...
# ssc.stop() or ssc.awaitTermination()
```

Note that just as sc and sqlContext are common conventions for object instantiations of the SparkContext and SQLContext or HiveContext classes, respectively, ssc is a common convention for an instance of the StreamingContext. Unlike the former entry points, however, the StreamingContext is not automatically instantiated in the interactive shells pyspark and spark-shell.

Introduction to DStreams

Discretized streams (DStreams) are the basic programming object in the Spark Streaming API. A DStream represents a continuous sequence of RDDs created from a continuous stream of data, with each underlying RDD representing a time window within the stream.

DStreams are created from streaming data sources such as TCP sockets, messaging systems, streaming APIs (such as the Twitter streaming API), and more. As an RDD abstraction, DStreams are also created from transformations performed on existing DStreams, such as map(), flatMap(), and other operations.

DStreams support two types of operations:

- Transformations
- Output operations

Output operations are analogous to RDD actions. DStreams execute lazily upon the request of an output operation, which is similar to lazy evaluation with Spark RDDs.

Figure 7.2 represents a DStream, with each *t* interval representing a window of time specified by the `batchDuration` argument in the `StreamingContext` instantiation.

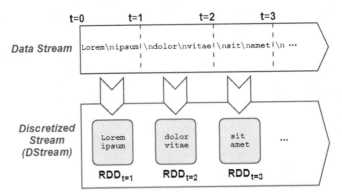

Figure 7.2   Spark discretized streams (DStreams).

DStream Sources

DStreams are defined within a `StreamingContext` for a specified input data stream, much the same way that RDDs are created for input data sources within a `SparkContext`. Many common streaming input sources are included in the Streaming API, such as sources to read data from a TCP socket or for reading data as it is written to HDFS.

The basic input data sources for creating DStreams are described in the following sections.

socketTextStream()

Syntax:

```
StreamingContext.socketTextStream(hostname,
        port,
        storageLevel=StorageLevel(True, True, False, False, 2))
```

Use the `socketTextStream()` method to create a DStream from an input TCP source defined by the `hostname` and `port` arguments. The data received is interpreted using UTF8 encoding, and new line termination is used to define new records. The `storageLevel` argument that defines the storage level for the DStream defaults to `MEMORY_AND_DISK_SER`. Listing 7.2 demonstrates the use of the `socketTextStream()` method.

Listing 7.2   **socketTextStream() Method**

```
from pyspark.streaming import StreamingContext
ssc = StreamingContext(sc, 1)
lines = ssc.socketTextStream('localhost', 9999)
counts = lines.flatMap(lambda line: line.split(" ")) \
                .map(lambda word: (word, 1)) \
                .reduceByKey(lambda a, b: a+b)
```

```
counts.pprint()
ssc.start()
ssc.awaitTermination()
```

textFileStream()

Syntax:

```
StreamingContext.textFileStream(directory)
```

Use the textFileStream() method to create a DStream by monitoring a directory from an instance of HDFS, as specified by the current system or application configuration settings. textFileStream() listens for the creation of new files in the directory specified by the directory argument and captures the data written as a streaming source. Listing 7.3 shows the use of the textFileStream() method.

Listing 7.3 **textFileStream() Method**

```
from pyspark.streaming import StreamingContext
ssc = StreamingContext(sc, 1)
lines = ssc.textFileStream('hdfs:///data/incoming/')
counts = lines.flatMap(lambda line: line.split(" ")) \
              .map(lambda x: (x, 1)) \
              .reduceByKey(lambda a, b: a+b)
counts.pprint()
ssc.start()
ssc.awaitTermination()
```

There are built-in sources for common messaging platforms such as Apache Kafka, Amazon Kinesis, Apache Flume, and more. We look at some of them shortly. You can also create custom streaming data sources by implementing a custom receiver for your desired source. At this stage, custom receivers must be written in Scala or Java.

DStream Transformations

The DStream API contains many of the transformations available through the RDD API. DStream transformations, like RDD transformations, create new DStreams by applying functions to existing DStreams. Listing 7.4 and Figure 7.3 show a simplified example of DStream transformations.

Listing 7.4 **DStream Transformations**

```
from pyspark.streaming import StreamingContext
ssc = StreamingContext(sc, 30)
lines = ssc.socketTextStream('localhost', 9999)
counts = lines.map(lambda word: (word, 1)) \
              .reduceByKey(lambda a, b: a+b)
counts.pprint()
ssc.start()
ssc.awaitTermination()
```

```
# output:
# --------------------------
# Time: 2017-10-21 19:57:30
# --------------------------
# (u'Lorem',1)
# (u'ipsum',1)
# --------------------------
# Time: 2017-10-21 19:58:00
# --------------------------
# (u'dolor',1)
# (u'vitae',1)
# --------------------------
# Time: 2017-10-21 19:58:30
# --------------------------
# (u'sit',1)
# (u'amet',1)
# --------------------------
# Time: 2017-10-21 19:59:00
# --------------------------
# ...
```

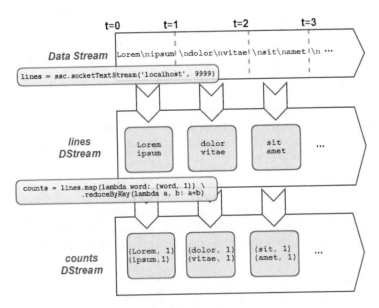

Figure 7.3   DStream transformations.

DStream Lineage and Checkpointing

The lineage of each DStream is maintained for fault tolerance much the same way that RDDs and DataFrames maintain their lineage. Because streaming applications are by definition long-lived applications, checkpointing is often necessary. Checkpointing with DStreams is similar to that in the RDD and DataFrame APIs. The methods are slightly different, however, and to make things confusing, the methods have the same names but are members of two separate classes. These are discussed in the following sections.

StreamingContext.checkpoint()

Syntax:

```
StreamingContext.checkpoint(directory)
```

The `StreamingContext.checkpoint()` method enables periodic checkpointing of DStream operations for durability and fault tolerance. The application DAG is checkpointed at each batch interval, as defined in the `StreamingContext`. The `directory` argument configures the directory, typically in HDFS, where the checkpoint data persists.

DStream.checkpoint()

Syntax:

```
DStream.checkpoint(interval)
```

The `DStream.checkpoint` method can enable periodic checkpointing of RDDs of a particular DStream. The `interval` argument is the time, in seconds, after which the underlying RDDs in a DStream are checkpointed.

Note that the `interval` argument must be a positive multiple of the `batchDuration` set in the `StreamingContext`.

Listing 7.5 demonstrates the use of the functions to control checkpointing behavior in Spark Streaming.

Listing 7.5   **Checkpointing in Spark Streaming**

```
from pyspark.streaming import StreamingContext
ssc = StreamingContext(sc, 30)
ssc.checkpoint('file:///opt/spark/data')
lines = ssc.socketTextStream('localhost', 9999)
counts = lines.map(lambda word: (word, 1)) \
              .reduceByKey(lambda a, b: a+b)
counts.checkpoint(30)
counts.pprint()
ssc.start()
ssc.awaitTermination()
```

Caching and Persistence with DStreams

DStreams support caching and persistence using interfaces with the same name and usage as their RDD counterparts, `cache()` and `persist()`. These options are especially handy for DStreams used more than once in downstream processing operations. Storage levels work the same with DStreams as they do with RDDs.

Broadcast Variables and Accumulators with Streaming Applications

Broadcast variables and accumulators are available for use in Spark Streaming applications in the same way they are implemented in native Spark applications. Broadcast variables are useful for distributing lookup or reference data associated with DStream RDD contents. You can use accumulators as counters.

There are some limitations with recovery when using broadcast variables or accumulators with checkpointing enabled. If you are developing production Spark Streaming applications and using broadcast variables or accumulators, consult the latest Spark Streaming programming guide.

DStream Output Operations

Output operations with DStreams are similar in concept to actions with RDDs. DStream output operations write data, results, events, or other data to a console, a filesystem, a database, or another destination, such as a messaging platform like Kafka. The basic DStream output operations are described in the following sections.

pprint()

Syntax:

```
DStream.pprint(num=10)
```

The `pprint()` method prints the first number of elements specified by the `num` argument for each RDD in the DStream (where `num` is 10 by default). Using `pprint()` is a common way to get interactive console feedback from a streaming application. Figure 7.4 shows the console output from a `pprint()` operation.

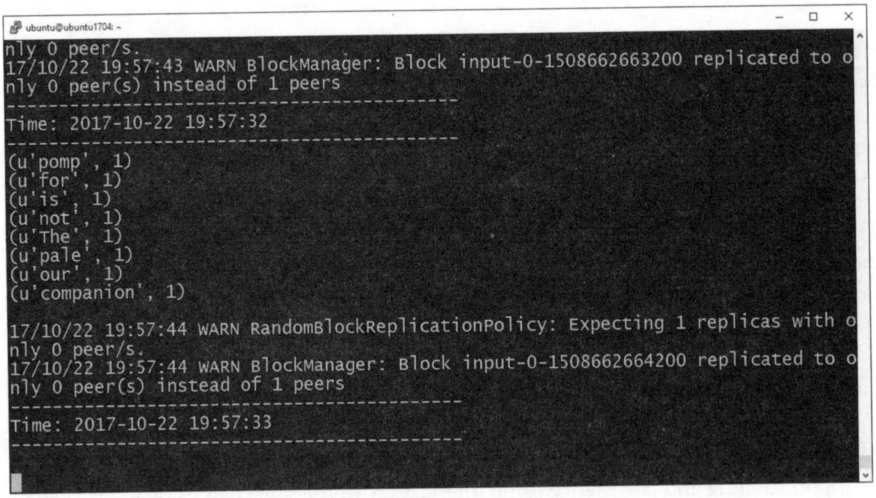

Figure 7.4 `pprint()` DStream console output.

saveAsTextFiles()

Syntax:

```
DStream.saveAsTextFiles(prefix, suffix-=None)
```

The saveAsTextFiles() method saves each RDD in a DStream as a text file in a target filesystem, local HDFS, or other filesystem. A directory of files is created with string representations of the elements contained in the DStream. Listing 7.6 shows the use of the saveAsTextFiles() method and the output directory created. Figure 7.5 provides a look at the file contents.

Listing 7.6 **Saving DStream Output to Files**

```
from pyspark.streaming import StreamingContext
ssc = StreamingContext(sc, 30)
lines = ssc.socketTextStream('localhost', 9999)
counts = lines.map(lambda word: (word, 1)) \
              .reduceByKey(lambda a, b: a+b)
counts.saveAsTextFiles("file:///opt/spark/data/counts")
ssc.start()
ssc.awaitTermination()
```

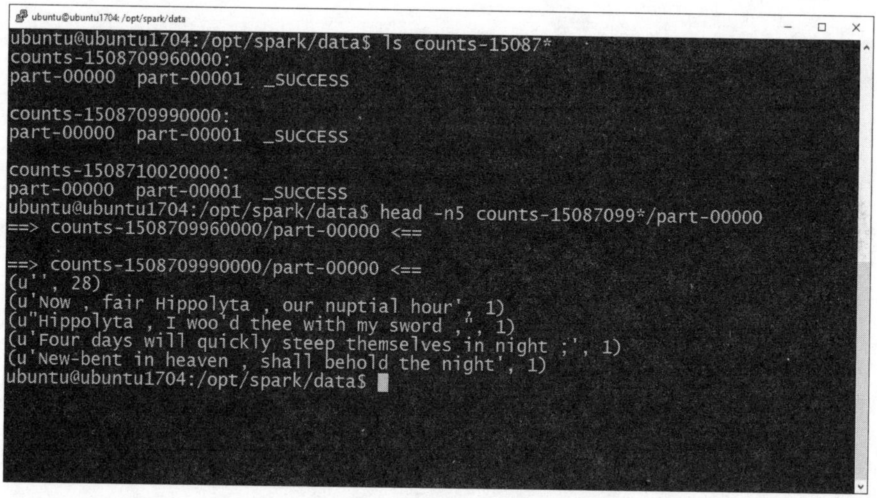

Figure 7.5   Output from the saveAsTextFiles() DStream method.

foreachRDD()

Syntax:

```
DStream.foreachRDD(func)
```

The foreachRDD() output operation is similar to the foreach() action in the Spark RDD API. It applies the function specified by the func argument to each RDD in a DStream. The foreachRDD() method is executed by the Driver process running the streaming application and usually forces the computation of the DStream RDDs. The function used can be a named one or an anonymous lambda function, as with foreach(). Listing 7.7 shows a simple example of the foreachRDD() method.

Listing 7.7 **Performing Functions on Each RDD in a DStream**

```
from pyspark.streaming import StreamingContext
def printx(x): print("received : " + x)
ssc = StreamingContext(sc, 30)
lines = ssc.socketTextStream('localhost', 9999)
lines.foreachRDD(lambda x: x.foreach(lambda y: printx(y)))
ssc.start()
ssc.awaitTermination()
# output:
# received : Lorem
# received : ipsum
# received : dolor
# received : vitae
# received : sit
# received : amet
```

Exercise: Getting Started with Spark Streaming

This exercise shows how to stream lines from a Shakespeare text and consume the lines with the Spark Streaming application. It also shows how to perform a streaming word count against the incoming data, much like word count examples shown earlier in this book. Follow these steps:

1. Use wget or curl to download the shakespeare.txt file from https://s3.amazonaws.com/sparkusingpython/shakespeare/shakespeare.txt to a local directory such as /opt/spark/data.

2. Open a pyspark shell. Note that if you're using Local mode, you need to specify at least two worker threads, as shown here:

   ```
   $ pyspark --master local[2]
   ```

3. Enter the following commands, line by line, in the pyspark shell:

   ```
   import re
   from pyspark.streaming import StreamingContext
   ssc = StreamingContext(sc, 30)
   lines = ssc.socketTextStream('localhost', 9999)
   wordcounts = lines.filter(lambda line: len(line) > 0) \
                  .flatMap(lambda line: re.split('\W+', line)) \
                  .filter(lambda word: len(word) > 0) \
                  .map(lambda word: (word.lower(), 1)) \
                  .reduceByKey(lambda x, y: x + y)
   ```

```
wordcounts.pprint()
ssc.start()
ssc.awaitTermination()
```

Note that until you start a stream on the defined socket, you see exceptions appear in the console output. This is normal.

4. In another terminal, using the directory containing the local `shakespeare.txt` file from step 1 as the current directory, execute the following command:

```
$ while read line; do echo -e "$line\n"; sleep 1; done \
 < shakespeare.txt | nc -lk 9999
```

This command reads a line from the `shakespeare.txt` file every second and sends it to the `netcat` server.

You should see that every 30 seconds (the batchInterval set on the StreamingContext in step 3), the lines received from the latest batch are transformed into key/value pairs and counted, with output to the console similar to the output shown here:

```
-----------------------------------------
Time: 2017-10-21 20:10:00
-----------------------------------------
(u'and', 11)
(u'laugh', 1)
(u 'old', 1)
(u'have', 1)
(u'trifles', 1)
(u'imitate', 1)
(u'neptune', 1)
(u'is', 2)
(u'crown', 1)
(u'changeling', 1)
...
```

Find the complete source code for this exercise in the `streaming-wordcount` folder at https://github.com/sparktraining/spark_using_python.

State Operations

So far, the examples of Spark Streaming applications in this chapter have dealt with data statelessly processing each batch during a batch interval, independent of any other batches in a stream. Often you want or need to maintain state across batches of data, with the state updated as each new batch is processed. You can accomplish this by using a *state* DStream.

State DStreams are created and updated using the special `updateStateByKey()` transformation. This is preferred over using accumulators as shared variables in streaming applications because `updateStateByKey()` is automatically checkpointed for integrity, durability, and recoverability.

updateStateByKey()

Syntax:

```
DStream.updateStateByKey(updateFunc, numPartitions=None)
```

The updateStateByKey() method returns a new state DStream, where the state for each key updates by applying the function specified by the updateFunc argument against the previous state of the key and the new values of the key.

The updateStateByKey() method expects key/value pair input and returns a corresponding key/value pair output, with the values updated according to the updateFunc setting.

The numPartitions argument can repartition the output similarly to the RDD methods with this argument.

Note that checkpointing must be enabled using ssc.checkpoint(directory) in the StreamingContext before you can use the updateStateByKey() method and create and update state DStreams.

Consider this input stream:

```
Lorem ipsum dolor
<pause for more than 30 seconds>
Lorem ipsum dolor
```

Listing 7.8 shows how to use updateStateByKey() to create and update the counts for the words received on the stream.

Listing 7.8 **State DStreams**

```
from pyspark.streaming import StreamingContext
ssc = StreamingContext(sc, 30)
ssc.checkpoint("checkpoint")
def updateFunc(new_values, last_sum):
return sum(new_values) + (last_sum or 0)
lines = ssc.socketTextStream('localhost', 9999)
wordcounts = lines.map(lambda word: (word, 1)) \
                  .updateStateByKey(updateFunc)
wordcounts.pprint()
ssc.start()
ssc.awaitTermination()
# output:
#...
# -------------------------------------------
# Time: 2016-03-31 00:02:30
# -------------------------------------------
# (u'Lorem', 1)
# (u'ipsum', 1)
# (u'dolor', 1)
#...
```

```
# -------------------------------------------
# Time: 2016-03-31 00:03:00
# -------------------------------------------
# (u'Lorem', 2)
# (u'ipsum', 2)
# (u'dolor', 2)
```

Sliding Window Operations

The state operations you learned about in the previous section apply to all RDDs in the DStream. It is useful to look at aggregations over a specific window, such as the last hour or day. Because this window is relative to a point in time, it's called a *sliding* window.

Sliding window operations in Spark Streaming span RDDs within a DStream over a specified duration (the window length) and are evaluated at specific intervals (the slide interval). Consider Figure 7.6. If you want to count the words in the last two intervals (window length) every two intervals (slide interval), you can use the reduceByKeyAndWindow() function to create "windowed" RDDs.

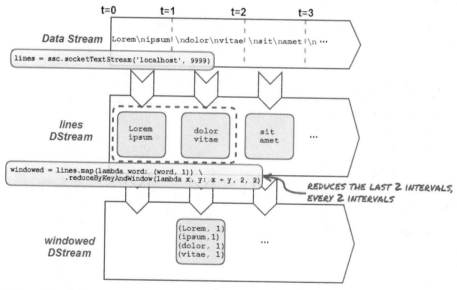

Figure 7.6   Sliding windows and windowed RDDs in Spark Streaming.

Sliding window functions available in the Spark Streaming API include window(), countByWindow(), reduceByWindow(), reduceByKeyAndWindow(), and count ByValueAndWindow(). The following sections cover a couple of these basic functions.

window()

Syntax:

```
DStream.window(windowLength, slideInterval)
```

The window() method returns a new DStream from specified batches of the input DStream. window() creates a new DStream object every interval, as specified by the slideInterval argument, consisting of elements from the input DStream for the specified windowLength.

Both slideInterval and windowLength must be multiples of the batchDuration set in the StreamingContext. Listing 7.9 demonstrates the use of the window() function.

Listing 7.9 **window() Function**

```
# send date to netcat every second:
# while sleep 1; do echo 'date'; done | nc -lk 9999
from pyspark.streaming import StreamingContext
ssc = StreamingContext(sc, 5)
dates = ssc.socketTextStream('localhost', 9999)
windowed = dates.window(10,10)
windowed.pprint()
ssc.start()
ssc.awaitTermination()
# output:
# ...
# -------------------------------------------
# Time: 2017-10-23 09:28:15
# -------------------------------------------
# Mon 23 Oct 09:28:05 AEDT 2017
# Mon 23 Oct 09:28:06 AEDT 2017
# Mon 23 Oct 09:28:07 AEDT 2017
# Mon 23 Oct 09:28:08 AEDT 2017
# Mon 23 Oct 09:28:09 AEDT 2017
# Mon 23 Oct 09:28:10 AEDT 2017
# Mon 23 Oct 09:28:11 AEDT 2017
# Mon 23 Oct 09:28:12 AEDT 2017
# Mon 23 Oct 09:28:13 AEDT 2017
#...
# -------------------------------------------
# Time: 2017-10-23 09:28:25
# -------------------------------------------
# Mon 23 Oct 09:28:14 AEDT 2017
# Mon 23 Oct 09:28:15 AEDT 2017
# Mon 23 Oct 09:28:16 AEDT 2017
# Mon 23 Oct 09:28:17 AEDT 2017
# Mon 23 Oct 09:28:18 AEDT 2017
# Mon 23 Oct 09:28:19 AEDT 2017
# Mon 23 Oct 09:28:20 AEDT 2017
```

```
# Mon 23 Oct 09:28:21 AEDT 2017
# Mon 23 Oct 09:28:22 AEDT 2017
# Mon 23 Oct 09:28:24 AEDT 2017
```

reduceByKeyAndWindow()

Syntax:

```
DStream.reduceByKeyAndWindow(func,
                            invFunc,
                            windowDuration,
                            slideDuration=None,
                            numPartitions=None,
                            filterFunc=None)
```

The reduceByKeyAndWindow() method creates a new DStream by performing an associative reduce function, as specified by the func argument, to a sliding window, as defined by the windowDuration and slideDuration arguments. The invFunc argument is an inverse function to the func argument. invFunc is included for efficiency to remove (or subtract) counts from the previous window; numPartitions is an optional argument supported for repartitioning the output DStream. The optional filterFunc argument can filter expired key/value pairs; in this case, only key/value pairs that satisfy the function are retained in the resultant DStream. Listing 7.10 demonstrates the use of the reduceByKeyAndWindow() function.

Note that checkpointing must be enabled when using the reduceByKeyAndWindow() function.

Listing 7.10 **The reduceByKeyAndWindow() Function**

```
from pyspark.streaming import StreamingContext
ssc = StreamingContext(sc, 5)
ssc.checkpoint("checkpoint")
lines = ssc.socketTextStream('localhost', 9999)
windowedWordCounts = lines.map(lambda word: (word, 1)) \
                    .reduceByKeyAndWindow(lambda x, y: x + y, \
                        lambda x, y: x - y, 30, 10)
windowedWordCounts.pprint()
ssc.start()
ssc.awaitTermination()
```

Structured Streaming

Stream processing in Spark is not limited to the RDD API; by using *Structured Streaming*, Spark Streaming is fully integrated with the Spark DataFrame API as well. Using Structured Streaming, streaming data sources are treated as an unbounded table that is continually appended to. SQL queries can run against these tables much as they are able to run from tables representing static DataFrames. Figure 7.7 shows a high-level overview of Structured Streaming with Spark.

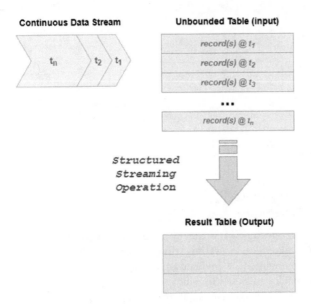

Figure 7.7   Structured Streaming.

Structured Streaming Data Sources

The DataFrameReader (detailed in Chapter 6) includes several built-in sources designed to ingest streaming data. These data sources include support for file, socket, and Kafka—which we discuss shortly—data streams. The DataFrameReader.readStream() method, available through the SparkSession object, includes a format() member used to define the streaming source.

File Sources

The file source reads new files written in a directory as a stream of data. Most of the file formats supported by the DataFrameReader are supported as Structured Streaming sources, including CSV, text, JSON, and Parquet ORC. Listing 7.11 demonstrates how to use a file source (CSV in this case) for a Structured Streaming application. Note that you must supply a schema unless there are existing files in the input directory from which the schema can be inferred.

Listing 7.11   **Structured Streaming Using a File Source**

```
from pyspark.sql.types import *
tripsSchema = StructType() \
        .add("TripID", "integer") \
        .add("Duration", "integer") \
        .add("StartDate", "string") \
        .add("StartStation", "string") \
        .add("StartTerminal", "integer") \
        .add("EndDate", "string") \
```

```
        .add("EndStation", "string") \
        .add("EndTerminal", "integer") \
        .add("BikeNo", "integer") \
        .add("SubscriberType", "string") \
        .add("ZipCode", "string")
csv_input = spark \
    .readStream \
    .schema(tripsSchema) \
    .csv("/tmp/trips")
...
```

Socket Sources

The socket source reads text data in UTF8 format from a socket connection in much the same way as the `socketTextStream()` method in the Spark Streaming RDD API. Listing 7.12 demonstrates the use of a socket data source to perform a Structured Streaming word count.

Listing 7.12   **Structured Streaming Using a Socket Source**

```
socket_input = spark \
    .readStream \
    .format("socket") \
    .option("host", "localhost") \
    .option("port", 9999) \
    .load()
...
```

Structured Streaming Data Sinks

As discussed earlier in this chapter, each data item arriving on a stream is treated like a new record appended to a table, referred to as the *Input Table*. The output from a Structured Streaming operation—that is, what is written out—is referred to as the *Result Table*. Output from Structured Streaming operations is written out by the `DataFrameWriter` object and, in particular, the `DataFrameWriter.writeStream()` method.

Output sinks in Spark's Structured Streaming define where the Result Table is written to. Output sinks themselves are defined using the `format()` member of the `DataFrameWriter.writeStream()` method.

There are built-in output sinks for writing data to files, memory, or the console.

File Sink

The file sink stores the Result Table in a directory in a supported filesystem (HDFS, local filesystem, S3, and so on). Listing 7.13 demonstrates the file sink.

Listing 7.13   **File Output Sink**

```
...
output.writeStream \
    .format("parquet") \
    .option("path", "/tmp/streaming_output") \
    .start()
# could also be "orc", "json", "csv"
```

To use a file output sink, you need to set a checkpoint location; this can be done as shown here:

```
spark.conf.set("spark.sql.streaming.checkpointLocation", "/tmp/checkpoint_dir")
```

Console Sink

The console sink prints the Result Table to the console. This is useful for debugging but could be impractical for large output sets. Listing 7.14 demonstrates the console sink.

Listing 7.14   **Console Output Sink**

```
...
output.writeStream \
    .format("console") \
    .start()
```

Memory Sink

The memory stores the Result Table as a table in memory; this type of sink is also useful for debugging but should be used with caution for larger output data sets. Listing 7.15 demonstrates the memory sink.

Listing 7.15   **Memory Output Sink**

```
...
output.writeStream \
    .format("memory") \
    .queryName("trips") \
    .start()
spark.sql("select * from trips").show()
```

Output Modes

Just as output sinks define *where* to send the output of a Structured Streaming operation, output modes define *how* the output is treated. There are several different output modes:

- **append:** Outputs only new rows added to the Result Table since the last trigger. This mode, which is the default, is useful for operations that are simply projecting or filtering new data, including where(), select(), and filter().

- **complete:** Outputs the entire Result Table, including all updates and transformations, after each trigger. This is useful for aggregate functions such as count(), sum(), and so on.

- **update:** Outputs only rows in the Result Table that have updated since the last trigger are output.

The output mode is specified using the outputMode() member of the writeStream() method.

Structured Streaming Operations

Because Structured Streaming builds on the DataFrame API, most DataFrame operations are available, including the following:

- Filtering records

- Projecting columns

- Performing column-level transformations using built-in or user-defined functions

- Grouping records and aggregating columns

- Joining streaming DataFrames with static DataFrames (with some limitations)

However, some operations in the DataFrame API are not available with streaming DataFrames, including the following:

- limit and take(n) operations

- distinct operations

- sort operations (supported only in complete output mode after an aggregation)

- Full outer join operations

- Any type of join between two streaming DataFrames

- Additional conditions on left and right outer join operations

Listing 7.16 puts together all the Structured Streaming concepts and showcases various operations that perform on streaming DataFrames.

Listing 7.16 **Structured Streaming Operations**

```
# declare a schema for a streaming source
from pyspark.sql.types import *
tripsSchema = StructType() \
        .add("TripID", "integer") \
        .add("Duration", "integer") \
        .add("StartDate", "string") \
        .add("StartStation", "string") \
        .add("StartTerminal", "integer") \
        .add("EndDate", "string") \
        .add("EndStation", "string") \
```

```
         .add("EndTerminal", "integer") \
         .add("BikeNo", "integer") \
         .add("SubscriberType", "string") \
         .add("ZipCode", "string")
# read from an input stream
trips = spark \
    .readStream \
    .schema(tripsSchema) \
    .csv("/tmp/trips")
# perform a streaming DataFrame aggregation
result = trips.select(trips.StartTerminal, trips.StartStation) \
         .groupBy(trips.StartTerminal, trips.StartStation) \
         .agg({"*": "count"})
# write out the result table to the console
result.writeStream \
    .format("console") \
    .outputMode("complete") \
    .start()
# returns:
# <pyspark.sql.streaming.StreamingQuery object at 0x7fb1c5c2a0f0>
# -------------------------------------------
# Batch: 0
# -------------------------------------------
# +-------------+--------------------+--------+
# |StartTerminal|        StartStation|count(1)|
# +-------------+--------------------+--------+
# |            7|Paseo de San Antonio|     856|
# |           65|       Townsend at 7th|   13752|
# |           26|Redwood City Medi...|     150|
# |           38|        Park at Olive|     376|
# ...
```

Using Spark with Messaging Platforms

Messaging systems originally formed to provide middleware functionality—more specifically, message-oriented middleware (MOM). This area saw rapid expansion in the 1980s, in integrating legacy systems with newer systems, such as mainframe and early distributed systems. Today messaging systems and platforms provide much more functionality than just simple integration. They are a critical part of the mobile computing and Internet of Things (IoT) landscape. Projects such as JMS (Java Message Service), Kafka, ActiveMQ, ZeroMQ (ØMQ), RabbitMQ, Amazon SQS (Simple Queue Service), and Kinesis have added to the existing landscape of more established commercial solutions such as TIBCO EMS (Enterprise Message Service), IBM WebSphere MQ, and Microsoft Message Queuing (MSMQ).

The following sections look at some messaging systems commonly used with Big Data and Spark implementations.

Apache Kafka

Originally developed at LinkedIn, Apache Kafka is a popular open source project written in Scala and designed for message brokering and queuing between various Hadoop ecosystem projects.

Kafka Architecture

Kafka is a distributed, reliable, low-latency, pub-sub messaging platform. Conceptually, Kafka acts as a write-ahead log (WAL) for messages, much the same way a transaction log or journal functions in an ACID data store. This log-based design provides durability, consistency, and the capability for subscribers to replay messages.

Publishers, called *producers*, write data to topics. Subscribers, called *consumers*, read messages from specified *topics*. Figure 7.8 summarizes the relationships among producers, topics, and consumers. Messages themselves are uninterpreted byte arrays that can represent any object or primitive datatype. Common message content formats include JSON and *Avro*, an open source Hadoop ecosystem data-serialization project.

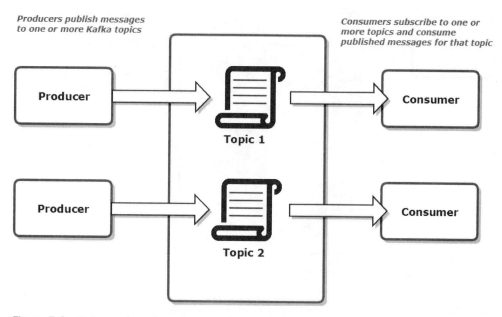

Figure 7.8   Kafka producers, consumers, and topics.

Kafka is a distributed system that consists of one or more *brokers*, typically on separate nodes of a cluster. Brokers manage *partitions*, which are ordered, immutable sequences of messages for a particular topic. Partitions replicate across multiple nodes in a cluster to provide fault tolerance. A topic may have many partitions.

Each topic in Kafka is treated as a log—a collection of messages—with a unique offset assigned to each message. Topics are ordered within a partition. Consumers can access messages from a topic based on these offsets, which means a consumer can replay previous messages.

Kafka retains messages for only a specified period of time. After the specified retention period, messages are purged, and consumers no longer have access to these messages.

Kafka uses *Apache ZooKeeper* to maintain state between brokers. ZooKeeper is an open source distributed configuration and synchronization service used by many other Hadoop ecosystem projects, including HBase. ZooKeeper is typically implemented in a cluster configuration called an *ensemble*, and it's typically deployed in odd numbers, such as three or five.

A majority of nodes, or a *quorum* of nodes, successfully performing an action (such as updating a state) is required. A quorum must "elect" a leader, which in a Kafka cluster is the node responsible for all reads and writes for a specific partition; every partition has a leader.

Other nodes are considered followers. *Followers* consume messages and update their partitions. If the leader is unavailable, Kafka elects a new leader.

Figure 7.9 presents the Kafka cluster architecture.

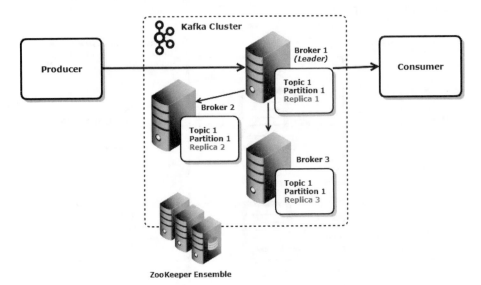

Figure 7.9   Kafka cluster architecture.

More detailed information about Kafka is available at http://kafka.apache.org/.

Using Spark with Kafka

Spark's support for Kafka closely aligns with the Spark Streaming project. Kafka's performance and durability make it a platform that's well suited to servicing Spark Streaming processes.

Common usage scenarios for Kafka and Spark include Spark Streaming processes reading data from a Kafka topic and performing event processing on the data stream or a Spark process serving as a producer and writing output to a Kafka topic.

There are two approaches to consuming messages from a Kafka topic using Spark:

- Using receivers

- Accessing messages directly from a broker (referred to as *Direct Stream Access*)

Receivers are processes that run within Spark Executors. Each receiver is responsible for an input DStream created from messages from a Kafka topic. Receivers query the ZooKeeper quorum for information about brokers, topics, partitions, and offsets. In addition, receivers implement a separate WAL—typically stored in HDFS—for durability and consistency. Messages and offsets are committed to the WAL, and then receipt of the message is acknowledged with an update of the consumed offset in ZooKeeper. This ensures that messages process once and only once across multiple receivers, if this guarantee is required.

The WAL implementation ensures durability and crash consistency in the event of receiver failure. Figure 7.10 summarizes the operation of Spark Streaming Kafka receivers.

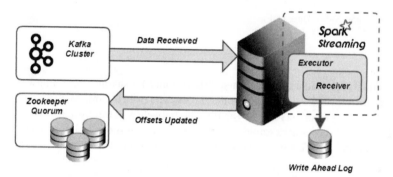

Figure 7.10   Spark Streaming Kafka receivers.

Although the receiver method for reading messages from Kafka provides durability and once-and-only-once processing, the blocking WAL write operations impact performance. A newer, alternative approach to stream consumption from Kafka is the direct approach. The direct approach does not use receivers or WAL. Instead, the Spark Driver queries Kafka for updates to offsets for each topic and directs application Executors to consume specified offsets in topic partitions directly from Kafka brokers.

The direct approach uses the SimpleConsumer Kafka API as opposed to the high-level ConsumerConnector API that is used with the receiver approach. The direct method provides durability and recoverability, and it enables "once-and-only-once" (transactional) processing semantics equivalent to the receiver approach without the WAL overhead. Figure 7.11 summarizes the operation of the Spark Streaming Kafka Direct API.

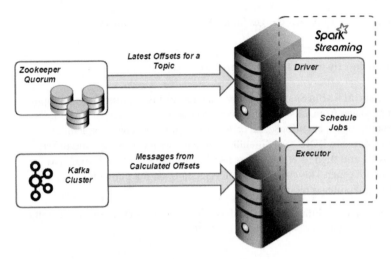

Figure 7.11   Spark Streaming Kafka Direct API.

KafkaUtils

In both the receiver and direct approaches to stream acquisition from a Kafka topic, you can use the KafkaUtils package with the Scala, Java, or Python API. First, you need to download or compile the spark-streaming-kafka-assembly.jar file; alternatively, you can use a ready-made Spark package. Listing 7.17 shows an example of starting a pyspark session, including the spark-streaming-kafka package. The same process applies for spark-shell or spark-submit.

Listing 7.17   **Using Spark KafkaUtils**

```
$SPARK_HOME/bin/pyspark \
        --packages org.apache.spark:spark-streaming-kafka-0-8_2.11:2.2.0
```

With the spark-streaming-kafka-assembly.jar file or Spark package included in a Spark session and a StreamingContext available, you can access methods from the KafkaUtils class, including methods to create a stream using the receiver approach or direct approach. The following sections describe these methods.

createDirectStream()

Syntax:

```
KafkaUtils.createDirectStream(ssc,
                              topics,
                              kafkaParams,
                              fromOffsets=None,
                              keyDecoder=utf8_decoder,
                              valueDecoder=utf8_decoder,
                              messageHandler=None)
```

Use the `createDirectStream()` method to create a Spark Streaming DStream object from a Kafka topic or topics. The DStream consists of key/value pairs, where the key is the message key, and the value is the message itself. The `ssc` argument is a `StreamingContext` object. The `topics` argument is a list of one or more Kafka topics to consume. The `kafkaParams` argument passes additional parameters to Kafka, such as a list of Kafka brokers to communicate with. The `fromOffsets` argument specifies the reading start point for the stream. If it is not supplied, the stream is consumed from either the smallest or largest offset available in Kafka (controlled by the `auto.offset.reset` setting in the `kafkaParams` argument). The optional `keyDecoder` and `valueDecoder` arguments decode message key and value objects, defaulting to doing so using UTF8. The `messageHandler` argument is an optional argument for supplying a function to access message metadata. Listing 7.18 demonstrates the use of the `createDirectStream()` method.

Listing 7.18 **`KafkaUtils.createDirectStream()` Method**

```
from pyspark.streaming import StreamingContext
from pyspark.streaming.kafka import KafkaUtils
ssc = StreamingContext(sc, 30)
stream = KafkaUtils.createDirectStream \
    (ssc, ["my_kafka_topic"], {"metadata.broker.list": "localhost:9092"})
```

There is a similar direct method in the `KafkaUtils` package, `createRDD()`, which is designed for batch access from a Kafka buffer; with it, you specify start and end offsets for a topic and partition.

createStream()

Syntax:

```
KafkaUtils.createStream(ssc,
                        zkQuorum,
                        groupId,
                        topics,
                        kafkaParams=None,
                        storageLevel=StorageLevel(True, True, False, False, 2),
                        keyDecoder=utf8_decoder,
                        valueDecoder=utf8_decoder)
```

The `createStream()` method creates a Spark Streaming DStream object from a Kafka topic or topics using a high-level Kafka consumer API and receiver, including a WAL. The `ssc` argument is a `StreamingContext` object instantiation. The `zkQuorum` argument specifies a list of ZooKeeper nodes for the receiver to interact with. The `groupId` argument specifies the group ID for the consumer. The `topics` argument is a dictionary consisting of the topic name to consume and the number of partitions to create; each partition is consumed using a separate thread. The `kafkaParams` argument specifies additional parameters to pass to Kafka. The `storageLevel` argument is the storage level to use for the WAL; the default is `MEMORY_AND_DISK_SER_2`. The `keyDecoder` and `valueDecoder` arguments specify functions to decode message keys and values, respectively. Both default to the `utf8_decoder` function. Listing 7.19 demonstrates the use of the `createStream()` method.

Listing 7.19 `KafkaUtils.createStream()` (Receiver) Method

```
from pyspark.streaming import StreamingContext
from pyspark.streaming.kafka import KafkaUtils
ssc = StreamingContext(sc, 1)
stream = KafkaUtils.createStream(ssc, \
        "localhost:2181", \
        "spark-streaming-consumer", \
        {"mykafkatopic": 1})
```

Exercise: Using Spark with Kafka

This exercise shows how to install a single-node Kafka system. You can use this platform to create messages through a producer and consume these messages as a DStream in a Spark Streaming application. For this exercise requires you need to have ZooKeeper installed, and it shows you how to do it. ZooKeeper is a requirement for installing HBase, so if you have an installation of HBase, you can use it. More information about ZooKeeper is available at https://zookeeper.apache.org/.

1. Download the latest release of Apache ZooKeeper (in this case, release 3.4.10) from https://zookeeper.apache.org/releases.html.

2. Unpack the ZooKeeper release:

    ```
    $ tar -xvf zookeeper-3.4.10.tar.gz
    ```

3. Change directories into your unpacked ZooKeeper release directory:

    ```
    $ cd zookeeper-3.4.10
    ```

4. Create a simple ZooKeeper config file (`zoo.cfg`) in the ZooKeeper configuration directory, using a text editor such as `vi`:

    ```
    $ vi conf/zoo.cfg
    ```

5. Add the following configuration to the `zoo.cfg` file:

    ```
    tickTime=2000
    dataDir=/tmp/zookeeper
    clientPort=2181
    ```

    Save the file and then exit the text editor

6. Start the ZooKeeper Server service:

    ```
    $ bin/zkServer.sh start
    ```

7. Download the latest Kafka release (in this case, Kafka release 1.0.0) from http://kafka.apache.org/downloads.html.

8. Unpack the `tar.gz` archive and create a Kafka home:

    ```
    $ tar -xvf kafka_2.11-1.0.0.tgz
    $ sudo mv kafka_2.11-1.0.0/ /opt/kafka/
    $ export KAFKA_HOME=/opt/kafka
    ```

9. Start the Kafka server:

```
$KAFKA_HOME/bin/kafka-server-start.sh \
$KAFKA_HOME/config/server.properties
```

You need to open several terminals concurrently for this exercise; refer to this terminal as terminal 1.

10. Open a second terminal (terminal 2) and create a test topic named mykafkatopic:

```
export KAFKA_HOME=/opt/kafka
$KAFKA_HOME/bin/kafka-topics.sh \
--create \
--zookeeper localhost:2181 \
--replication-factor 1 \
--partitions 1 \
--topic mykafkatopic
```

11. In terminal 2, list the available topics, and you should see the topic you just created:

```
$KAFKA_HOME/bin/kafka-topics.sh \
--list \
--zookeeper localhost:2181
```

12. In terminal 2, create a consumer process to read from your Kafka topic:

```
$KAFKA_HOME/bin/kafka-console-consumer.sh \
--bootstrap-server localhost:9092 \
--topic mykafkatopic \
--from-beginning
```

13. Open a new terminal (terminal 3) and use this terminal to start a new producer process to write to your Kafka topic:

```
export KAFKA_HOME=/opt/kafka
$KAFKA_HOME/bin/kafka-console-producer.sh \
--broker-list localhost:9092 \
--topic mykafkatopic
```

14. Enter messages, such as this is a test message, in your producer in terminal 3; you should see these messages appear in your consumer in terminal 2.

15. Use Ctrl+C to close the consumer process running in terminal 2 and the producer process running in terminal 3.

16. Using terminal 2, create a new topic named shakespeare:

```
$KAFKA_HOME/bin/kafka-topics.sh \
--create \
--zookeeper localhost:2181 \
--replication-factor 1 \
--partitions 1 \
--topic shakespeare
```

17. In terminal 2, open a pyspark session using the Spark Streaming assembly package (which is required for Kafka support):

```
$SPARK_HOME/bin/pyspark --master local[2] \
--jars spark-streaming-kafka-0-10-assembly_2.11-2.2.0.jar
```

This example uses Local mode; however, you can use a Standalone or YARN Cluster mode (if you have a YARN cluster available).

18. In the pyspark session, enter the following statements:

```
from pyspark.streaming import StreamingContext
from pyspark.streaming.kafka import KafkaUtils
ssc = StreamingContext(sc, 30)
brokers = "localhost:9092"
topic = "shakespeare"
stream = KafkaUtils.createDirectStream \
(ssc, [topic], {"metadata.broker.list": brokers})
lines = stream.map(lambda x: x[1])
counts = lines.flatMap(lambda line: line.split(" ")) \
            .map(lambda word: (word, 1)) \
            .reduceByKey(lambda a, b: a+b)
counts.pprint()
ssc.start()
ssc.awaitTermination()
```

19. In terminal 3, run the following command to send the contents of the shakespeare.txt file to your Kafka topic:

```
while read line; do echo -e "$line\n"; sleep 1; done \
< /opt/spark/data/shakespeare.txt \
| $KAFKA_HOME/bin/kafka-console-producer.sh \
--broker-list localhost:9092 \
--topic shakespeare
```

20. Check terminal 2; you should see results similar to the following:

```
-------------------------------------------
Time: 2017-11-03 05:24:30
-------------------------------------------
('', 37)
('step', 1)
('bring', 1)
('days', 2)
('quickly', 2)
('four', 1)
('but', 1)
('pomp', 2)
('thy', 1)
('dowager', 1)
...
```

The complete source code for this exercise is in the kafka-streaming-wordcount folder at https://github.com/sparktraining/spark_using_python.

Amazon Kinesis

Amazon Kinesis from Amazon Web Services is a fully managed distributed messaging platform inspired by, or at least very similar to, Apache Kafka. Kinesis is the AWS next-generation message queue service, and it introduces real-time stream processing at scale as an additional messaging alternative to the company's original SQS offering.

The AWS Kinesis product family includes Amazon Kinesis Analytics, which enables SQL queries against streaming data, and Amazon Kinesis Firehose, which provides the capability to capture and load streaming data directly into Amazon S3, Amazon Redshift (an AWS cloud-based data warehouse platform), and other services. The Kinesis component we discuss here is Amazon Kinesis Streams.

Kinesis Streams

A Kinesis Streams application involves producers and consumers in the same way as the other messaging platforms already discussed in this chapter. Producers and consumers can be mobile applications or other systems within AWS (or note).

A Kinesis stream is an ordered sequence of data records; each record has a sequence number and is assigned to a shard (similar to a partition) based on a partition key. Shards are distributed across multiple instances in the AWS environment. Producers put data into shards, and consumers get data from shards. See Figure 7.12.

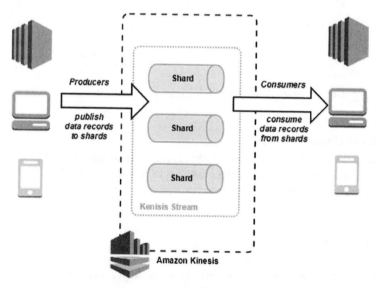

Figure 7.12   Amazon Kinesis streams.

You can create these streams by using the AWS console, the CLI, or the Streams API. Figure 7.13 demonstrates creating a stream using the AWS Management Console.

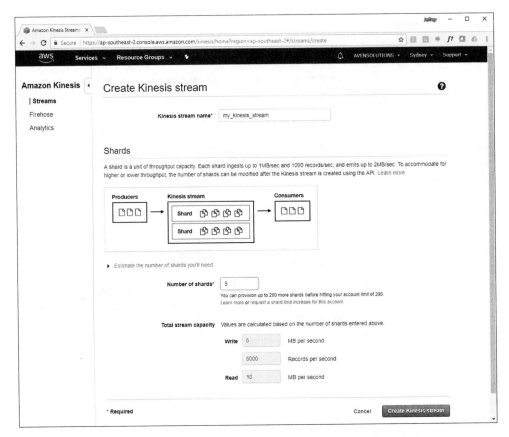

Figure 7.13   Creating a Kinesis stream by using the AWS Management Console.

Amazon Kinesis Producer Library

The *Amazon Kinesis Producer Library* (*KPL*) is the set of API objects and methods used for producers to send records out to a Kinesis stream. The KPL enables producers to put records into Kinesis with the capability to buffer records, receive the result of a put as an asynchronous callback, write to multiple shards, and more.

Amazon Kinesis Client Library

The *Amazon Kinesis Client Library* (*KCL*) is the consumer API to connect to a stream and consume data records. The KCL is typically an entry point for record processing, such as event stream processing using Spark Streaming, from a Kinesis stream. The KCL also performs important functions, such as checkpointing processed records, using Amazon's DynamoDB key/value store to maintain a durable copy of the Stream application's state. This table appears automatically in the same region as your Streams application, using your AWS credentials. The KCL is available in various common languages, including Java, Node.js, Ruby, and Python.

Using Spark with Amazon Kinesis

You can access Kinesis Streams from a Spark Streaming application by using the `createStream()` method and the `KinesisUtils` package (`pyspark.streaming.kinesis.KinesisUtils`). The `createStream()` method creates a receiver using the KCL and returns a DStream object.

Note that the KCL is licensed under the Amazon Software License (ASL). The terms and conditions of the ASL scheme vary somewhat from the Apache, GPL, and other open source licensing frameworks. Find more information at https://aws.amazon.com/asl/.

To use the `KinesisUtils.createStream()` function, you need an AWS account and API access credentials (Access Key ID and Secret Access Key); you also need to create a Kinesis Stream, though that process is beyond the scope of this book. You also need to supply the necessary Kinesis libraries, which you do by supplying the required `jar` using the `--jars` argument. Listing 7.20 shows an example of how to submit an application with Kinesis support.

Listing 7.20   **Submitting a Streaming Application with Kinesis Support**

```
spark-submit \
--jars /usr/lib/spark/external/lib/spark-streaming-kinesis-asl-assembly.jar
...
```

Given these prerequisites, the following section shows a description and an example of the `KinesisUtils.createStream()` method.

createStream()

Syntax:

```
KinesisUtils.createStream(ssc,
                          kinesisAppName,
                          streamName,
                          endpointUrl,
                          regionName,
                          initialPositionInStream,
                          checkpointInterval,
                          storageLevel=StorageLevel(True, True, False, True, 2),
                          awsAccessKeyId=None,
                          awsSecretKey=None,
                          decoder=utf8_decoder)
```

The `createStream()` method creates an input stream that pulls messages from a Kinesis stream using the KCL and returns a DStream object. The `ssc` argument is an instantiated Spark `StreamingContext`. The `kinesisAppName` argument is a unique name used by the KCL to update state in the DynamoDB backing table. The `streamName` is the Kinesis stream name assigned when the stream was created. The `endpointUrl` and `regionName` arguments are references to the AWS Kinesis service and region—for example, `https://kinesis.us-east-1.amazonaws.com` and `us-east-1`. The `initialPositionInStream` is the initial starting position for messages in the stream; if checkpointing information is available, this argument is not used. The `checkpointInterval` is the interval for Kinesis checkpointing. The `storageLevel` argument is the RDD storage level to use for storing received objects; it defaults to `StorageLevel.MEMORY_AND_DISK_2`. The `awsAccessKeyId` and `awsSecretKey` arguments are your AWS API credentials. The decoder is the function used to decode message byte arrays, and it defaults to `utf8_decoder`. Listing 7.21 shows an example of using the `createStream()` method.

Listing 7.21   **Spark Streaming Using Amazon Kinesis**

```
from pyspark.streaming import StreamingContext
from pyspark import StorageLevel
from pyspark.streaming.kinesis import KinesisUtils
from pyspark.streaming.kinesis import InitialPositionInStream
ssc = StreamingContext(sc, 30)
appName = "KinesisCountApplication"
streamName = "my_kinesis_stream"
endpointUrl = "https://kinesis.ap-southeast-2.amazonaws.com"
regionName = "ap-southeast-2"
awsAccessKeyId = "YOURAWSACCESSKEYID"
awsSecretKey = "YOURAWSSECRETKEY"
# connect to Kinesis Stream
records = KinesisUtils.createStream(
          ssc, appName, streamName, endpointUrl, regionName,
          InitialPositionInStream.LATEST, 2,
          StorageLevel.MEMORY_AND_DISK_2,
          awsAccessKeyId, awsSecretKey)
# do some processing
output.pprint()
ssc.start()
ssc.awaitTermination()
```

Much more information about Kinesis is available at https://aws.amazon.com/kinesis/.

Summary

Spark Streaming is a key extension to the Spark core API, and it introduces objects and functions designed to process streams of data. One such object is the discretized stream (DStream), which is an RDD abstraction comprising streams of data batched into RDDs based on time intervals. Transformations applied to DStreams provide functions to each underlying RDD in the DStream. DStreams also have the capability to maintain state, which is accessible and updatable in real time—a key capability in stream processing use cases. Spark DStreams also support sliding window operations, which operate on data "windows" (such as the last hour, day, and so on).

This chapter covers some of the key open source messaging systems, such as Apache Kafka, which enable disparate systems to exchange messages, such as control messages or event messages, in an asynchronous yet reliable manner. The Spark Streaming project provides out-of-the-box support for Kafka, Kinesis, and other messaging platforms. When you use the messaging platform consumer libraries and utilities provided with the Spark Streaming subproject, Spark Streaming applications can connect to message brokers and consume messages into DStream objects.

Messaging systems are common data sources in complex event-processing pipelines powered by Spark applications. As the universe of connected devices continues to expand and machine-to-machine (M2M) data exchange proliferates, Spark Streaming and messaging will become even more important.

8

Introduction to Data Science and Machine Learning Using Spark

When the facts change, I change my mind.

John Maynard Keynes, British economist

In This Chapter:

- Introduction to R and SparkR
- Statistical functions and predictive models with SparkR
- Machine learning and Spark using Spark MLlib
- Notebooks with Spark

Machine learning and data science are exciting areas of computer science. As more storage and computing capability become available at lower costs, we can harness the true power of machine learning to help make better decisions. Spark and the wider Big Data ecosystem are great enablers and accelerators of this capability.

Spark and R

R is a powerful programming language and software environment for statistical computing, visual analytics, and predictive modeling. For data analysts, statisticians, mathematicians, and data scientists already using R, Spark provides a scalable runtime engine for R: *SparkR*. For developers and analysts new to R, this chapter provides an introduction and shows how R can seamlessly integrate with Spark.

Introduction to R

R is an open source language and runtime environment for statistical computing and graphics, based on a language called S originally developed at Bell Labs in the late 1970s. The R language is widely used among statisticians, data analysts, and data scientists as a popular alternative to SAS, IBM SPSS, and other similar commercial software packages.

Native R is primarily written in C and compiled into machine code for the targeted platform. Precompiled binary versions are available for various operating systems, including Linux, macOS, and Windows. R programs can run from the command line as batch scripts or through the interactive shell. In addition, there are several graphical user interfaces available for R, including desktop applications and web-based interfaces, discussed later in this chapter. R's graphical rendering capabilities combine its mathematical modeling strength with the capability to produce visual statistics and analytics, as shown in Figure 8.1.

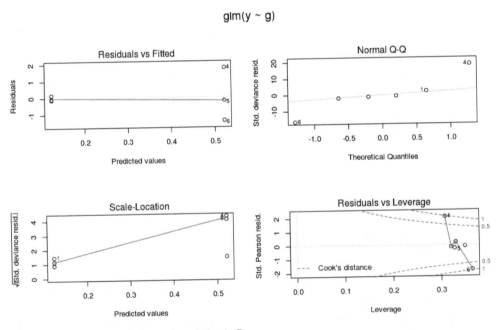

Figure 8.1   Visual statistics and analytics in R.

R is a case-sensitive, interpreted language. R code is generally easy to spot by its non-conventional assignment operator (`<-`), as in the following example:

```
y <- x + 2
```

The following sections look at some of the building blocks of the R programming language.

R Basic Datatypes

R has several basic datatypes used to represent data elements held within the data structures. The main R datatypes used to represent data elements are summarized in Table 8.1.

Table 8.1   **Primary R Datatypes**

Datatype	Description	Example
Logical	Boolean value	TRUE, FALSE
Numeric	Double-precision numeric value	3, 1.4, 1.1e+10
Integer	32-bit signed integer	3L, 384L
Character	String value of arbitrary length	'spark', '123', 'A'

Integers can cause some confusion, especially because the L notation declares them in R. R integer types are a subset of the Numeric type. At the time of this writing, an R integer is a 32-bit (or 4-byte) signed integer, in contrast to a long type in most programming languages, which is a 64-bit or 8-byte signed integer, often declared using the nL syntax. For conventional long numbers, you typically use the Numeric type in R, which is a double-precision number capable of storing much larger numbers.

Listing 8.1 shows the use of system functions to display the maximum values for Integer and Numeric (double) types in R.

Listing 8.1   **Max Values for R Integer and Numeric (Double) Types**

```
> .Machine$integer.max
[1] 2147483647
> .Machine$double.xmax
[1] 1.797693e+308
```

There are also more obscure types for complex numbers and raw byte arrays. However, they are beyond the scope of this book.

Data Structures in R

R's data model is based on the concept of vectors. A *vector* is a sequence of data elements of the same type. The members of a vector are called *components*. More complex structures are built on vectors, such as matrices, which are two-dimensional data structures with data elements of the same type, and arrays, which are multidimensional objects (with more than two dimensions).

Importantly, R has an additional data structure called a *data frame*. Data frames in R are conceptually similar to DataFrames in Spark SQL. In fact, the Spark SQL DataFrame was inspired by the data frame construct in R. R data frames are two-dimensional data structures where columns may be of different types, but all the values within a column are of the same type. Basically, this is tantamount to a table object in a relational database.

Figure 8.2 shows a representation of the basic data structures in R with sample data.

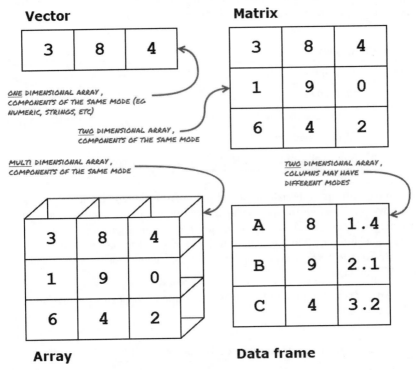

Figure 8.2   Data structures in R.

R has no concept of scalar values, akin to primitive types available in most common programming languages. The equivalent of a scalar variable is represented as a vector with a length of 1 in R. Consider Listing 8.2. If you want to create a simple variable, var, with a scalar-like assignment equal to 1, var is created as a vector with one component.

Listing 8.2   **A Simple R Vector**

```
> var <- 1
> var
[1] 1
```

A multivalued vector is created using the combine, or c(), function, as demonstrated in Listing 8.3.

Listing 8.3   **Using the c() Function to Create an R Vector**

```
> vec <- c(1,2,3)
> vec
[1] 1 2 3
```

A two-dimensional matrix is created using the `matrix` command. An example of creating a 3×3 matrix using the `c()` function is shown in Listing 8.4. By default, elements fill in by column. However, you can specify `byrow=TRUE` to fill in a matrix row by row.

Listing 8.4   **Creating an R Matrix**

```
> mat = matrix(
+       c(1,2,3,4,5,6,7,8,9),
+       nrow=3,
+       ncol=3)
> mat
      [,1] [,2] [,3]
[1,]    1    4    7
[2,]    2    5    8
[3,]    3    6    9
```

Elements of a matrix are accessible using subscripts and brackets. For instance, x[i,] is a reference to the *i*th row of the matrix x; x[,j] is a reference to the *j*th column of a matrix x; and x[i,j] refers to the intersection of the *i*th row and *j*th column. An example of this is shown in Listing 8.5.

Listing 8.5   **Accessing Data Elements in an R Matrix**

```
> mat[1,]
[1] 1 4 7
> mat[,1]
[1] 1 2 3
> mat[3,3]
[1] 9
```

Creating and Accessing R Data Frames

Arguably, the most important data structure in R is the data frame. Think of data frames in R as data tables, with rows and columns, where columns can be of mixed types. The important difference between data frames and other data structures in R is that data frames allow for column and row-specific operations such as projections and filtering. The R data frame is the primary data structure used to interact with SparkR, as discussed shortly.

You create data frames from column vectors by using the `data.frame` function, as shown in Listing 8.6.

Listing 8.6   **Creating an R Data Frame from Column Vectors**

```
> col1 = c("A", "B", "C")
> col2 = c(8,9,4)
> col3 = c(1.4,2.1,3.2)
> df = data.frame(col1,col2,col3)
```

```
> df
  col1 col2 col3
1    A    8  1.4
2    B    9  2.1
3    C    4  3.2
```

You can also create R data frames from external sources by using the `read` command; `read` supports different sources, summarized in Table 8.2.

Table 8.2 **Functions to Create an R Data Frame from an External Source**

Function	Description
`read.table()`	Reads a new line–terminated file with fields delimited by whitespace in table format and creates a data frame.
`read.csv()`	Same as `read.table()` using commas (,) as field separators.
`read.fwf()`	Reads a table of fixed-width formatted data, a common extract format for many mainframe and other legacy systems.

There are several other SparkR-specific methods for creating distributed data frames in SparkR from external sources, as discussed shortly.

In R, several methods can be used to inspect and access data from within a data frame. Some of these are demonstrated in Listing 8.7, using the sample data frame created in Listing 8.6.

Listing 8.7 **Accessing and Inspecting Data in R Data Frames**

```
> # get element in row 1, col 2
> df[1,2] [1] 8
> # get number of cols in the dataframe
> ncol(df) [1] 3
> # get number of rows in the dataframe
> nrow(df) [1] 3
> # display first row from the dataframe
> head(df, 1)
  col1 col2 col3
1    A    8  1.4
```

R Functions and Packages

Most R programs involve manipulating data elements or data structures using functions. R, like most other languages, includes many common built-in functions. Table 8.3 provides a sampling of the available built-in functions.

Table 8.3 **Sample Built-in R Functions**

Category	Examples of Functions
Numeric	`abs()`, `sqrt()`, `ceiling()`, `floor()`, `log()`, `exp()`
Character	`substr()`, `grep()`, `strsplit()`, `toupper()`
Statistical	`mean()`, `sd()`, `median()`, `quantile()`, `sum()`, `min()`
Probability	`dnorm()`, `pnorm()`, `qnorm()`, `dpois()`, `ppois()`

The true power of R, however, is in libraries and packages written for R. *Packages* are collections of R functions, data, and compiled code in a well-defined and well-described format. The directory on the system where the packages reside is the *library*.

R ships with a standard set of packages, including several sample datasets, which we will look at shortly. You can also obtain custom R packages from a publicly available collection of packages from an R user community called *CRAN*. Find more information about the R packages available from CRAN at https://cran.r-project.org/.

If you cannot find a built-in function, an included package, or a CRAN package to do what you need, you can author your own packages.

You install by using the R CMD INSTALL <package> command on the system running the R program. After a package is installed, you can load into the current R session by using the library(<package>) command.

You can use the library() function with no arguments to view all the packages loaded and available in the current R session, as shown in Listing 8.8.

Listing 8.8 **Listing R Packages Installed and Available in an R Session**

```
> library()
Packages in library '/opt/spark/R/lib':

SparkR                  R Frontend for Apache Spark

Packages in library '/usr/lib/R/library':

base                    The R Base Package
boot                    Bootstrap Functions (Originally by Angelo Canty
                        for S)
class                   Functions for Classification
cluster                 "Finding Groups in Data": Cluster Analysis
                        Extended Rousseeuw et al.
codetools               Code Analysis Tools for R
compiler                The R Compiler Package
datasets                The R Datasets Package
foreign                 Read Data Stored by Minitab, S, SAS, SPSS,
                        Stata, Systat, Weka, dBase, ...
graphics                The R Graphics Package
...
```

As you can see in Listing 8.8, SparkR itself is an R package, as discussed in the next section.

Using Spark with R

The SparkR package for R provides an interface to access Spark from R, including the implementation of distributed data frames and large-scale statistical analysis, probability, and predictive modeling operations. SparkR comes with the Spark release. The package library is available in $SPARK_HOME/R/lib/SparkR. SparkR provides an R programming environment that enables R programmers to use Spark as a processing engine. Specific documentation about the SparkR API is available at https://spark.apache.org/docs/latest/api/R/index.html.

Accessing SparkR

Using the sparkR shell is the easiest way to get started with Spark and R. The command to launch the sparkR shell is sparkR, which is available in the bin directory of your Spark installation (the same directory as the other interactive shells, including pyspark, spark-sql, and beeline); sparkR starts an R session using the SparkR package with the Spark environment defaults for the specific system, such as spark.master and spark.driver.memory. Figure 8.3 shows an example of the sparkR shell.

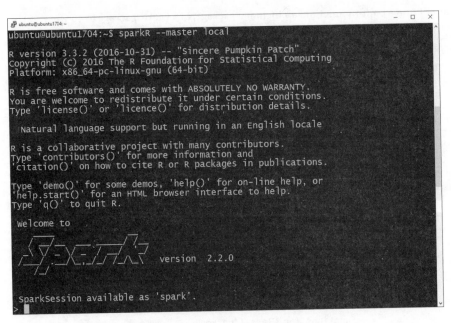

Figure 8.3   The sparkR shell.

Notice that, as with pyspark, a SparkSession object named spark is created automatically. Likewise, a SparkContext is available as sc. The SparkContext and SparkSession objects are required as entry points to connect your R program to a Spark cluster and to be able to use data frames.

You can also use the sparkR command to run R programs in batch mode, using spark-submit, which recognizes an R program by its file extension (.R). Given an R program named helloworld.R, Figure 8.4 demonstrates how to run the program in batch mode, using spark-submit.

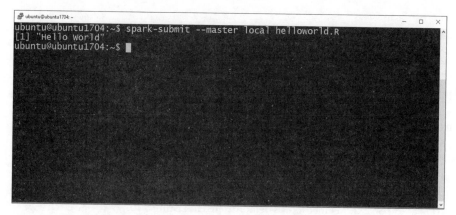

Figure 8.4   Running R programs in batch mode by using sparkR.

Creating Data Frames in SparkR

You can create SparkR data frames in a number of ways.

You can easily convert native R data frames into distributed data frames in SparkR. To demonstrate this, you can use the built-in R dataset mtcars, which consists of data extracted from the 1974 issues of the American magazine *Motor Trend*, including fuel consumption and 10 aspects of automobile design and performance for 32 automobiles (1973–1974 models).

The R datasets Package

One of the packages included with R is the datasets package. This package includes more than 100 diverse datasets from worldwide contributors, ranging from airline passenger numbers to air quality measurements to road casualties and violent crime rates. The datasets package also includes the famous Edgar Anderson's Iris Data dataset, which provides the measurements of sepal and petal length and width for 50 flowers from three species of irises—the "Hello, World" of data mining. You can view a complete list of the sample R datasets available in the datasets package by entering the following in your R or sparkR interactive shell:

```
> library(help = "datasets")
```

The mtcars sample dataset is an R data frame with 32 observations on 11 variables. In Listing 8.9, using a sparkR session, the mtcars sample dataset is loaded into an R data frame named df, and then the nrow(), ncol(), and head() functions inspect the data frame.

Listing 8.9 **mtcars Data Frame in R**

```
> r_df <- mtcars
> nrow(r_df)
[1] 32
> ncol(r_df)
[1] 11
> head(r_df, 2)
               mpg cyl disp  hp drat    wt  qsec vs am gear carb
Mazda RX4       21   6  160 110  3.9 2.620 16.46  0  1    4    4
Mazda RX4 Wag   21   6  160 110  3.9 2.875 17.02  0  1    4    4
```

Note that because R is a scientific and modeling language, the data terminology used to refer to elements and constructs has an experimental science and mathematical modeling context. For instance, in the sample mtcars datasets, rows are *observations*, and fields within rows representing columns are *variables*.

The R data frame, r_df, created in Listing 8.9 can help create a SparkR data frame using the createDataFrame() SparkR API method, as demonstrated in Listing 8.10.

Listing 8.10 **Creating a SparkR Data Frame from an R Data Frame**

```
> spark_df <- createDataFrame(r_df)
> spark_df
SparkDataFrame[mpg:double, cyl:double, disp:double, hp:double, drat:double,
wt:double, qsec:double, vs:double, am:double, gear:double, carb:double]
```

Another common requirement is to create SparkR data frames from comma-separated value (CSV) files. The simplest method for loading a SparkR data frame from a CSV file is to use the SparkR read.df() method, as shown in Listing 8.11.

Listing 8.11 **Creating a SparkR Data Frame from a CSV File**

```
> csvPath <- 'file:///usr/lib/spark/examples/src/main/resources/people.txt'
> df <- read.df(csvPath, 'csv', header = 'false', inferSchema = 'true')
> head(df)
       _c0 _c1
1 Michael  29
2    Andy  30
3  Justin  19
```

The approach shown in Listing 8.11 results in an inferred schema for the resultant data frame. You can also explicitly define the schema for data in a CSV file by creating a schema object and supplying it to the schema argument in the read.df() method, as demonstrated in Listing 8.12.

Listing 8.12   **Defining the Schema for a SparkR Data Frame**

```
> csvPath <- 'file:///usr/lib/spark/examples/src/main/resources/people.txt'
> people_schema <- structType(structField("Name", "string"),
+ structField("age", "double"))
> df <- read.df(csvPath, 'csv', header = 'false', schema = people_schema)
> head(df)
    Name age
1 Michael  29
2   Andy   30
3 Justin   19
```

There are also purpose-built functions in the SparkR API to create SparkR data frames from other common Spark SQL external data sources, such as read.parquet() and read.json().

You can also create SparkR data frames from Hive tables. The sparkR.session() function creates a connection to the configured Hive metastore; once this connection is available within a sparkR session, the sql() function in R can populate a SparkR data frame with the results of a Hive query. The sql() function can also be used to execute any Spark SQL statement, such as querying views and tables directly. Listing 8.13 shows an example of creating a SparkR data frame from a table in Hive.

Listing 8.13   **Creating a SparkR Data Frame from a Hive Table**

```
> sparkR.session()
> results <- sql("FROM stations SELECT station_id, lat, long")
  station_id       lat       long
1          2 37.32973 -121.9018
2          3 37.33070 -121.8890
3          4 37.33399 -121.8949
4          5 37.33141 -121.8932
5          6 37.33672 -121.8941
6          7 37.33380 -121.8869
```

After creating a SparkR data frame, you can reference columns by using the <dataframe>$<column_name> syntax. An example of this is shown in Listing 8.14.

Listing 8.14   **Accessing Columns in a SparkR Data Frame**

```
> head(filter(results, results$station_id > 10.0), 2)
  station_id       lat       long
1         11 37.33588 -121.8857
2         12 37.33281 -121.8839
```

SparkR and Predictive Analytics

Predictive analytics at scale is one of the key functional drivers of Big Data platforms. Retailers want to better understand customers and predict their buying behavior and propensity, credit providers want to assess risk involved with products and applicants, utilities companies want to predict and preempt customer churn, and so on.

The primary cases for using SparkR, like R, are performing statistical analysis of data and building predictive models from observations and variables. SparkR provides the ability to do this at a much greater scale than R itself because it capitalizes on Spark's powerful distributed computing framework.

Introduction to Data Mining and Predictive Modeling

If you're a data scientist, feel free to skip the next few paragraphs. If you're not a data scientist, the next few paragraphs will give you a soft introduction to data science and how the processes and methods data scientists use can be extended to leverage Spark.

Data mining is the process of discovering patterns within data that can be combined to predict an outcome. The process of discovering the inputs to these predictions is called *predictive modeling*. Predictive modeling usually falls into one of two categories: supervised learning or unsupervised learning.

Supervised learning observations receive labels such as "spam," "notspam," and "defaulted." This label is then used when observing patterns in the associated data to determine the influence that these patterns have on the outcome (the label). You "teach" the system what a desirable (or undesirable) outcome looks like—hence the name *supervised*.

In contrast, *unsupervised learning* does not involve classified observations. Typically, unsupervised learning involves identifying similarity between observations or clustering instances, which can also facilitate identifying outliers or detecting anomalies. In either case, the process of building a model typically follows the workflow pictured in Figure 8.5.

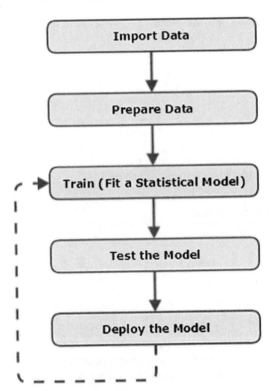

Figure 8.5 Steps involved in predictive modeling.

In this book, we have looked at how to import data and spent a considerable amount of time on the preparation and curation of data. The following process is what R is exceptionally good at:

- Fitting a statistical model to the data (or training the model)
- Testing the model against a known set of data not used in the training phase
- Deploying the model to predict outcomes for new data observations

Linear Regression

One of the simplest forms of a predictive model is the linear regression model. Without going into the mathematics behind this type of model, a linear regression model assigns coefficients (weights) to variables and creates a generalized linear function, the result of which is a prediction.

After being trained, tested, and deployed, the regression function performs against new data (observations) to predict outcomes, given the known variables. The general linear model is defined as follows:

$$y_i = \beta_0 + \beta_1 x_1 + \cdots + \beta_p x_p + \varepsilon$$

In this model, y_i is the response (or predicted outcome), β represents the coefficients or weight, and ε represents error.

R and SparkR include the function glm(), which creates a generalized linear model; glm() builds a model from observations in a data frame using an input formula in the following form:

$$y \sim x_1 + x_2 \dots$$

Where y is the response, and x_1 and x_2 are continuous or categorical variables. Listing 8.15 shows the use of the glm() function in SparkR to create a generalized linear model to predict sepal length from the iris dataset. The summary() function can describe the model after it is built.

Listing 8.15   **Building a Generalized Linear Model with SparkR**

```
> # prepare data frame and build model
> iris_df <- createDataFrame(iris)
> training <- sample(iris_df, FALSE, 0.8)
> test <- sample(iris_df, FALSE, 0.2)
> model <- glm(Sepal_Length ~ Sepal_Width + Species, data = training, family =
"gaussian")
> summary(model)
Deviance Residuals:
(Note: These are approximate quantiles with relative error <= 0.01)
    Min        1Q     Median        3Q        Max
-1.31166   -0.25586   -0.05586    0.17351    1.40303
```

```
Coefficients:
                 Estimate  Std. Error  t value   Pr(>|t|)
(Intercept)       2.08211    0.43376    4.8001   4.7693e-06
Sepal_Width       0.85317    0.12417    6.8708   3.3820e-10
Species_versicolor 1.47019   0.12693   11.5830   0.0000e+00
Species_virginica  1.99662   0.11553   17.2827   0.0000e+00

(Dispersion parameter for gaussian family taken to be 0.1969856)

    Null deviance: 82.826  on 119  degrees of freedom
Residual deviance: 22.850  on 116  degrees of freedom
AIC: 151.5

Number of Fisher Scoring iterations: 1
```

After you've built your model in SparkR, you can apply it to new data to make predictions by using the predict() function (see Listing 8.16).

Listing 8.16 **Using a GLM to Make Predictions on New Data**

```
> # predict new data
> predictions <- predict(model, test)
> head(select(predictions, "Sepal_Length", "prediction"))
  Sepal_Length prediction
1          5.1   5.068201
2          4.9   4.641617
3          4.7   4.812251
4          4.8   4.641617
5          4.3   4.641617
6          4.8   4.982885
```

Using SparkR with RStudio

So far, you have interacted with SparkR by using the sparkR shell interface. Although this exposes all the key functions in R for data manipulation, preparation, analysis, and modeling, it lacks the rich visualization capabilities of a desktop or browser-based interface.

RStudio is an open source Integrated Development Environment (IDE) for R. RStudio is available as a desktop application, RStudio Desktop, and as a server-based application, RStudio Server. RStudio Server enables clients to connect and interact with an R environment using a web browser. Figure 8.6 shows the RStudio client interface.

RStudio provides the full set of capabilities available from the command line interface, including built-in functions and packages, as well as the capability to create and export publication-quality visual analytic outputs.

RStudio is easily configurable for using SparkR as its runtime engine for execution.

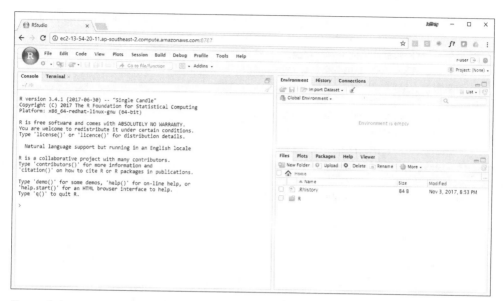

Figure 8.6   RStudio web interface.

Exercise: Using RStudio with SparkR

This exercise shows how to install RStudio alongside your Spark installation and configure RStudio to use SparkR as its processing engine. This example uses a Spark installation on a Red Hat/Centos system. RStudio is a compiled application with builds for various platforms. To obtain the specific build for your platform, go to www.rstudio.com/products/rstudio/download-server/ and follow these steps:

1. From your system, download and install your specific build of RStudio:

   ```
   $ wget https://download2.rstudio.org/...x86_64.rpm
   $ sudo yum install --nogpgcheck rstudio-server-rhel-....rpm
   ```

2. To ensure that RStudio is available on port 8787 of your server, go to http://<yourserver>:8787/.

3. Create a new R user:

   ```
   $ sudo useradd -d /home/r-user -m r-user
   $ sudo passwd r-user
   ```

   R users require a home directory because R automatically saves the user's "workspace" to this directory. Note that you also need to create a home directory for the user in HDFS if you are running RStudio on a Hadoop cluster.

4. Log in to RStudio by using the r-user account created in step 3.

5. From the console window on the left side of the RStudio interface, at the R prompt, enter the following commands to load the SparkR package and initialize a SparkR session:

```
> Sys.setenv(SPARK_HOME = "/opt/spark")
> library(SparkR, lib.loc = c(file.path("/opt/spark/R/lib")))
> sparkR.session()
```

6. Test some simple visualizations using the built-in iris dataset by entering the following at the console prompt:

```
> hist(iris$Sepal.Length,xlim=c(4,8),col="blue",freq=FALSE)
> lines(density(iris$Sepal.Length))
```

In the Plots window, you should see the histogram shown in Figure 8.7.

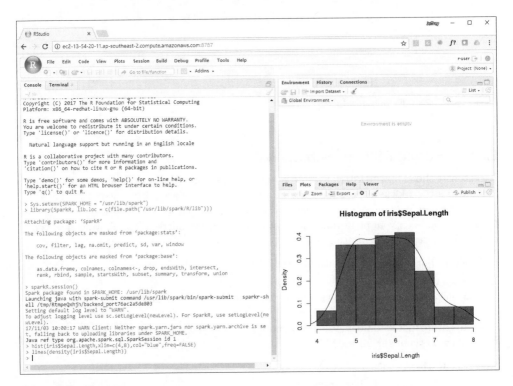

Figure 8.7   Histogram

7. Try creating a SparkR data frame from one of the included R datasets. Recall that you can see information about available datasets by using the following command:

```
> library(help = "datasets")
```

Then use functions from the SparkR API to manipulate, analyze, or create and test a model from the data. Documentation for the SparkR API is available at https://spark.apache.org/docs/latest/api/R/index.html.

Machine Learning with Spark

Machine learning is the science of creating algorithms capable of learning based on the data provided to them. Common applications of machine learning are around every day, from recommendation engines to spam filters to fraud detection and much more. Machine learning is the process of automating data mining. Spark includes two purpose-built libraries, MLlib and ML, to make practical machine learning scalable, easy, and seamlessly integrated into Spark.

Machine Learning Primer

Machine learning is a specific discipline within the field of predictive analytics, which refers to programs that leverage the data they collect to influence the program's future behavior. In other words, the program "learns" from the data rather than relying on explicit instructions.

Machine learning is often associated with data at scale. As more data is observed in the learning process, the higher the accuracy of the model, or the better it is at making predictions.

You can see practical examples of machine learning in everyday life, including recommendation engines in ecommerce websites, optical character recognition, facial recognition, spam filtering, fraud detection, and so on.

Three primary techniques are used in machine learning:

- Classification
- Collaborative filtering
- Clustering

The following sections take a high-level look at each of these techniques.

Classification

Classification is a supervised learning technique that takes a set of data with known labels and learns how to label new data based on that information. Consider a spam filter on an email server that determines whether an incoming message should be classified as "spam" or "not spam." The classification algorithm trains itself by observing user behavior to discover what's classified as spam. Learning from this observed behavior, the algorithm classifies new mail accordingly. The classification process for this example is pictured in Figure 8.8.

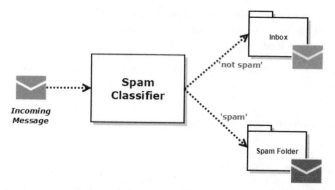

Figure 8.8   Classification of incoming email messages.

Classification techniques appear in a wide variety of applications across various domains, ranging from oncology, where a classifier may be trained to distinguish benign tumors from malignant tumors, to credit risk analysis, where a classifier may be trained to identify a customer at risk of defaulting on a credit product.

Collaborative Filtering

Collaborative filtering is a technique for making recommendations. It is commonly denoted by the "You might also like..." or similar sidebars or callouts on shopping websites. The algorithm processes large numbers of data observations to find entities with similar traits or characteristics and then makes recommendations or suggestions to newly observed entities based on the previous observations.

Collaborative filtering, unlike classification, is an unsupervised learning technique. And unlike with supervised learning, unsupervised learning algorithms can derive patterns in data without supplied labels.

Collaborative filtering is domain agnostic. It can be used in a wide variety of cases, from online retailing to streaming music and video services to travel sites to online gaming and more. Figure 8.9 depicts the process of collaborative filtering for the purpose of generating recommendations.

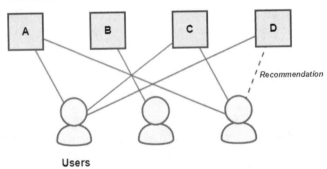

Figure 8.9   Collaborative filtering.

Clustering

Clustering is the process of discovering structure within collections of data observations, especially where a formal structure is not obvious. Clustering algorithms discover, or "learn," what groupings naturally occur in the data provided to them.

Clustering is another example of an unsupervised learning technique often used for exploratory analysis. You can determine clusters in several ways, including by density, proximity, location, levels of connectivity, or size.

Some examples of clustering applications include the following:

- Market or customer segmentation
- Finding related news articles, tweets, or blog posts

- Image-recognition applications where clusters of pixels cohere into discernible objects

- Epidemiological studies, such as identifying "cancer clusters"

Figure 8.10 clearly shows three clusters when you look at the relationship between sepal length and sepal width in the iris dataset. The center of each cluster is the centroid. The centroid is a vector representing the mean of a variable for the observations in the cluster that are usable for approximating distances between clusters.

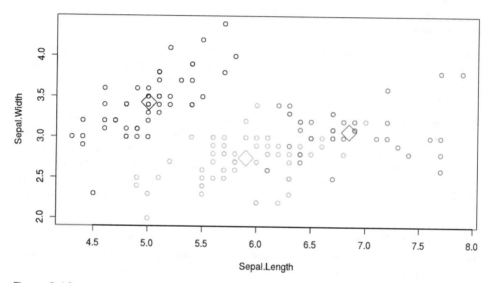

Figure 8.10   Clustering.

Features and Feature Extraction

In machine learning, a *feature* is a measurable attribute or characteristic of an observation. Variables for developing models are sourced from a pool of features. Examples of simple features for building a retail or financial services propensity or risk model are annual income, total amount spent in the past 12 months in a particular category, and a three-month moving-average credit card balance.

Often features don't present in the data itself; they derive from the data, historical data, or other available data sources. Moreover, features can be aggregated or summarized from the underlying data. Creating the set of features used by an algorithm in a machine learning program is the process of *feature extraction*. Selecting and extracting an appropriate set of features is as important as, if not more important than, algorithm selection or tuning.

Features often represent as numeric vectors. Sometimes it is necessary to represent text-based data as feature vectors. There are many established techniques for doing so, including TF-IDF (Term Frequency–Inverse Document Frequency). TF-IDF measures the significance of an element relevant to other elements within a set. This technique is common in text mining and search. For instance, you could assess how important the term "Spark" is in this book compared to all the other books available on Amazon.com.

Machine Learning Using Spark MLlib

Spark MLlib is a Spark subproject that provides machine learning functions that can be used with RDDs. MLlib, like Spark Streaming and Spark SQL, is an integral component in the Spark program and has come with Spark since the 0.8 release.

Classification Using Spark MLlib

Common approaches or algorithms used for classification in machine learning include decision trees and naive Bayes. Both techniques learn from previous observations and make classification judgments based on probability.

Decision trees are an intuitive form of classification in which a decision process is represented as a tree. Nodes of the tree signify decisions that usually compare an attribute from the dataset with a constant or a label. Each decision node creates a fork in the structure until the end of the tree is reached and a classification prediction is made.

A simple example used to describe decision trees is a golf (or weather) dataset. This simple example is often cited in data mining textbooks as a sample dataset for generating a decision tree. This small dataset, shown in Table 8.4, contains 14 instances (or observations) and 5 primary attributes: outlook, temperature, humidity, windy, and play. The temperature and humidity attributes appear in nominal and numeric formats. The last attribute, play, is the class attribute, which can have a value of "Yes" or "No."

Table 8.4 **Golf/Weather Dataset**

Outlook	Numeric Temp	Nominal Temp	Numeric Humidity	Nominal Humidity	Windy	Play?
Overcast	83	Hot	86	High	False	Yes
Overcast	64	Cool	65	Normal	True	Yes
Overcast	72	Mild	90	High	True	Yes
Overcast	81	Hot	75	Normal	False	Yes
Rainy	70	Mild	96	High	False	Yes
Rainy	68	Cool	80	Normal	False	Yes
Rainy	65	Cool	70	Normal	True	No
Rainy	75	Mild	80	Normal	False	Yes
Rainy	71	Mild	91	High	True	No
Sunny	85	Hot	85	High	False	No
Sunny	80	Hot	90	High	True	No
Sunny	72	Mild	95	High	False	No
Sunny	69	Cool	70	Normal	False	Yes
Sunny	75	Mild	70	Normal	True	Yes

The weather dataset is also included in the *WEKA* (Waikato Environment for Knowledge Analysis) machine learning software package, a popular free software package developed at the University of Waikato, New Zealand. Although not directly related to Spark, this is a recommended package for those who wish to explore machine learning algorithms in more detail.

After using a machine learning decision tree classification algorithm against a set of input data, the model produced evaluates each attribute and progresses through the tree until a decision node is reached. Figure 8.11 shows the decision tree that results for the sample weather dataset using the nominal (or categorical) features.

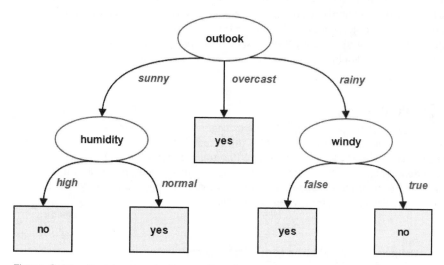

Figure 8.11   Decision tree for the weather dataset.

Spark MLlib supports decision trees for both continuous (numeric) and categorical features. The training process parallelizes instances from a training dataset and iterates over these instances to develop the resultant decision tree.

Splitting Data into Training and Test Datasets

In supervised machine learning model development, it's generally recommended that you split your input dataset into two subsets: a training dataset and a test dataset. The training dataset trains the model and usually comprises 60% or more of the overall input dataset. The test dataset comprises the remaining data from the input dataset and makes predictions to validate the accuracy of the trained model. Spark includes the randomSplit() function to split a dataset into multiple datasets for training and testing; randomSplit() accepts as input argument weights—that is, a list of weightings for the respective output datasets. Listing 8.17 shows an example of the randomSplit() function.

Listing 8.17 **Splitting Data into Training and Test Datasets**

```
data = sc.parallelize([1,2,3,4,5,6,7,8,9,10])
training, test = data.randomSplit([0.6, 0.4])
training.collect()
# returns: [1, 2, 5, 6, 9, 10]
test.collect()
# returns: [3, 4, 7, 8]
```

To construct an example of a decision tree classifier using the training dataset, you first need to create an RDD consisting of LabeledPoint (pyspark.mllib.regression.LabeledPoint) objects. A LabeledPoint object contains the label or class attribute for an instance, along with the associated instance attributes. Listing 8.18 shows an example of creating an RDD containing LabeledPoint objects. For brevity, this section shows how to use this RDD in some of the examples.

> ## NumPy and Pandas
>
> NumPy is a Python library used for scientific computing. Its special-purpose array objects are used by PySpark MLlib internally and, therefore, it is a required package if you are using MLlib with Python. NumPy is easily installed using pip (for example, pip install numpy). More information about NumPy is at http://www.numpy.org/. Pandas is another useful Python library; although not required for MLlib, Pandas is useful for structuring and analyzing data. More information about Pandas is at http://pandas.pydata.org/.

Listing 8.18 **Creating an RDD of LabeledPoint Objects**

```
from pyspark.mllib.regression import LabeledPoint
outlook = {"sunny": 0.0, "overcast": 1.0, "rainy": 2.0}
labeledpoints = [
    LabeledPoint(0.0,[outlook["sunny"],85,85,False]),
    LabeledPoint(0.0,[outlook["sunny"],80,90,True]),
    LabeledPoint(1.0,[outlook["overcast"],83,86,False]),
    LabeledPoint(1.0,[outlook["rainy"],70,96,False]),
    LabeledPoint(1.0,[outlook["rainy"],68,80,False]),
    LabeledPoint(0.0,[outlook["rainy"],65,70,True]),
    LabeledPoint(1.0,[outlook["overcast"],64,65,True]),
    LabeledPoint(0.0,[outlook["sunny"],72,95,False]),
    LabeledPoint(1.0,[outlook["sunny"],69,70,False]),
    LabeledPoint(1.0,[outlook["sunny"],75,80,False]),
    LabeledPoint(1.0,[outlook["sunny"],75,70,True]),
    LabeledPoint(1.0,[outlook["overcast"],72,90,True]),
    LabeledPoint(1.0,[outlook["overcast"],81,75,False]),
    LabeledPoint(0.0,[outlook["rainy"],71,91,True])
    ]
data = sc.parallelize(labeledpoints)
```

LabeledPoint object attributes must be float values or objects that can be converted to float values, such as Boolean or int. With a categorical feature (outlook), you need to create a dictionary or map to associate the float value used in the LabeledPoint with a categorical key.

Input Data Formats for Machine Learning in Spark

Spark's machine learning libraries support many input formats commonly used in classification or regression modeling. An example is the libsvm file format, a format from a library designed for support vector classification. Many other data structures from popular scientific and statistical packages, such as NumPy and SciPy, are supported in Spark's machine learning libraries as well.

Using the RDD containing LabeledPoint objects created in Listing 8.18, you can now train a decision tree model by using the DecisionTree.trainClassifier() function in the Spark mllib package, as shown in Listing 8.19.

Listing 8.19 **Training a Decision Tree Model with Spark MLlib**

```
from pyspark.mllib.tree import DecisionTree
model = DecisionTree.trainClassifier(data=data,
        numClasses=2,
        categoricalFeaturesInfo={0: 3})
print(model.toDebugString())
# returns:
# DecisionTreeModel classifier of depth 3 with 9 nodes
#   If (feature 0 in {0.0,2.0})
#     If (feature 2 <= 80.0)
#      If (feature 1 <= 65.0)
#       Predict: 0.0
#      Else (feature 1 > 65.0)
#       Predict: 1.0
#     Else (feature 2 > 80.0)
#      If (feature 1 <= 70.0)
#       Predict: 1.0
#      Else (feature 1 > 70.0)
#       Predict: 0.0
#   Else (feature 0 not in {0.0,2.0})
#     Predict: 1.0
```

The DecisionTree.trainClassifier() function creates a model by training the data, a parallelized collection of LabeledPoint objects. The numClasses argument specifies how many discrete classes to predict; in this case, it is two because the example simply predicts a binary outcome of yes/no. The categoricalFeaturesInfo argument is a dictionary or map that specifies which features are categorical and how many categorical values each of those features can take. In this case, you need to direct the trainClassifier() method that the values representing the outlook category are discrete—for example, "sunny" or "rainy" or "overcast". Any features not specified in the categoricalFeaturesInfo argument are treated as continuous.

When you have a model, what is next? Now you need a method to predict the class attribute from new data that does not include the class attribute. Spark MLlib provides the predict() function to do this. Listing 8.20 demonstrates the use of the predict() method.

Listing 8.20   **Using a Spark MLlib Decision Tree Model to Classify New Data**

```
model.predict([outlook["overcast"],85,85,True])
# returns: 1.0
```

As you can see in Listing 8.20, given the inputs outlook="overcast", temperature=85, humidity=85, and windy=True, the decision to play is 1.0, or yes. This follows the logic from the decision tree you created.

Naive Bayes is another popular technique for classification in machine learning. Naive Bayes is based upon Bayes' theorem, which describes how the conditional probability of an outcome can be evaluated from the known probabilities of its causes. Bayes' theorem is modeled mathematically as shown here:

$$P(A|B) = \frac{P(B|A)P(A)}{P(B)}$$

In this case, *A* and *B* are independent events; *P(A)* and *P(B)* are the probabilities of *A* and *B* without regard to each other; *P(A|B)* is the probability of observing event *A* given that *B* is true; and *P(B|A)* is the probability of observing event *B* given that *A* is true.

You implement naive Bayes classification by using Spark MLlib with the NaiveBayes.train() method from the pyspark.mllib.classification.NaiveBayes package.

NaiveBayes.train() takes an input RDD consisting of LabeledPoint objects, as in the decision tree example, and includes an optional smoothing parameter, lambda_. The output is a NaiveBayesModel (pyspark.mllib.classification.NaiveBayesModel) that can classify new data using the predict() method.

Listing 8.21 uses the weather dataset to create a model using the naive Bayes algorithm implementation in Spark MLlib and then uses this model to predict the class attribute of new data.

Listing 8.21   **Implementing a Naive Bayes Classifier Using Spark MLlib**

```
from pyspark.mllib.classification import NaiveBayes, NaiveBayesModel
model = NaiveBayes.train(data=data, lambda_=1.0)
model.predict([1.0,85,85,True])
# returns: 1.0
```

Collaborative Filtering Using Spark MLlib

Collaborative filtering is one of the most common applications of machine learning in use in many different domains. Spark uses the *ALS* (or *Alternating Least Squares*) technique in its collaborative filtering or recommendation module. ALS is an algorithm for performing matrix factorization. *Matrix factorization* is the process of factorizing a matrix into a product of matrixes. A simple example is shown in Figure 8.12.

recommendations

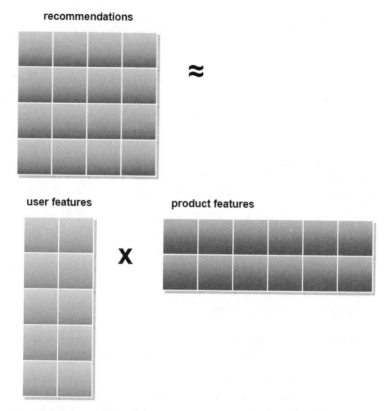

Figure 8.12   Matrix factorization.

A deep dive into matrix factorization and the ALS algorithm is beyond the scope of this book. However, ALS is the preferred implementation method for machine learning in Spark because it is a fully parallelizable algorithm.

The exercise that follows shows an implementation of a recommender using Spark MLlib and ALS.

Exercise: Implementing a Recommender Using Spark MLlib

This exercise uses a subset of the Movielens dataset, which originated at the University of Minnesota as a data exploration and recommendation project. The Movielens dataset captures movie ratings by user, along with user and movie attributes, and can be used for collaborative filtering exercises. The website for the Movielens project is https://movielens.org/. You can download the subset of data used for this exercise at https://s3.amazonaws.com/sparkusingpython/movielens/movielens.dat. This dataset contains 100,000 ratings by 943 users on 1,682 items, with each user having rated at least 20 movies. The ratings data (`movielens.dat`) is a tab-delimited, new line–terminated text file with this structure:

```
user id | item id | rating | timestamp
```

For the following exercise you need to be running Spark on a Hadoop cluster and must have the movielens.dat file saved to a directory named /data/movielens. Follow these steps:

1. Start a pyspark shell.

2. Import the required MLlib libraries:

```
from pyspark.mllib.recommendation \
import ALS, MatrixFactorizationModel, Rating
```

3. Load the Movielens dataset and create an RDD containing Rating objects:

```
data = sc.textFile("hdfs:///data/movielens")
ratings = data.map(lambda x: x.split('        ')) \
    .map(lambda x: Rating(int(x[0]), int(x[1]), float(x[2])))
```

Rating is a special tuple Spark uses and represents (user, product, rating). Note also that you filter the timestamp field because it is not necessary in this case.

4. Train a model using the ALS algorithm:

```
rank = 10
numIterations = 10
model = ALS.train(ratings, rank, numIterations)
```

Note that rank and numIterations are algorithm tuning parameters; rank is the number of latent factors in the model, and numIterations is the number of iterations to run.

5. Now you can test the model against the same dataset without the rating (use the model to predict this attribute). Then compare the results of the predictions with the actual ratings to determine the mean squared error, measuring the accuracy of the model:

```
testdata = ratings.map(lambda p: (p[0], p[1]))
predictions = model.predictAll(testdata) \
    .map(lambda r: ((r[0], r[1]), r[2]))
ratesAndPreds = ratings.map(lambda r: ((r[0], r[1]), r[2])) \
    .join(predictions)
MSE = ratesAndPreds.map(lambda r: (r[1][0] - r[1][1])**2) \
    .mean()
print("Mean Squared Error = " + str(MSE))
# returns: Mean Squared Error = 0.482478475145
```

As discussed earlier in this chapter, a good practice is to divide your input dataset into two discrete sets, one for training and another for testing. This helps avoid overfitting your model.

6. To save the model for use with new recommendations, use the model.save() function, as shown here:

```
model.save(sc, "ratings_model")
```

This saves the model to a folder named ratings_model in your current user's home directory in HDFS.

7. To reload the model in a new session—for instance, to deploy the model against real-time data from a Spark DStream—use the `MatrixFactorizationModel.load()` function, as shown here:

```
from pyspark.mllib.recommendation \
import MatrixFactorizationModel
reloaded_model = MatrixFactorizationModel.load \
                (sc, "ratings_model")
```

The complete source code for this exercise is in the `recommendation-engine` folder at https://github.com/sparktraining/spark_using_python.

Clustering Using Spark MLlib

As discussed earlier in this chapter, clustering algorithms discover groups or clusters of associated instances within a collection of data. A common approach to clustering is the *k-means* technique.

By definition, k-means clustering is an iterative algorithm used in machine learning and graph analysis. Consider a set of data in a plane—which could represent a variable and an independent variable on an x, y axis, for simplicity. The objective of the k-means algorithm is to find the center of each cluster (the centroid) presented in the data, as pictured in Figure 8.13.

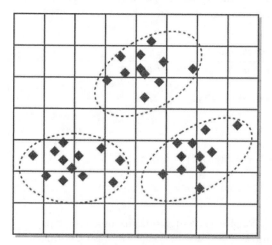

Figure 8.13   k-means clustering.

The k-means approach works as follows:

- Select *k* random points as starting center points (centroids).

- For each point, find the closest *k* and allocate the point to the cluster associated with *k*.

- Calculate the mean (center) of each cluster by averaging all the points in that cluster.

- Iterate until no points reassign to new clusters.

As you can see, this is a brute-force, parallelizable, iterative routine, which makes it very well suited to Spark.

To implement k-means in Spark, use the `pyspark.mllib.clustering.KMeans` package. Listing 8.22 demonstrates how to train a k-means clustering machine learning model using the sample `kmeans_data` dataset provided as part of the Spark release.

Listing 8.22   **Training a k-Means Clustering Model Using Spark MLlib**

```
from pyspark.mllib.clustering import KMeans, KMeansModel
from numpy import array
from math import sqrt
# Load and parse the data
data = sc.textFile("file:///opt/spark/data/mllib/kmeans_data.txt")
parsedData = data.map(lambda line: array( \
             [float(x) for x in line.split(' ')]))
# Build the model (cluster the data)
clusters = KMeans.train(parsedData, 2, maxIterations=10,
    initializationMode="random")
```

Notice that this example uses the NumPy library mentioned earlier. When you have a k-means clustering model, you can evaluate the error rate within each cluster, as shown in Listing 8.23.

Listing 8.23   **Evaluating a k-Means Clustering Model**

```
# Evaluate clustering by computing Within Set Sum of Squared Errors
def error(point):
    center = clusters.centers[clusters.predict(point)]
    return sqrt(sum([x**2 for x in (point - center)]))
WSSSE = parsedData.map(lambda point: error(point)) \
    .reduce(lambda x, y: x + y)
print("Within Set Sum of Squared Error = " + str(WSSSE))
# returns:
# Within Set Sum of Squared Error = 0.692820323028
```

As with the collaborative filtering and classification models, with a k-means model you typically need to persist the model so it can load into a new session to evaluate new data. Listing 8.24 demonstrates the use of the `save` and `load` functions to accomplish this.

Listing 8.24   **Saving and Reloading a Clustering Model**

```
# Save and load model
clusters.save(sc, "kmeans_model")
reloaded_model = KMeansModel.load(sc, "kmeans_model")
```

Machine Learning Using Spark ML

Spark ML extends the MLlib library and functions to Spark SQL DataFrames. Spark ML may be a more natural choice for machine learning if you use Spark SQL DataFrames for data processing.

Classification Using Spark ML

Spark ML supports various classification methods, including logistic regression, binomial logistic regression, multinomial logistic regression, decision trees, random forest, gradient-boosted tree, multilayer perceptron, linear support vector machine, one-versus-rest, and naive Bayes.

Just as Spark MLlib classification algorithms require an RDD of LabeledPoint objects, Spark ML algorithms require a DataFrame of Row objects, including labels and features. The label column specifies the classification for the observation, and the features column contains either a SparseVector or a DenseVector object. A DenseVector is used when each observation contains the same features, whereas a SparseVector is used when features may vary from instance to instance—that is, some features may be null or not populated for certain instances. The main advantage of SparseVector is that it only stores features that have a value, which requires less space in datasets that contain null values.

Listing 8.25 demonstrates a Spark ML implementation of a decision tree classifier example using the golf/weather dataset from earlier in this chapter.

Listing 8.25 **Decision Tree Classifier Using Spark ML**

```
from pyspark.ml.linalg import DenseVector
from pyspark.ml.classification import DecisionTreeClassifier
from pyspark.ml.evaluation import MulticlassClassificationEvaluator
from pyspark.sql import Row

# Prepare DataFrame of labeled observations
outlook = {"sunny": 0.0, "overcast": 1.0, "rainy": 2.0}
observations = [
Row(label=0, features=DenseVector([outlook["sunny"],85,85,False])),
Row(label=0, features=DenseVector([outlook["sunny"],80,90,True])),
Row(label=1, features=DenseVector([outlook["overcast"],83,86,False])),
Row(label=1, features=DenseVector([outlook["rainy"],70,96,False])),
Row(label=1, features=DenseVector([outlook["rainy"],68,80,False])),
Row(label=0, features=DenseVector([outlook["rainy"],65,70,True])),
Row(label=1, features=DenseVector([outlook["overcast"],64,65,True])),
Row(label=0, features=DenseVector([outlook["sunny"],72,95,False])),
Row(label=1, features=DenseVector([outlook["sunny"],69,70,False])),
Row(label=1, features=DenseVector([outlook["sunny"],75,80,False])),
Row(label=1, features=DenseVector([outlook["sunny"],75,70,True])),
Row(label=1, features=DenseVector([outlook["overcast"],72,90,True])),
Row(label=1, features=DenseVector([outlook["overcast"],81,75,False])),
Row(label=0, features=DenseVector([outlook["rainy"],71,91,True]))
]
```

```
rdd = sc.parallelize(observations)
data = spark.createDataFrame(rdd)

# Split data into training and test sets
(trainingData, testData) = data.randomSplit([0.7, 0.3])

# Train decision tree model
dt = DecisionTreeClassifier()
model = dt.fit(trainingData)
# returns:
# DecisionTreeClassificationModel (uid=DecisionTreeClassifier_495f9e5bcc6aaffa81c5)
of depth 4 with 13 nodes

# Make predictions using the test  dataset
predictions = model.transform(testData)
predictions.show()
# returns:
# +-------------------+-----+-------------+-----------+----------+
# |            features|label|rawPrediction|probability|prediction|
# +-------------------+-----+-------------+-----------+----------+
# |[0.0,75.0,80.0,0.0]|    1|    [0.0,4.0]|  [0.0,1.0]|       1.0|
# +-------------------+-----+-------------+-----------+----------+

# Evaluate model accuracy
evaluator = MulticlassClassificationEvaluator(
    labelCol="label", predictionCol="prediction", metricName="accuracy")
accuracy = evaluator.evaluate(predictions)
print("Test Error = %g " % (1.0 - accuracy))
# returns: Test Error = 0
```

Collaborative Filtering Using Spark ML

As with Spark MLlib, the Spark ML collaborative filtering implementation uses the ALS algorithm. Listing 8.26 demonstrates collaborative filtering using Spark ML.

Listing 8.26 **Collaborative Filtering Example Using Spark ML**

```
from pyspark.ml.evaluation import RegressionEvaluator
from pyspark.ml.recommendation import ALS
from pyspark.sql import Row

# load and prepare data, split data into training and test  datasets
ratings_rdd = sc.textFile("/opt/spark/data/movielens") \
    .map(lambda x: x.split('     ')) \
    .map(lambda x: Row(userId=int(x[0]), movieId=int(x[1]),
         rating=float(x[2]), timestamp=int(x[3])))
```

```
ratings = spark.createDataFrame(ratings_rdd)
(training, test) = ratings.randomSplit([0.7, 0.3])

# train model
als = ALS(maxIter=5, regParam=0.01, userCol="userId", itemCol="movieId",
ratingCol="rating",
          coldStartStrategy="drop")
model = als.fit(training)

# evaluate model
predictions = model.transform(test)
evaluator = RegressionEvaluator(metricName="rmse", labelCol="rating",
    predictionCol="prediction")
rmse = evaluator.evaluate(predictions)
print("Root-mean-square error = " + str(rmse))
# returns: Root-mean-square error = 1.093931162606997

# movie recommendations for each user
model.recommendForAllUsers(3).show(3)
# returns:
# +------+--------------------+
# |userId|     recommendations|
# +------+--------------------+
# |   471|[[1206,9.413772],...|
# |   463|[[1206,6.576718],...|
# |   833|[[853,5.8933687],...|
# +------+--------------------+

# user recommendations for each movie
model.recommendForAllItems(3).show(3)
# returns:
# +-------+--------------------+
# |movieId|     recommendations|
# +-------+--------------------+
# |   1580|[[475,1.8473656],...|
# |    471|[[628,5.776228], ...|
# |   1591|[[777,8.130051], ...|
# +-------+--------------------+
```

Clustering Using Spark ML

Clustering techniques supported in Spark ML include k-means, bisecting k-means, latent Dirichlet allocation (LDA), and Gaussian mixture model (GMM). Listing 8.27 demonstrates k-means clustering using Spark ML.

Listing 8.27   **k-Means Clustering with Spark ML**

```
from pyspark.ml.clustering import KMeans

# load data
dataset =
spark.read.format("libsvm").load("/opt/spark/data/mllib/sample_kmeans_data.txt")

# train a k-means model
kmeans = KMeans().setK(2).setSeed(1)
model = kmeans.fit(dataset)

# evaluate using Within Set Sum of Squared Errors
wssse = model.computeCost(dataset)
print("Within Set Sum of Squared Errors = " + str(wssse))
# returns:
# Within Set Sum of Squared Errors = 0.11999999999994547

# show results
centers = model.clusterCenters()
print("Cluster Centers: ")
for center in centers:
    print(center)
# returns:
# [ 0.1  0.1  0.1]
# [ 9.1  9.1  9.1]
```

libsvm Format

LIBSVM (library for support vector machines) provides a format specification for files containing training data. The libsvm format allows for sparse data. The Spark DataFrameReader and DataFrameWriter include native support for the libsvm format, as shown in Listing 8.27. The libsvm format provides a useful way to store and process training data for machine learning algorithms using Spark ML.

ML Pipelines

Spark ML introduces support for machine learning *pipelines*. The *Scikit-learn* project (Python machine learning library) inspired the pipeline concept. Pipelines allow you to chain data preparation and feature extraction steps with models to encapsulate all of your workflow. Pipeline components include *transformers*, *estimators*, and *parameters*.

A Transformer object transforms a DataFrame into another DataFrame by implementing a transform() method. An Estimator object is an algorithm that can fit on a DataFrame to produce a model by implementing a fit() method. A Pipeline object chains multiple Transformer and Estimator objects together to encapsulate a Spark ML workflow. The Parameter API provides a uniform mechanism for Transformer and Estimator objects to specify parameters. Listing 8.28 demonstrates a Spark ML pipeline for classifying text.

Listing 8.28 **Spark ML Pipelines**

```python
from pyspark.ml import Pipeline
from pyspark.ml.classification import LogisticRegression
from pyspark.ml.feature import HashingTF, Tokenizer

# Prepare training documents from a list of (id, text, label) tuples.
training = spark.createDataFrame([
    (0, "a b c d e spark", 1.0),
    (1, "b d", 0.0),
    (2, "spark f g h", 1.0),
    (3, "hadoop mapreduce", 0.0)
], ["id", "text", "label"])

# Configure an ML pipeline, which consists of 3 stages: tokenizer, hashingTF, and lr.
tokenizer = Tokenizer(inputCol="text", outputCol="words")
hashingTF = HashingTF(inputCol=tokenizer.getOutputCol(), outputCol="features")
lr = LogisticRegression(maxIter=10, regParam=0.001)
pipeline = Pipeline(stages=[tokenizer, hashingTF, lr])

# Fit the pipeline to training documents.
model = pipeline.fit(training)

# Make predictions on test documents ...
```

Using Notebooks with Spark

Notebooks have become popular tools in the Spark development community. Notebooks provide the capability to combine different languages along with visualization, rich text, and markup and markdown facilities, making it easy to explore and visualize data in an interactive environment. Importantly, notebooks allow you to use data to tell a story and can encapsulate data preparation, model training and testing, and visualization in a single, succinct document, making it easy to follow or reproduce your thought process.

Using Jupyter (IPython) Notebooks with Spark

Jupyter, formally known as the IPython notebook, provides a web-based notebook experience that includes extensions for Ruby, R, and other languages. Jupyter notebook files are an open document format using JSON. Notebook files contain source code, text, markup, media content, metadata, and more. Notebook contents are stored in cells in a document. Figure 8.14 and Listing 8.29 show an example of a Jupyter notebook and an excerpt from the associated JSON document.

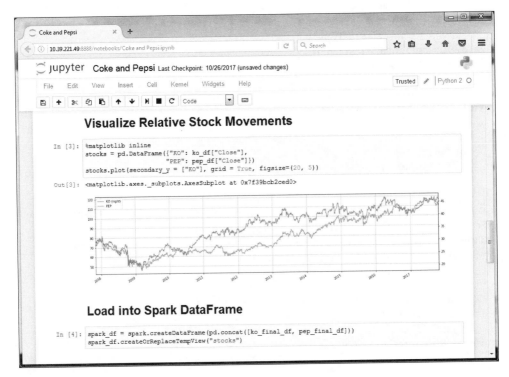

Figure 8.14   Jupyter notebook.

Listing 8.29   **Jupyter Notebook JSON Document**

```
{"cells": [
  {
   "cell_type": "markdown",
   "metadata": {},
   "source": [
    "# Calculate Pearson Coefficient"
   ]
  },
  {
   "cell_type": "code",
   "execution_count": null,
   "metadata": {},
   "outputs": [],
   "source": [
    "import numpy as np\n",
    "from pyspark.mllib.stat import Statistics\n",
    "spark_df = spark.read.parquet('hdfs://namenode:8020/data/closingprices/')\n",
    "seriesX = spark_df.select('Close').where(\"Stock='KO'\").rdd.map(lambda x:
```

```
float(x.Close))\n",
    "seriesY = spark_df.select('Close').where(\"Stock='PEP'\").rdd.map(lambda x:
float(x.Close))\n",
    "correlation = str(Statistics.corr(seriesX, seriesY, method=\"pearson\"))\n",
    "printmd('# Pearson Correlation between KO and PEP is: <span
style=\"color:red\">' + correlation + '</span> ')"
   ]
  },
  {
   "cell_type": "code",
   "execution_count": null,
   "metadata": {
    "collapsed": true
   },
   "outputs": [],
   "source": []
  }
 ],
 "metadata": {
  "kernelspec": {
   "display_name": "Python 2",
   "language": "python",
   "name": "python2"
  },
  "language_info": {
   "codemirror_mode": {
    "name": "ipython",
    "version": 2
   },
   "file_extension": ".py",
   "mimetype": "text/x-python",
   "name": "python",
   "nbconvert_exporter": "python",
   "pygments_lexer": "ipython2",
   "version": "2.7.13"
  }
}}
```

Jupyter/IPython notebooks communicate with back-end systems using kernels. *Kernels* are processes that run interactive code in a particular programming language and return output to the user. Kernels also respond to tab completion and introspection requests. Kernels communicate with notebooks using the Interactive Computing Protocol, which is an open network protocol based on JSON data over ZMQ and WebSocket.

Kernels are currently available for Scala, Ruby, JavaScript, Erlang, Bash, Perl, PHP, PowerShell, Clojure, Go, Spark, and many other languages. Of course, there is a kernel to communicate with IPython (which was the basis of the Jupyter project). The IPython kernel is known as Kernel Zero, and it is the reference implementation for all other kernels.

Using Apache Zeppelin Notebooks with Spark

Apache Zeppelin is a web-based, multilanguage, interactive notebook application with native Spark integration. Zeppelin provides a query environment for Spark, and it provides data-visualization capabilities.

Figure 8.15 shows a Zeppelin notebook running a PySpark program.

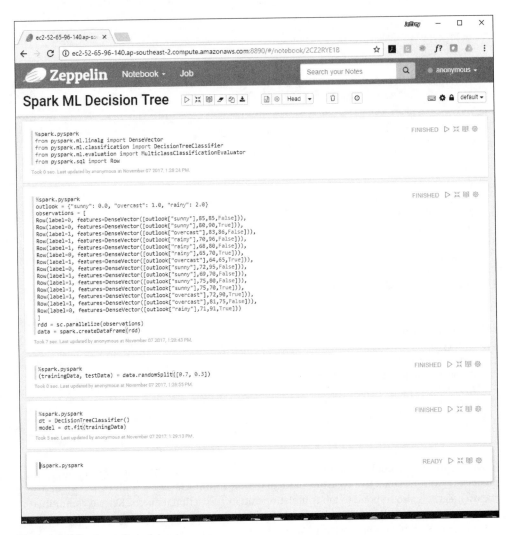

Figure 8.15   Zeppelin notebook.

> **Zeppelin Interpreters**
>
> Zeppelin interpreters are analogous to the Jupyter kernels just discussed. Interpreters allow Zeppelin to use various programming interfaces and runtimes. As an example, to use the PySpark language and runtime in Zeppelin, you need the `%spark.pyspark` interpreter. Other available interpreters include `%md` (Markdown), `%angular` (AngularJS), `%python`, `%sh` (Shell commands), `%spark.sql`, `%spark` (Spark using the Scala API), and many others.

Summary

Predictive analytics and machine learning are core use cases for Spark. Spark provides seamless integration to R through the SparkR API, a package that provides access to Spark and distributed data frame operations from an R environment using the R programming language.

SparkR provides various methods for creating data frames, including loading data from external sources such as flat files in a local or distributed file system or from a Hive table. SparkR enables the use of R data frames for distributed operations with Spark, including statistical analysis and building, testing, and deployment of simple linear regression models. SparkR is accessible from an integrated REPL shell environment, `sparkR`, and through the graphical RStudio programming interface.

R continues to grow in popularity; it is finding its way from researchers at universities to business and data analysts in commercial and government organizations. As R becomes the standard for statistical analysis and modeling in many organizations, SparkR and the Spark distributed processing runtime become compelling features for analysis at scale.

Machine learning is a rapidly emerging area of computer science that enables systems and models to "learn" from observations and data. The three primary techniques used in machine learning are classification, collaborative filtering, and clustering. This chapter examines all of these approaches, using Spark's built-in machine learning libraries (MLlib and ML), including their specific applications and common uses and implementations.

MLlib is built on the Spark core RDD API, and ML is built on the DataFrame API. Both the MLlib and ML packages include many common machine learning algorithms and utilities to perform data preparation, feature extraction, model training, and testing. MLlib and ML are designed for succinct, user-friendly yet functionally rich, powerful, and scalable machine learning abstraction on top of Spark.

This chapter looks at using notebooks with Spark; notebooks are a popular development interface for researchers and data scientists. The IPython notebook Jupyter and Apache Zeppelin both enable you to combine multiple languages with visualizations, rich text, and markdown.

You have finished the first part of your journey of learning Spark using Python. I hope this book has helped you in building solid foundations as a Spark and Python practitioner. Thank you for your time, and I wish you all the best in your career!

Index

D

G